# *ABOUT THE EDITORS*

**Miss Amrita Grover,** sister of late Professor B.R. Grover, is a distinguished historian in her own right. She is well versed with Professor Grover's writings as they always discussed and exchanged their historical views with each other, even from their student days. Upon obtaining her master's degree in History Honours with distinction and a Roll of Honour from Government College, Lahore, Punjab University, she initially taught at Inderprastha College and Miranda House for a few years and then joined the Indian Audit and Accounts Service. A graduate of National Defence College, New Delhi, Miss Grover retired as Accountant General and ex-officio Member, Audit Board. For more than two decades now, she has devoted full time to historical studies and research in history. She has attended various national and international history conferences and has presented several research papers at international conferences held at Croatia, Montreal, Berlin, Sri Lanka, Moscow, etc.

**Dr. Anju Grover Chaudhary,** niece of Professor Grover, journalist and historian, is also well versed with Professor Grover's works. She is professor of journalism at Howard University, U.S.A., where she teaches courses in history of journalism, international press and news reporting. She obtained her master's degree in history from Howard University and a master's degree and Ph.D in journalism from University of Maryland, U.S.A. An author and editor of several books and journal articles, she has presented numerous papers at international conferences throughout the world.

**Dr. J.C. Dua,** Reader, Department of History and TTM, Dyal Singh Evening College (University of Delhi), New Delhi, has had academic association with late Professor B.R. Grover since the IHC Session 1961. Professor Grover was his teacher, mentor and the one who taught him how to locate, decipher and analyse the sources on history. Dr. Dua has contributed a large number of research papers in national and international seminars and has published numerous books. The Peoples Republic of Bulgaria awarded him Georgi Dimitrov Gold Medal in 1983 and was also invited to deliver the prestigious Dr. Kalaignar Thiru M. Karunanidhi Endowment Lectures by Madras University, Chennai, in 1995.

Collected Works of Professor B. R. Grover Vol. VII

# Historiography of the Mughal Age

*Edited by*
Amrita Grover
Dr. Anju Grover Chaudhary
Dr. J.C. Dua

Originals
Delhi

First Published 2014

ISBN 10: 81-8454-140-6

ISBN 13: 978-81-8454-140-3

*Published by*

**Originals**

A-6, 2nd Floor, Nimri Commercial Centre,
Ashok Vihar Phase 4, Delhi 110052 (INDIA)
tel.: +91-11-27302453 fax.: +91-11-47061936
e-mail: info@LPPindia.com url: www.LPPindia.com



PRINTED IN INDIA

***Dedicated to the Memory of my Esteemed Brother Professor B.R. Grover***

*Amrita Grover*

# Table of Contents

# About the Author

**(b. 1923- d. 2001)**

Professor B.R. Grover, former Chairman of the Indian Council of Historical Research, with an academic and administrative career spanning more than 55 years, has left an indelible mark as one of India's most eminent and dedicated historians. He has left behind a massive wealth of historical research based on original Persian, Urdu, Ottoman Turkish, Punjabi and English sources. Known for doing intensive research in the archives and libraries of India, several European countries and the United States of America, Professor Grover had carved out a distinct position for himself as a moving encyclopaedia of source material on agrarian history of the Mughals, especially the land revenue administration.

Upon his death on May 10, 2001, the then Prime Minister Atal Behari Vajpayee paid him a rich tribute, stating: "He would always be remembered for his formidable legacy of excellence, erudition, and dedication to historical research and academic administration." Dr. Murli Manohar Joshi, then Minister of Human Resources and Scientific Research, paid him a personal homage and called him a real "Karma Yogi". He said, "He lived like a Yogi and died like a Yogi." Former Vice President of India, Justice Hidayatullah, had also applauded him for his research. His colleagues described him as "a man of sterling qualities of head and heart"; and "a dynamic and objective head of country's premier historical Institute who has left a rich legacy of his outstanding achievements in the world of historical research," among other things.

Born on February 10, 1923, Professor Grover started his career in teaching in 1946 in Lahore and later taught at the University of Punjab and various universities in Delhi until 1974, including Delhi University, Jawahar Lal Nehru University and Jamia Milia Islamia, where he also served as head of the Department of Indian History and Culture. In 1974, he was called upon to join as Director cum Member-Secretary of the newly established Indian Council of Historical Research (ICHR), a premier historical research Institute, where he served from 1974 to 1985 as Director and was later appointed as Chairman in 1999. For his long association with ICHR, his colleague, Prof. A.R. Khan, wrote in his obituary: "On account of his long association with the Council and the services rendered by him to it, Professor Grover became an institution by himself and he and the Council became a synonymy, as the latter came to be identified, both in India and abroad, with Professor Grover, even when he was not holding any office in the Council.

Initially having received training at Paris under the auspices of UNESCO for the promotion of history as a means of international understanding, Professor Grover wrote and published books in British history. Later, because of his deep interest in the study of original sources and his proficiency in Persian language, his research interests shifted to the medieval period of Indian history. His interest later widened to the study and research in regard to the social, cultural and economic impact of the Indian immigrants in West Asia and East European countries. As an avid researcher, Professor Grover wrote and published copiously on various aspects of the Mughal Agrarian System, Patterns of Rural Trade, The Concept of Village Community and a host of other topics. His writings, mostly published in prestigious journals, like the journals of the Delhi School of Economics and the proceedings of various conferences, became nodal points for the scholars of his generation. His published writings in *The Indian Economic and Social History Review, Proceedings of the Indian Historical Records Commission, Indian Archives, Proceedings of the Punjab History Conference, Punjab Past and Present* and *The Proceedings of the Indian History Congress,* among others, brought him national and international recognition. At an early stage of Professor Grover's career, Prof. M.M. Pearson of Pennsylvania University, U.S.A., wrote about his Mughal Agrarian writings as "...an impressive start...brilliant, which makes fundamental contribution in this area." Prof. C.A. Bailey of Cambridge University, complimented him for "comprehensive listing of materials" and "excellent bibliographies."

Because of his expertise in historical manuscripts/documents and objects, Professor Grover was nominated by the Government of India for several honorary positions such as member of the Indian Historical Records Commission, member of the Historical Documents Purchase Committee of the National Archives of India, member of the Committee on Preservation and Development of Cultural Heritage of Delhi, and an expert member of the Verification Committee of National Museum, India. Professor Grover was also a member of the Publication Committee of the "Comprehensive History of India". For the Indian History Congress, he served intermittently as a Joint Secretary, a Treasurer and Sectional President (Medieval India). Professor Grover also edited the well-known Time Capsule in 1978, and advised the Government to display it in the National Museum instead of inserting it again underground. He also served on the Editorial Board constituted by the Government of India for the production of documentaries on "Freedom Struggle for India's Independence, 1984-2001." Under this scheme, more than 75 documentaries were published by the Films Division, Ministry of Information and Broadcasting.

Professor Grover represented India at several international organizations, including UNESCO in 1951; Indian delegate to West Germany, 1957; delegate to the International Conference in History, Bucharest, 1980; delegate to the International Conference on the Bulgarian Studies, Sofia, 1986; and delegate to the World Archaeological Congress, Croatia, 1998, among others. Besides participating in numerous Indo-European cultural exchange programmes, presiding over innumerable regional/national/international seminars and conferences and contributing papers to various national/international seminars and conferences, he also lectured widely in West Germany (1957), Bulgaria (1986), Zagreb (1998), UK (1998), Holland (1998), and United States (1998 and 2000).

Professor Grover received several honours and awards for his historical research. For his writings on Georgi Dimitrov, the "Role of the Indian Immigrants in the Culture and Economy of the West Asian and East European Countries During the Medieval Age," and "The Social, Religious and Agrarian Aspects in East Europe, especially Bulgaria under the Ottoman-Turkish Rule (14th-19th centuries)," he was awarded Georgi Dimitrov Gold Medal by the Peoples Republic of Bulgaria. For his work on Punjab History, Professor Grover was awarded Saropa Roll of Honour by the Punjabi University, Patiala, in 1996. A life-long scholar of medieval and Islamic India, Professor Grover again came in limelight in 2001 when (upon the demolition of Buddhist statues at Bamiyan by the Taliban government), his expert opinion was sought by the Indian media to determine whether there was any parallel between Bamiyan and Ayodhya.

As a distinguished historian and a scholar with an integrated and scientific approach to the analysis of the historical process, Professor Grover, being a liberal thinker, was a great believer in the social cohesion and national integration in India and made an immense contribution in this regard.

# Preface

The papers presented in this seventh volume of **The Collected Works of Professor B. R. Grover** contain the writings of Professor Grover on historiography in a holistic manner. He consulted original sources, hitherto unknown, in Persian and other languages in numerous libraries of the world and highlighted the different approaches to the writing of medieval Indian history. Earlier historians have relied upon political, social and economic history to interpret the events of medieval India. To make further breakthrough in the analysis of social and economic history, Professor Grover advocated an examination of the regional areas remaining untapped hitherto. He strongly believed that in India, "One has to concentrate on rural society, the agrarian set-up, the tribal structure, the role of the tribes, clans, castes and landed intermediaries, the condition of the peasantry, the concept of the village community, handicrafts and industries in the rural and urban society." He wrote copiously on these subjects. Moreover, earlier historians did not have much access to the Persian manuscripts and contemporary original records due to their limited knowledge of the Persian language.

Some of the important articles on historiography being published in this volume include (i)Approach to the Writing of Medieval Indian History; (ii) Mughal Age: An Overview; (iii) Source Material for the Agrarian History of Mughal India; (iv) Agrarian System of the Punjab during the 18$^{th}$ Century; (v) Amir Khusrau as a Source of Indian Culture; (vi) The Role of Political, Diplomatic and Military History versus Social, Economic and Cultural History; (vii) Indo-German Understanding as a Means for Promoting International Stability; (vii) Russian Authors on Indian History; (viii) Indo-Soviet Relations: An Approach to Indian History; (ix) The Relevance and Importance of the Ottoman Documents to the Study of Agrarian System in Medieval India; (x) A Note on source Material in Persian Language; (xi) Modern Writers on the Mughal Land Revenue Administration: From Philip Francis to Moreland; and (xii) Distortions of History.

Professor Grover believed that one of the biggest challenges facing the Indian history is the "reconstruction of Indian history." He attributed this to a variety of factors, including: the vastness of the Indian subcontinent that offers regional variations because of diversities of language, culture and habits of people settled in different regions; the socio-economic and political phases that have affected the growth of different regions in numerous ways during the course of the century; and the scattered source materials in different regions instead of their availability at one central location.

In the paper on "Approach to the Writing of Medieval Indian History," Professor Grover stipulated that we have inherited the popular division of Indian history into Hindu, Muslim and British periods from the British times. He termed this division as "extremely illogical and arbitrary." He believed that this division is no longer applicable. According to him, the medieval concept of Indian culture comprised from $7^{th}$ - $8^{th}$ century A.D. to the late $18^{th}$ century, and that the medieval ages end when modern industrialization begins. Further, Professor Grover wrote in this paper that "With the Mughal age, we enter a period of centralization and integration. This is an age of grand vision. It is during this time that we start getting huge archival source material and documents of the centre as well as different regions which enable us to reconstruct the entire socio-economic and political set up." He believed that with the availability of such tremendous source material, it was possible to "reconstruct the rural agrarian society, the role of the caste in the agrarian holdings and that of the landed intermediaries. " He further believed that the disintegration of the Mughal Empire cannot be explained only on religious factors. He iterated: "The rise of the Marathas, Sikhs, Jats and other clans can be explained only against the socio-economic background.

This alone can explain the crisis of the medieval order and the stagnation of the Indian scene, decadence of the urban culture, impoverishment of peasantry, decline in crafts and industries, etc., the failure to develop industrial revolution which ultimately paved the way for foreign domination in India. It is only with this pragmatic approach that we can reconstruct the medieval Indian history."

In one of his articles, "Modern Writers on the Mughal Land Revenue Administration", Professor Grover pointed out that the origins of the historical writings on land revenue problems of Mughal India lie in the official memoranda and minutes of the British revenue experts, administrators and scholars. He believed that a thorough study of the modern writings on the Mughal land revenue administration is possible only when the official reports of the administrators on the regional land revenue problems as well as the works of the professional historians are taken into consideration. In fact, his paper on "Nature of Land Rights in Mughal India," based upon the official reports and original memoranda in Persian and other languages, gave a new direction to the writing of medieval Indian history.

Professor Grover was also deeply concerned with the problems in the method of the study of the social and economic history of India." He believed in exploiting the full range of available source material to reconstruct a proper perspective of the socio-economic development at regional and all-India level. He stipulated: "With an objective approach and disciplined methodology of research, we can construct a fairly accurate and dependable picture of the social and economic life of the people at various levels of historical development in the course of the centuries."

To give importance to the social, economic and cultural history was of utmost importance to Professor Grover. In the paper on "The Role of Political, Diplomatic and Military History versus Social, Economic and Cultural History," he told the historians that if they were eager to seek the truth about the causes of evolution and wanted to use history teaching as a means of developing international understanding, it was imperative to give more importance to social, economic and cultural history. Moreover, he strongly believed that it was the historian's job to seek truth concerning the past and to explain it without bias. He stipulated that "suppressing the truth" could lead to the "falsification or misunderstanding the past".

A very valuable contribution of Professor Grover to this volume is a listing of all the Persian sources for the Agrarian History of Mughal India. In the article titled, "Source Material for the Agrarian History of Mughal India," Professor Grover lists some *Dastur ul amls* and recently discovered Persian manuscripts. He wrote: "Undoubtedly, *Ain-i-Akbari*, *Akbar Nama*, *Badauni's Muntkhibut Tawarikh* and other contemporary chronicles from the reign of Akbar to Aurangzeb continue with their original importance but the interpretation of many a technical terms and languages hitherto wrongly analyzed by the previous scholars has become clearer in the light of the recently discovered *Dastur ul amls* and original documents which explain and exemplify the various terms and vocabulary. For the early Mughal period, *Tuzk-i-Baburi* by Zamud Din Khawaf provides us with details of topical, geographical and various means of irrigation of land. In the provincial histories for Akbar's reign, *Tarikh-i-Sind* and *Mirat-i-Ahemedi* are significant. " He also wrote: "The working of the land revenue administration and the agrarian policies can be well noted from the importance of *Dastur-ul-amls*, *Raqbabandi* documents of Akbar's reign and the original *Firmans* and *Sanads* from the time of Akbar onwards. " He also stated that "there are other original *pargana* land revenue papers of various categories, both in Hindi and Persian, starting from the year 1069."

Another forte of Professor Grover was the agrarian system of the Punjab during the 18th century. He considered this period very crucial in the agrarian history of the Punjab. He believed that historians of agrarian history needed to be familiar with the connotation of the technical revenue terminologies in order to understand the agrarian system of the 18th century. He himself was fully conversant with these terminologies and the source material that was available in the libraries at that time. Regarding the source material, he wrote: "Apart from the Persian chronicles, *dastur ul amls*, travelogues, there is archival source material in

Persian, Hindi, Marathi, Rajasthani in various State Archives throughout India."

Professor Grover was very open about examining the trends of historiography in other cultures as well. He believed that "culture exists in society and not outside it" and alleged that "the understanding of the concept of culture for a proper scientific study of history is essential." He was one of the few historians who examined the documents in Persian language instead of relying solely on the translated versions of historical literature. Because of his expertise in Persian, he was able to examine the Persian sources in various libraries and archives in India that throw a flood of light on the socio-economic life of India, especially from the 16$^{th}$ to 18$^{th}$ centuries. Through the various source-materials in Persian language, including the *Farmans, Sanads* and *madad-i-maash* (charitable grants), he was able to decipher the socio-economic and political trends of the times. In the article entitled: "A Note on Source Material in Persian Language", Professor Grover lists the documents and manuscripts that provide a detailed discussion on the 18$^{th}$ century administrative history and land revenue problems of various territories, including Bengal, Bihar and Orissa.

Further, his knowledge of the Persian language enabled him to understand at least one of the Soviet languages and culture of some people of Central Asian region. As a result, he was able to approach the study of Indian history through other perspectives as well. One big factor that contributed to Professor Grover's understanding of Indian history was the connection that he was able to make with the Soviet historians and their history. In the paper on "Indo-Soviet Relations—An Approach to Indian History", he wrote: "... my discussions with various Soviet scholars both at personal and symposia levels have greatly benefitted me in having a perspective and an approach to the Soviet historians, to the study of history, more so of Indian history." He wrote that "the trends in the historiography may be equally examined in the context of Indo-Soviet relations," since the Soviet writings have emphasized the impact on the social and cultural history of medieval India. In another paper on "Russian Authors on Indian History", he concluded: "For the medieval ages and the pre-British era, the

Soviet writers have rightly emphasized the identical social values on the part of the Hindu and Muslim communities and have struck down the two-nation theory."

Similarly, Professor Grover examined the documents in the libraries of Germany to understand the Indo-German relations as well as the German contributions to the scholarship in India's ancient and medieval culture. In the article on "Indo-German Understanding as a Means for Promoting International_Stability", he wrote: "A proper understanding amongst the countries is not possible unless their respective histories were to be read in proper and balanced perspectives."

Professor Grover examined the Ottoman documents as well to enhance his understanding of the agrarian system in medieval India. He researched at the oriental unit of the Cyril and Methodius National Library in Sofia that has a very rich collection of the documents from the 15th century onwards. His paper, entitled "The Relevance and Importance of the Ottoman Documents to the Study of Agrarian_System in Medieval India", is based upon "the study of the archival sources in Bulgaria which remained under the Ottoman rule for nearly five centuries, i.e. from the closing years of the 14th century to 1878 A.D."

The articles included in this volume that were earlier presented at various conferences and seminars have been appreciatively referred to and frequently quoted by the leading historians in India and other countries for more than four decades. The editors hope that this retrospective collection of Professor B. R. Grover's work will prove to be a treasured source material for the students of Mughal history. The editors also express their sincere thanks to Shri Pradeep Mittal, Proprietor of Originals (Publishers), for publishing this book.

Ms. Amrita Grover
Dr. Anju Grover Chaudhary
Dr. J.C. Dua

# Introduction

The term "historiography" generally referred to as "the body of techniques and principles of historical research and presentation" (Webster's College Dictionary) more specifically refers to the "narrative presentation of history based on a critical examination, evaluation and selection of material from primary and secondary sources and subject to scholarly criteria." (Dictionary.com) Over the years, scholars of history have been critically examining and analyzing the past events based upon their own understanding and particular criteria. Professor Grover went a step further in defining the term "historiography". According to him, historiography pertains to the "changing interpretation of the past events in the works of individual historians" and he believed that constant research is needed to uncover more facts and offer new interpretations. He also alleged that the study of historiography mandates an unbiased, critical approach that goes beyond the mere examination of historical facts.

The present volume, seventh in the series of The Collected Works of Professor B. R. Grover, deals with "Historiography", a subject about which Professor Grover wrote profusely and lectured passionately. The term "historiography" not only refers to the study of past events but deals with the theory and methodology of historical writing. Based on the critical examination of various sources, different historians have recorded and interpreted the events, over time, according to their own understanding. The collection of papers contained in this Volume reflects how Professor Grover approached, understood, and analyzed various historical events.

Professor Grover often stated that "history plays a vital role in the understanding of the ways of life, cultures and religions of people, their contribution to human civilization through the ages and their present day interdependence. It presents the vast panorama of man's progress through the ages. It is a continuous social process." Besides being a social process, history is also considered a science. According to Professor Grover, "the term 'history' today is generally used for that field of study which treats history as 'actuality' or history as a 'science'. It has been defined as the 'science of man in time'". "In so far as it seeks truth, history is a science," concluded Professor Grover. He also believed that an objective and scientific writing of history ought to be encouraged. He was of the firm belief that in the selection of facts, "a historian should avoid bias and prejudice but the selected facts in history might be interpreted in an analytical manner...." The study of historiography thus demands a critical approach that goes beyond the mere examination of historical facts. Studies about historiography consider the source, often by researching the author, his or her position in society, and the type of history being written at the time because the ways in which history is studied and recorded necessarily impacts on the ways in which a culture understands the past. The concept is important to those concerned with the subject of history. Explaining the importance of the past in history, Professor Grover stipulated that "the past is observed not for its relation with the present, or from which the present is evolved. It is important only because it furnishes examples and lessons which the present generation can imbibe. History, therefore, is in the hands of the writers, annalistic, didactic, theocratic and an instrument to transmit the facts of the past."

Contemporary historiography mostly deals with social history, gender history, and the history of non-Western societies, and especially the importance or influence of history to and/or, on society. The meaning is useful to historians because it allows them to invoke an entire body of work in a meaningful manner. Over the years, historical writing has become more rigorous and imaginative in its use of evidence. Today, history as a discipline is alive and growing, telling its story of change but telling also how tenaciously the past survives in the present. In its broadest sense then, history is the story of humanity's past. It also refers to the recording of that past. The diverse sources of history include books, newspapers, printed documents, personal papers, and other archival records, artifacts, and oral accounts. Historians use these materials to uncover linked sequences and patterns in past events and form coherent narratives.

Historiography does not pertain strictly to the study of the events of the past directly, but pertains to changing interpretations of those events in the works of individual historians. "Constant research is needed to uncover more facts and offer new interpretations," believed Professor Grover. According to him, "critical investigation of the work of others can result in the formulation of more correct interpretations. Every age brings with it some new ideas about the historical thinking on the part of the people in respect of their past life. Thus history is to be rewritten not only because new facts and data have been discovered but because the life and culture of the people has to be looked upon from a different and proper angle than done in the past and new aspects have to be taken into account." Moreover, Professor Grover was of the firm belief that in addition to the continuation of work on traditional line of political history, it is necessary to make further breakthrough in the analysis of social and economic history, more so at the regional level." Further, he was of the strong opinion that in countries like India, "one has to concentrate on rural society, the agrarian set-up, the tribal structure, the role of the tribes, clans, castes and landed intermediaries, the condition of the peasantry, the concept of the village community, handicrafts and industries in the rural and urban society." He put these ideas into practice by writing copiously on these subject matters and in fact, came to be known as an authority on these subjects through his monumental works on "The Concept of Village Community in North India...", "Classification of Agrarian Land," "Elements of Continuity and Change in Land Ownership," "Land Revenue System in Ancient and Early Medieval India," etc.

In ancient India, although learning and literature flourished at different levels and concerned almost all broad disciplines of knowledge, there is a total absence not only of ancient historical works or even any reference to them, said Professor Grover. However, despite the absence of historical literature up to the end of the 10th century, it is possible to draw a picture of the changing ideas of history on ancient India from *Ashwameghas* by Narassamsi and the two great epics of Ramayana and Mahabharata. Although these did not lead to the growth of historical writing, for centuries, they were considered the nearest thing to history. According to Professor Grover, the first definite pronouncement on Itihasa is to be found in Kautilya's *Arthashastr*a – the historical chronicles outside the sphere of religion. In the 7th century, the work of Hsuan-tsang gave much valuable information about India. Then around the 10th century, Arab works on India, notably those of Al Beruni, began to appear. The historical literature produced under Arabic inspiration or Persian tradition was replete with religious fervour, and Islamic historiography has remained clerical in nature while books written by Muslims on world history, Islamic history, general history, dynastic history, or histories of countries and regions, aimed at delineating the achievements of Islam.

With the establishment of Muslim rule in India, official and non-official chroniclers produced works covering all the dynasties of the Central Sultanate of Delhi (C. 1200-1526) as well as the dynasties of the various Muslim kingdoms. Some of the writers, though religious bigots like Ziyauddin Barani and Abdul Qadir Badaoni, were geniuses in their own way. Barani's contemporary Amir Khusrau, too, wrote historical works. However, medieval Muslim chroniclers wrote with a strong religious bias. Persian chroniclers, by and large, wrote at the command of Kings and nobles. Moreover, almost all Persian writers have exaggerated the achievements of their contemporary rulers, especially in the spheres of conquest and crushing of infidelity. Even their acts of cruelty and atrocities have been painted as virtuous deeds. Those who wrote independently suffered from racial pride and prejudice. Unlike the later historians, like Abul Fazl, Badaoni and Khafi Khan, who tried to understand the social and cultural milieu of the country, chroniclers like Hasan Nizami and Ziyauddin Barani do not refer to the vast majority of the Hindus at all. Of regular historical works, of course, there is no dearth. Scholars like Abul Fazl, Abdul Hamid Lahori and Khafi Khan wrote in a style and with the comprehension of Edward Gibbon and Thomas Babington Macaulay. Sir Henry Elliot's work was appreciated the most. He rightly arrived at the conclusion that medieval histories were "recorded by writers who seem to sympathise with no virtues and to abhor no vices." Practically all historians refer to Elliot's works for interpreting medieval Indian history.

In the early phase, the main task of historians was to translate medieval historical works from Arabic and Persian into English and other European languages. Assisted by the translations of Muslim chroniclers by the first generation scholars, foreign and Indian historians embarked on writing of medieval Indian history. The first comprehensive history of India entitled 'History of British India' (1818) was attempted by James Mill. On the basis of chronicles available in Persian, Arabic and Hindi, the study of medieval Indian history in modern times began in the 1860s, under the patronage of the Asiatic Society of Bengal. The Indo-Persian chronicles of the medieval period began to be printed in the *Bibliotheca Indica* series. Elliot and Dowson's *History of India as Told by its Own Historians* appeared in 1866-77. James Tod's monumental classic, *Annals and Antiquities of Rajasthan*, was also well known. Padmanabh's *Kanhadde-Prabandh*, Bhandu's *Vyas,* Hammirayan *Nainsi's Khyat*, Vidyapati's *Purush Pariksha* and Kirtilata and Kaviraj Shymaldas' *Vir Vinod* are other historical works of Hindus through the centuries.

Indian historiography of today owes much to the nationalist schools of history that developed before Independence. The prefix "nationalist" by no means disqualifies them from being counted as unbiased or scientific historians. Tara Chand, author of the *Influence of Islam on Indian Culture* (first published, 1922), and Mohammad Habib, author of *Mahmud of Ghazni* (published 1924), did not by any means give an unqualified endorsement to either the culture or the character described; yet their texts were treated as important works of the nationalist schools.

Soon after independence, the Hindu and Muslim communal schools found their standard statements in two series on either side of the border of the partitioned subcontinent.

The 19th and 20th centuries saw the development of modern

methods of historical investigation based on the use of primary source materials. Moreover, in the 19th century, the history of the nation-sate became the dominant form of history writing. The theories of Karl Marx not only set in motion a continuing series of interpretations of history from the Marxist economic point of view but also affected historians of all other schools. Within nationalist historiography, there developed in time the Marxist trend. Its early products were *India Today* (1940) by R. P. Dutt, dealing with India under British rule. Other influential group of historians, including Eric Hobsbawm, E. P. Thompson, and Herbert Gutman, who were influenced by Marxist class analysis, wrote histories of working people and the popular classes. Full-scale Marxist writing came only later. D. D. Kosambi's *Introduction to the Study of Indian History (*1956) was essentially a Marxist interpretation of ancient India. In the second line came R. S. Sharma, with his many papers pursuing Marxist analysis of ancient social phenomena, culminating in *Indian Feudalism* (1965) and Irfan Habib's *Agrarian System of Mughal India* (1963). The body of Marxist writing in India is now quite huge, including, among others, the writings of Suvira Jaiswal and Iqtidar A. Khan. Marxists works have thus added considerable dimensions to our study of economic and social history. However, Marx's view of India's past was quite Euro-centered.

Later, a branch of historiography grew essentially hostile to mainstream nationalism which has come to be described as communal. For instance, the *History and Culture of the Indian People*, edited by R. C. Majumdar and published by the Bhartiya Vidya Bhavan, and T*he Freedom Struggle of the Muslims* in the Indo-Pakistan Sub-continent, edited by I. H. Qureshi believed in the two-nation theory.

As far as medieval historiography is concerned, in the beginning, it remained confined to political history or biography writing. Thereafter, modern historians of medieval history tried to probe into the ideas behind human actions performed in the past. However, the partition of the country affected the historiography of medieval India since many distinguished scholars conversant with classical Persian shifted to Pakistan. Professor Grover was one of the very few historians in India who stood out for approaching the historiography of medieval Indian history in a holistic manner. As a prolific and meticulous researcher, Professor Grover would invariably break new ground by tapping original sources in Persian hitherto unknown as well as by reinterpreting the known sources. Neither subscribing to any particular school of thought nor ideology, he always appreciated the contributions made by his predecessors as well as contemporaries and rendered his own viewpoints based on contemporary and near contemporary original sources in Persian and other languages. He believed that the source-material in Persian language covering the period from the beginning of the $13^{th}$ century to the closing years of the $18^{th}$ century occupies an important place in medieval Indian historiography. By thus examining the original records in Persian, he earned a reputation for himself as a distinguished historian and scholar who took an integrated and scientific approach to the analysis of the historical process.

The editors hope that the scholars of history would find these original contributions of Professor Grover on "historiography" to be of great value. The editors also wish to thank Shri Pradeep Mittal, proprietor, **Originals**, for an excellent job in publishing this volume.

Ms. Amrita Grover
Dr. Anju Grover Chaudhary
Dr. J.C. Dua

# 1

# Medieval Period

## I. WHAT DO WE MEAN BY MEDIEVAL PERIOD?

1. In Indian History; the medieval period according to most of the historians started in the $7^{th}$ Century, with the fall of Harsha Kingdom, and goes upto the end of $17^{th}$ or mid $18^{th}$ century, although the symptoms of modern age had started even in the $16^{th}$ century. It is, however, difficult to precisely fix this medieval period. Even in Europe, it is very difficult to fix any dates for ascertaining medieval period.

2. Medieval villages in India covered a wide range. They still continue to exist and their condition, more or less, remains the same today as it existed in the $17^{th}$ or $18^{th}$ century. Generally, the way of living of people has not changed much in rural areas except in certain parts of the country.

## II. COMPARISON WITH THE EUROPEAN CIVILIZATIONS

3. In Europe, in the medieval period, there was no polity; there was no nationhood whatsoever. There was no such thing as State. This is due to the fact that there was no sovereignty, which is one of the very important attributes of a State. Nation is not complete without sovereignty. It is missing within, as well as without. The idea of Christianity was the main consideration. Pope, the head of the Christian religion, in those days, was most powerful. His superamacy was taken for granted in every European State. His order carried more weight than the orders of the King of the land. In a way, Christian States owed their allegiance to the Pope.

4. The advents of Columbus and Vasco Da Gama, were very important in so far as their respective discoveries were concerned. Columbus who actually started for India, had reached America–the New Land. Vasco-da-gama, however, reached the Western Coast of India. With the discovery of the sea-route to India, Portuguese colonies were established in India, on the Western Coast.

III. POLITY IN INDIA

5. Europe in the middle ages was dominated by the feudal lords, and there was negation of any centralised type of State. There was no concept of nationhood as we understand it in the modern age. The same state of affairs existed in our country in those days. After the fall of Harsha, fragmentation of North India into small Principalities took place. The Society was caste-ridden and divided into exclusive, water-fight compartments. As early as the 8th century, Mohammad-Bin-Kasim had established his rule in Sind. However, when Muslims came on the scene in a major way towards the close of the 12th Century, Rajputs were all-powerful. Even so, with separatist tendencies, they were fighting amongst themselves and, as such, not strong enough to meet the foreign challenge. The Rajput Chiefs, as they were called, were holding tiny states of their own, and had vested interests–landed, political and economic. They did not hold themselves responsible for the progress of their subjects, as they were least interested in them, except perhaps to the extent of collection of revenue. They were not bothered about the development of the land or anything else for the public good as such. Rajput Chiefs knew no proper art of warfare, were ill-equipped and had very defective policies. They were concerned only about their territory and ultimately came the ruin of the Indian society due mainly to their fault. None of those Rajput Chiefs had any aspirations to build up a centralised and strong government or administration system. This situation brought about total ruin of the Indian society.

6. Since the 8th century, several Muslim settlements had been established, particularly on the West Coast of India, and the petty Chiefs had not been successful in resisting various incursions which took place, not once, not twice, but on several occasions with a view to collecting loot to finance their projects for wars.

7. The invasions of Mahmud of Ghazni towards the close of the 12$^{th}$ century was a major event in India. Mahmud of Ghazni was a very fine soldier and the Rajputs were no match to him in the art of warfare. Historians have counted not less than seventeen campaigns waged by him between 1000-1023 AD. He invaded north-western India, looted several temples, and the sack of Somnath was the most devastating. Rajputs fought bravely but did not present a united front to the invaders, who were actually raiders. They had no intention of staying in India because they only wanted to loot India and go away. The invaders found the Rajput Chiefs very weak, and disunited, and incapable of putting up a united fight. They had no sense of nationalism or brotherhood, and there was no awakening on the part of the people in the face of common danger. Factional fights were the order of the day amongst the Rajput Chiefs, and the country's defence against possible foreign invasion had received no consideration at all. There was hardly any defence policy as such, no pre-planning or preparations to meet successive invasions which came at fragment intervals. The Rajput Chiefs would not take any initiative in defence matters. Foreign incursion on the neighbouring Chiefs territory would not worry other Chiefs, who concerned themselves merely with their own vested interests; nor did the common people show any interest in what was going on in the country. Such was the peculiar feature of the Indian polity in the middle ages. It is indeed strange that Mahmud of Gazni should go through the heart of Rajasthan and no Rajput Chief would stop him. No single Rajput had the courage to stop him while coming to the Somnath temple. Some of the Rajput Chiefs in Gujrat did show signs of putting up a fight against him. But Mahmud of Ghazni who came to know of these plans was shrewd enough to change his route.

8. After Mohd. Ghazni, came Mohammad of Ghori. Prithvi Raj Chauhan put up strong opposition and defeated him in the Ist battle of Tarain (1191 AD). But with this victory, he did not take any steps to further strengthen his frontiers. Prithvi Raj was defeated by Ghori in the second battle of Tarain (1192 AD) and later at Panipat, and the Muslim rule came to stay in India for centuries to come.

9. One major factor responsible for all this catastrophe was the social factor. Hindu society at that time was totally caste-ridden. Intellectual supremacy rested with the Brahmins. Kshatriyas were responsible only for government and defence of the State. Trade was in the hands of Vaishyas and to serve all the above castes was the lot of the Shudras. People were so caste- minded that they would not attempt to do any job which did not fall within the purview of their caste. Thus only one fourth of the population was responsible for the defence of the State, an arrangement which rendered three fourth of the population defenceless, not having been trained to wield arms. Hindu society had become very conservative, and their potential for resisting foreign invasion diminished thereby.

10. There was another problem also. The warriors who were taken prisoners in the battles, after their return to their respective States, were considered outcaste since they lived and ate with people outside their own caste. They were not allowed to again bear arms, and as such the fighting strength diminished greatly. Mohammad Ghori after his victory in the 2$^{nd}$ battle of Tarain in 1192 A.D., occupied the whole of north India. With complete inertia and lack of national consciousness, there was no attempt on the part of the Chiefs or the people to take back the area conquered by the Muslims.

## IV. COMING OF ISLAM:

11. Some historians have tried to defend the theory of conversions to Islam at the point of the sword. Others feel that Islam was purely and simply a missionary religion. Both can be true. As soon as the Muslim kings came into power, it was opportune for them to convert Hindus to their own religion — whether at the point of sword or otherwise. Same was the case with the Christian rulers in Europe, some of whom were quite harsh in their methods, even as the Muslims were. It is seen that even in Delhi and Agra, which were the centres of Muslim power, the places dominated by the Hindu population, who outnumbered them continued to be so. Even the use of sword does not seem to have succeeded in turning the whole of this population completely as Muslims. There may have also been social reasons assisting in

this conversion. The Hindu society being caste-ridden and Shudras being ill-treated, they might have opted for this conversion. In those days, these classes did not enjoy equal social rights. The poor people preferred to get converted and have the material benefits which the Muslims enjoyed. Similar reasons were responsible for the spread of Christianity in other countries.

12. Muslim Kings having come to power, levied the *Jazia* tax upon non-Muslims, and they were given equal civic rights as citizens only on payment of the tax. In early stages, this *Jazia* system was invoked for military purposes. Hindu generals were exempted from such payment. Invalid persons, women and children were, however, exempted from this penalty. The question arises, as to how far this imposition of *Jazia* actually helped in conversions to Islam.

13. 17th Century documents, which are still available in some of the Museums, show that if a person was not able to pay *Jazia* of even one anna, he was forced to accept Islam as his religion. This was a very significant factor. A low caste man, socially down-trodden and economically also poor, naturally fell into this trap and became a Muslim. There was no other alternative left for him. Only the lowest class of people joined Islam because even as Hindus they did not enjoy equal rights with people belonging to the higher classes and, as such, the advent of Islam was perhaps welcome. Thus it was mainly the social aspects which helped conversions to Islam and not only the military impositions. Islam preached universal brotherhood and this came as a noble idea to low class Hindus who stood socially degraded, and they accepted Islam gladly.

14. Aurangzeb went still further in promoting the conversions. He started another method. In order to become a Chaudhary of a village, one had to be a Muslim. So quite a number of Hindu elders accepted this dictum in order to hold on to their *Gaddi* and safeguard their own vested interests. It is obvious from this that either the richest people accepted Islam due to their vested interests, or the poorest accepted the same to avoid payment of *Jazia*, or else to get over (erstwhile) social injustice.

## V. THE SULTANATE PERIOD:

15. The Sultanate was purely and simply a theocratic state. Ala-ud-din khilji acted with extreme cruelty towards his Hindu population. He extorted the wealthy Hindus by forcing them to pay exhorbitant revenue. Mohammad Tughlak imposed *Jazia* upon high class Brahamins also, who were previously exempt from such payment. Muslim polity in early middle ages was wholly governed on theocratic lines.

16. There was a new way of looking at the old Indian History through the Vedas, through the Shastras and other Sacred Books. Hindus, not understanding the oneness of God in Hinduism, worshipped so many Gods whereas Islam believed in only one God, i.e., Allah. All things were governed by Allah. Hinduism was fast losing ground to Islamic ideology, and the 11$^{th}$ and 12$^{th}$ centuries saw a complete renaissance within Hinduism. Islam had been successful mostly in converting the lower population or the ruling classes to the Muslim fold. Islam was the dominant religion of the time. Even so it was not easy for Islam to completely exterminate Hinduism. Muslims were only a small minority among the majority of Hindus, and were mostly living in cities, being accustomed to urban life. India was a country of villages where most of the population was Hindu. Hinduism acted just like a shock absorber to the Islamic onslaught.

17. With the Hindu renaissance, the Bhakti Movement started. The leaders of the Bhakti Movement thus met the challenge of Islam. Hinduism had become stagnant; but man could attain *Mukti* with worshipping one God and love of people. Kabir, one of the exponents of the Bhakti Movement, pleaded that there is only one God – may be Allah for the Muslims, and Ram and others for the Hindus – these were essentially one and the same. He believed in a classless society. He said that God could be reached not only through worship but otherwise also, such as, through love. Kabir had a wider outlook. He said that to go to the temple or to the Masjid is one and the same thing. There is only one God, according to him, but that these could be many manifestations of HIM.

18. Seers and Saints like Kabir, Ramanand, Guru Nanak, brought about a change in Hinduism, with some blend of the

Islamic thought in it. These exponents preached to the public in the early 16th century. Hindus wished to preserve their own entity and were actually on the self-defence. Islam had assumed the aggressive path. Bhakti Movement confronted Islam as a counter blast, and soon spread through the whole of India including the South.

VI. THE MOGHUL PERIOD:

19. The establishment of Moghul dynasty brought about a big change in the early medieval history. Moghuls actually came from Mongolia. They started invading India in the 13th century A.D. and had been invading from time to time. In 1526, the Moghuls under the leadership of Babar invaded India and defeated Ibrahim, and Babar became the first King of the Moghul Dynasty. He liked himself to be called as Badshah (King), instead of as the Sultan, the title assumed by the previous Muslim rulers. The Sultan was however considered as the head of the Muslim community, in addition to his sovereign duties.

20. Akbar was the greatest King of the Moghul dynasty. He conquered most of the territories in North India. It was during his time that more or less a common pattern of administration was introduced in the various provinces of the Moghul Empire, and the power was centralised. From the point of view of polity, this was a very good thing, as it brought unity.

VII. INDIAN MAHARAJAHS AND RAJAHS:

21. We find that our medieval society was divided into a hierarchical pattern of Zamindari. There were Zamindars owning wide territories. They were known as Maharajahs and Rajahs. But the Moghuls would not allow them to be called as such lest it should reduce their status because there was only one Emperor. As such, the Moghuls called them as Zamindars. They had to submit to the central authority of the Moghul Emperor at the top. They were also forced to pay tributes to him. Akbar started a new system by which the Zamindars were encouraged to enroll themselves in the Imperial Army, in lieu of the payment of these tributes, thus eliminating the possibility of the Zamindars conspiring against the Imperial interests. To win them over further, the Zamindars were

actually given large *Jagirs,* and given titles such as Mansabdars. They were made responsible for maintaining peace in their respective *Jagirs,* as also for collecting land revenue. Some of these Mansabdars were also given salaries in cash. This system gave stability to the central authority–without that authority ever coming in direct conflict with the people.

VIII. SYSTEM OF ADMINISTRATION UNDER AKBAR:

Akbar's administration stood for Imperialism, and for annexation of any territory to its kingdom. Moghuls had very tight control over the Indian Chiefs. Akbar won over allegiance from the Rajput Chiefs, who served as high ranking generals in the Moghul armies. Administrative unity had been well established under the Moghuls.

22. Hindus under Akbar enjoyed equal civic rights, without having to pay the *Jazia.* According to Akbar, a king could not govern effectively if he discriminated between persons professing different religions. He also had liberal ideas and was able to establish a secular government in which all religions could flourish side by side in perfect harmony. There were no inhibitions on his Hindu subjects. But Akbar himself remained a staunch Muslim to the last.

23. Akbar was the first Muslim king who tried to unite Hindus and Muslims by propagating a common religion called *Din-i-Ilahi.* This religion took the best features from both the religions; this new concept of religion however, did not make much of a success, and it faded out soon after the death of Akbar. Both Jehangir and Shahjahan, who succeeded Akbar in turn, were capable rulers and generally pursued the policies of Akbar.

24. Then came Aurangzeb. During his reign *Jazia* was re-imposed, and Hindus were again denied civil rights, as also subjected to other similar hardships. His behaviour towards Hindu religion was very hateful. Hindus were also denied admission to government service, exceptions apart.

25. Aurangzeb wanted to establish heaven on earth by exterminating the Hindus. Forcible mass conversions to Islam also took place. This policy of (hate) however, soon brought about

a (counter) reaction and gave Aurangzeb endless troubles. There was no respect for the Rule of the Law, and no consequent respect for the king either.

IX. THE RISE OF SHIVAJI:

26. Revolts soon broke out everywhere. Marathas were the fore-runners in putting up strong opposition to the Muslim tyranny. Then Shivaji came on the scene, and Aurangzeb waged endless wars against the Marathas, who were determined to re-establish the Hindu rule. This anti-Muslim movement was not however, truely a nationalist movement with the sole aim of re-establishing the unity of Hinduism throughout the country. Shivaji, in his aggressive designs, had annexed territories and looted wealthy principalities even outside Aurangzeb's hold. Shivaji started his career at a very early age. He conquered Torna, Rajgarh, Purandhar and many other hill-forts and wade the strongholds from which, the Moghuls could be continuously harassed. The Marathas menace proved to be very costly for Aurangzeb.

27. In the North, Jats and Sikhs also started their revolt against Aurangzeb. The Jats, however, did not fight so much for a cause of Hinduism, but out of personal motives in seeking power and prestige. On the other hand, the Sikhs were motivated differently. Guru Tegh Bahadur sacrified his life in the cause of Hinduism. Guru Gobind Singh fought against Aurangzeb and had won many battles. He considered that it was not possible to safeguard the interests of Sikhism without gaining political power. At Anandpur, he endeavoured to establish a Sikh principality, but he did not succeed in his attempt as the Moghuls were still very powerful. However, the resistance offered by the Sikhs proved disastrous for Aurangzeb, as the whole population was against his rule. The *Jagir* system had become stagnant, and Zamindars had started to stop paying revenues to the state exchequer. Thus, it had become difficult to maintain the military set-up.

28. Due to his ruthless and disastrous policies, Aurangzeb's rule proved a complete failure, and soon after his death, both the Moghul ideology as also the Moghul Empire crumbled to its logical end.

## X. ECONOMIC LIFE UNDER THE MUGHALS:

29. The economic life of the people under the Mughals was however, not so bad. The agriculturists were quite well off. There was no fragmentation of holdings due to the joint family system, and large holdings proved very advantageous to the agriculturists. There was plenty of land available to grow crops as the population was not so dense as it is today. There was, however, considerable shortage of human labour to till all the land available and hardly one fourth of land was ever fully under the plough. 33% of the gross produce was to be paid to the State by way of land revenue. People generally lived in *kacha* houses.

30. The 18th century was, however, the darkest period in the Indian History. The disintegration of whole of the Moghul empire had taken place and there were internecine wars waged by various Chiefs over petty matters. These fratricidal feuds made it easy for the Europeans to establish and strengthen their position in India and in this they were fully successful.

31. Another feature of the Moghul period was that they started the policy of giving charity grants to Muslims living in villages. So, a lot of urban Muslims moved to the villages in order to avail of these charity grants. One effect of this was that Hindus and Muslims had developed better understanding amongst themselves and had generally learnt to live in mutual harmony. Muslims had got integrated to the Indian ways of life, even though the two communities actually lived apart as two separate and distinct communities.

32. The impact of Islam had not been much in India as in other countries where the advent of Islam resulted in total extinction of the local people as a separate community. In Indian villages, Hindus continued to constitute almost 80% of the total population. This situation, ironically enough, was later to be the prime cause for permanent division of the country into India and Pakistan.

# 2

# Mughal Age: An Overview

The Mughal age is one of the most distinctive phases in the history of India, the Indian people and their culture. It was after centuries that an all-Indian Mughal Empire was built on the tottering edifice of the Delhi Sultanate and on the local character of the provincial dynasties. The comparative peace and political stability established by the Great Mughals in the 16th and 17th centuries stand in glaring contrast to the insecurity of life, fissiparous tendencies, politically chaotic and torn Indian society during the $18^{th}$ century which saw the disintegration of the Mughal Empire. Apart from the political stability, the Mughal administration in its manifold aspects, the cultural achievements in the realm of art, architecture and literature, the attempt for the establishment of a secular concept of an Indian state, the emergence of the concept of mutual co-existence or the religious communities and their cultural assimilation tending towards social cohesion, the agricultural development, the fostering of an inland and international trade and commerce underline the main traits of the Mughal age.

The Mughal Empire was founded by Zahiruddin Muhammad Babur after his victories over Ibrahim Lodhi at Panipat (1526 A.D.) and Rana Sanga at Khanwa (1527 AD). Babur's reign was too short lived and he died in 1530 A.D., leaving an insecure state. His son, Humayun, could not withstand the Afghan attempt under Sher Khan's leadership for the recapture of the Delhi throne and remained in exile to Persia. Sher Shah (1540-45 A.D.) introduced administrative and revenue reforms, some of which served as useful basis for the administrative structure of the Mughal Empire. Sher Shah's successors were weak monarchs and the Sur dynasty ended in 1555 A.D. on Humayun's return to India. Humayun died shortly and was succeeded by his son, Jalaluddin Muhammad Akbar (1556-1605 A.D.), who expanded and consolidated the Mughal Empire. In fact, Akbar was the real founder of the Empire and he stood like a colossus over the kings who either preceeded or succeeded him. Jahangir (1605-1627 AD), Shah Jahan (1628-58 A .D.), and Aurangzeb (1658-1707) further expanded the Empire. Such is the irony of history that the Mughal Empire reached its largest territorial extent under Aurangzeb and yet it was during his regime that the process of its disintegration started. The Mughal Empire broke up in the 18th century though the last Mughal ruler Bahadur Shah Zafar lost his throne in 1857 A.D. after the revolt for independence was suppressed by the British Government.

To the popular mind, the most appealing aspects are the cultural contribution of the Mughal times and the development of the secular concept of State on Akbar's part. The Mughal Empire has vanished but the Mughal monuments and the development of the Indian literature still present a vivid picture of the Mughal glory whereas Akbar's concept of mind on the nature Indian state is a repeated rejoinder to the 20th century Indian politics.

The greatness of the Mughal Empire rests, to a considerable extent, on Akbar's reorganisation of the Empire and introduction of new principles of state policy based on liberalism and secularism. Akbar believed in the policy of *Sulh-i-kul* (Peace with all) whereby all religions showed paths to one God and that the state as an Institution stood above any particular religion. Akbar's concept of sovereignty stood for justice and equity. It was essentially non-sectarian in nature and, as such, refused to make any discrimination between different communities on religious ground when otherwise they owed full allegiance to the State. It was in pursuance of this concept that Akbar abolished the pilgrimage cess and *Jizya* (religious cess) upon the Hindus. Hitherto, the Muslim state in India had imposed *Jizya* with a view to appease the *Ulma* (Orthodox ecclesiastics) who in accordance with their interpretation of the *shariah* believed in the humilation of the Hindus and assertion of the Muslims as the ruling class thereby to give the State in India an Islamic colour. Akbar established the supremacy of the State over the Church and exercised rigid control over the financial and religious affairs of the State. The abolition of *Jizya* afforded to the Hindus equality of citizenship in the State and won over the political allegiance of the Rajput Rajas. Akbar's concept of State was essentially modern in outlook. Jahangir, more or less, maintained the status-quo but Shah Jahan tilted towards the Islamic character of the State. Aurangzeb was an orthodox Sunni and a puritan. Being highly religious minded, he had a concept or an ideal State based on his own understanding of the *Shariat*. At the same time, he did not want to totally surrender the practical concept of State polity based on expediency and traditional concept of Mughal polity. So in his actual State polity, he struck a delicate equipoise between his ideal and practical considerations. He re-imposed *Jizya* and destroyed some of the Hindu temples. He resumed some land grants from the Hindus and at the same time issued fresh grants to some of the important temples. But this policy was not a success. His religious intolerance caused aversion among the Hindu population. His religio-polity and staunch imperialism brought him in conflict with the Marathas in Deccan whom he was unable to crush till the end of his life. His constant wars in Deccan weakened the central authority in the North and led to the occasional Zamindari revolts in different parts of the Empire. This gave a rude shock to the entire land revenue machinery and wrecked the Empire. In the 18$^{th}$ century, Muhammad Shah abolished *Jizya* and reverted to pre-Aurangzeb State polity but by that time the damage had been done and the disintegration of the Empire had already started.

In the domain of art, ever since the Gupta age (4$^{th}$-5$^{th}$ centuries A.D.), India had not witnessed glorious proficiency as it did during the Mughal age. Throughout the medieval age, the indigenous characteristics of the Indian art had continued to develop on regional scale under the Delhi sultanate and the provincial dynasties. But under the Mughals, the vast resources and the wealth of the Empire as well as the personal aesthetic nature and patronage of the rulers gave unprecedented impetus to the growth of art and architecture. Even though affected by the local and Persian influences, it displayed the same uniformity in its architectural character and structural principles in practically throughout the Empire. Babur's main interest lay in the ornamental gardens. The traditions of Persian architecture left great impression on Humayun's mind during his exile in Persia and matured after his death in his own mausoleum constructed by his wife, Haji Begum. The Humayun tomb represents a combination of indigenous Indian architecture and Indian representation of Persian art. The red sand stone and white marble were admirably blended. The taut and rigid outlining gave an austere dignity to the entire conception. The double dome feature, borrowed from Persian architecture, appeared in the Indian architecture for the first time. It was only in the reign of Akbar that the Mughal style of architecture took a concrete form. Under him, it was chiefly executed in red sand stone with insertions of white marble frequently introduced for the purpose of emphasis. The concept was indigenous as it was already known in secular wooden arch type prevalent in Punjab and Kashmir. The dome of the 'Lodi' type, even when built hollow, was technically not of true double order. The pillar shafts were usually many-sided and capitals were in the form of bracket support. Ornamentation, carved or boldly inlaid, was common pattern whereas pointed designs were often introduced on the interior walls and ceilings. Akbar had to his credit the construction of palatial forts at Agra, Lahore, Allahabad, a fortress at Ajmer, and a capital city at Fatehpur Sikri. Jahangir had more interest in miniature painting but the outstanding architectural production is his own mausoleum at Shahdra near Lahore. The tomb of Itmad-ud-Daulah at Agra illustrates a fresh interpretation of architectural style and forms a connecting link between Akbari and Shah Jahani architecture. Shah Jahan's reign represents a second phase of the Mughal architecture which is characterised by the lavish use of marble, occasional plastic decoration and enrichment by means of inlaid patterns in coloured stone. The introduction of the foliated curves resulting in the formation of white marble arcades of engraved arches and the assumption of the Persian type dome, bulbous in its outline and constructed in its neck, the system of true Persian double doming, pillars with tapering, voluted bracket Capitals and foliated bases, the structural ornamental elements of a curvilinear order and fluidity of line sensuousness represent the main features of the architecture.

With his ever increasing resources and voluptuous taste, Shah Jahan was a great builder. He replaced the stone buildings in the palace-forts of Agra and Lahore by marble pavilions, built Red Fort and Jama Masjid at Delhi, Taj Mahal and Jama Masjid at Agra. The plan of the Taj Mahal, as of the other Mughal monuments, was fully indigenous–executed by the Indian mason-guilds and engineers. The marble of the Taj was brought from Makrana (in Rajasthan) which has the main characteristic of assuming subtle variations in tone and shade according to the changes in the light presenting the passing colour of the moment. At the same times, in the Punjab, an architecture of brick masonary with an insertion of sand stone and exterior decoration with brilliantly coloured glazed tiles was evolved. Wazir Khan's mosque in Lahore represents this phase. The decline of the Mughal style of architecture came in Aurangzeb's reign who did not have much taste for it. His only notable monuments are the Badshahi Masjid at Lahore, Moti Masjid within the premises of the Red Fort, the mosques at Benares and Mathura and some buildings at Aurangabad. During the 18th century, the centre of power shifted from Delhi. Lucknow became the centre of fresh architectural structure but the few monuments built in the Mughal style represent the melancholies of the times. The Safdar Jang mausoleum marks the downwards trend of the Mughal style and is no match to the Humayun tomb.

The Mughal age forms a creative period in the evolution of school of painting. This school integrated various elements known to the ancient classical age and Sultanate period of Indian History, the medieval Chinese and the contemporary European arts. Notwithstanding the introduction of the Persian influence during Humayun's reign, the indigenous elements, however rudimentary and crude, found expression in a refined and sophisticated manner in the final evolution of the art. Under Akbar, the illustration of the classics like Romance of Amir Hamza gradually gave way to greater humanism, interest in landscape, animal and bird life as well as a growing realism in female figures and trees. Under Jahangir, Mughal painting developed maturer and independent style. With the ever-growing local influence, there was tendency towards naturalism. Apart from the illustration of his own Memoirs, the brush of the painter concentrated on human beings, animals and plants. Trees with straight trunks, realistic branches and distinct leaves, mountains of solid conical masses and clouds with natural shapes began to dominate. The brilliant colours were avoided so as to leave soft and liquid effect. The Persian taste of blue, pink and white gave way to red, yellow and green. The western influence also exerted stronger impact on the Mughal art. Even though Shah Jahan was given more to architecture and Aurangzeb was much less aesthete, the Mughal miniature painting continued to find patronage both at the Royal court and with the nobles. The fresco paintings on the walls of the mosque of Wazir Khan in Lahore also show the Mughal interest in the mural paintings.

The Mughal period also marked considerable development in literature, calligraphy and education. Apart from Persian, which was the court language, the regional languages, especially Hindi found impetus. Good works were produced by literary persons, poets and historian both in Persian and Hindi. The Urdu language having evolved itself in Deccan found its way at the Mughal camp during the latter half of the 17$^{th}$ and the 18$^{th}$ centuries. In fact, education and learning found due place during this age. The schools for the Hindus named *pathshalas* and for the Muslims known as *maktabs* were attached to the temples and the mosques respectively. The latter met the educational expenditure from the State subsistence land grants and public charity. The higher seats of learning may be regarded as Universities of those times. Of the many places, the important higher seats of Hindu learning were located at Benares, Nadia, Tirhut, Paithan, Thatta, Multan and Sirhind.

The students from various parts of India gathered at these centres. The *madrasahs* were the secondary schools and colleges for higher learning for the Muslims. The main seats of Muslim learning were Agra, Delhi, Lahore, Jaunpur, Gujrat, Sialkot, and Ahmedabad and they attracted students from all over India. Notwithstanding the specialisation in different courses of study by the Hindu and the Muslim seat of learning, there were even mixed schools for Hindus and Muslims as Muslim students attended the classes of the Hindu teachers, specially in astronomy, astrology and mathematics while the Hindus attended the *madrasahas* for leaning Persian which was the court language. Despite manifold literary and educational developments during the Mughal age, it is regrettable that Akbar refused to accept the gift of a printing machine from the Portuguese. The introduction of the printing press would have brought revolutionary changes in the realm of thought and literature. It would have definitely escalated the process of change from the medieval to the modern concept and values of the Indian life. But the chance was missed and India lagged behind in this aspect by a few centuries.

As regards administrative set-up, at the centre, the King had a team of ministers who were put in-charge of different departments of the State. The ministers were responsible to the King and held office at his pleasure. The Empire was divided into *Subahs* (provinces). Every *Subah* was put under the charge of *Subahdar* (Governor) and his ministers with the charge of different departments. For the purposes of administration, the *Subah* was further divided into *Sarkars*, *Parganas*, *Tappahs* and *Mauzas* (villages). In Shah Jahan's reign, a new administrative-cum-fiscal division named *Chakla* smaller than the Sarkar or at times comprising *Parganas* from inter-*Sarkar* divisions was formed. A *Faujdar* and a *Diwan* administered the *Sarkar* and *Chakla* divisions whereas a *Shiqdar* and a *Thanadar* were put in-charge of the *Pargana*. The *Tappadars*, *Chaudharies* and the *Muqaddams* (headmen) were the local semi-officials responsible for the collection of land revenue and maintenance of law and order. Beneath the Imperial and uniform administrative polity lay the *Zamindari* territories and village communities resting essentially on clannish social structure and casteism. The institution of *Zamindari* played an important role in the Mughal land revenue administration and the agrarian set-up of the country. A *Zamindar* was responsible for the collection of revenue and maintenance of law and order. He was entitled to perquisites in lieu thereof. The *Tappahdars*, the *Chaudharies* and at times even *Muqaddams* belonged to the *Zamindari* class. Such villages which paid land revenues directly to the Government were known as *riayti* villages. Land revenue formed the main income of the State. The State demand was based on a detailed classification of the agricultural land. Under Akbar, the State charged 1/3 of the gross produce on the best quality of soil in respect of grain crops and much less on the inferior soils. The rate of the cash crops varied from 1/3 to 1/8th or even less in accordance with the nature of the crop. Later on, the incidence of State share on the grain crops seems to have been raised to 1/2 of gross produce on the best quality of land with full crops (i.e. when there was no crop failure) but the rates in respect of cash crops remained the same. However, there were always regional variations in respect of incidence of State share. The population of the Indian sub-continent was less than 1/5th of what it is today and the cultivable land was available in plenty. As such, the average holding of peasant land owning families was fairly large so as to lead a comfortable life in normal years of production. The occupancy and contracting tenants were always sought after and made a living of easy subsistence. The Mughal State encouraged the peasants to bring the maximum land under cultivation, offered agricultural loans (*taqavi*) for the purchase of seeds and maintenance of wells and extended the scope of artificial means of irrigation through the opening of the canals, especially in the North-West portions (*Subahs* of Delhi and Lahore) where they were badly needed. The Mughal State gave religious and subsistence revenue free grants of land to the Muslim and Hindu mendicants, poets, writers, teachers, the widows and needy persons, management staff of the mausoleums and temples. The Hindu chiefs also made such grants especially to the Hindu Brahman families. In the pre-Mughal age, the Muslim population in India was mostly urban minded. The large scale revenue free assignments to the Muslim families brought them in intimate touch with the Hindu agricultural population. It gave great impetus to the process of Muslim colonisation in the rural society. Notwithstanding initial acerbity in feelings, far from driving a wedge between the Hindus and the Muslims, it gradually helped the rural masses of the two communities in mutual understanding and appreciation of the two cultures. Many a Muslim families, whether local converts or otherwise settled, adopted the broad features of the Hindu society as well as the local customs and manners. This process of cultural assimilation, backed by the identical agricultural interests of the two communities however imperceptible, became a marked feature of the rural society in the $16^{th}$-$18^{th}$ centuries.

It is in the commercial sphere that Mughal India made spectacular progress. India had carried on brisk trade with Asiatic countries, the African coastal regions throughout ancient and early medieval ages. However, the European maritime activities, Vasco de Gama's contact with the Indian Malabar coast (1497 A.D.) and the establishment of the European trading companies on the Indian coasts with their inland network of branches towards the close of the $15^{th}$ and during the course of the $16^{th}$ & $17^{th}$ centuries, opened a new horizon in the commercial world. During this age, India was a great producer of the consumer goods and commanded an enviable position in the world of commerce and industry. Even though no regular economic theory was evolved by the Indians, looking it from the practical operation of the Indian trade with the outside world, it seems that the Mughal State believed in the mercantilist concept which equally governed the contemporary European thought. During the Mughal ages, India enjoyed a high degree of favourable balance of trade. India had trade relations with the Asiatic, African and European countries. She exported cotton textile goods and calicoes, indigo, iron and steel, sugar, rice, pepper, spices, pearls and diamonds.

As India produced most of essential commodities for self-consumption, she needed mostly luxury goods from outside in order to meet the needs of the elite and the State. As such, she imported raw silk, velvet of various colours, fine woolen cloth, oil, paintings and landscapes, carpets and horses. A class of merchants– rich as well as with average means constituting the middle class, controlled both the inland and foreign trade. This was the bourgeoisie class which carried on banking and money lending. It acted as distributor of goods. It provided artisans, especially the professional classes of weavers and jewellers to produce goods and paid them market wages for their subsistence. Some of the princes and princesses and the nobles also indulged in trade.

The development of trade and commerce had tremendous impact on the growth of urbanisation and the spread of money-economy in the urban centres and such rural areas which were well-connected with the local markets and cities. With comparative peace during this age, the population increased. The urban character of the society was escalated and many a big city like Agra, Delhi, Patna, Ahmedabad and Lahore had greater population than the contemporary big European cities. It goes without saying that the nobility led a rich and ostentatious life. Apart from Muslim merchants, the majority of the bourgeoisie class was Hindu–governed strictly by caste rules in its social relations. Only the known financing families lived an ostentatious life whereas others, even though economically well off, preferred a life of anonymity. There was a growing tendency on the part of the State and the merchants to acquire monopolistic rights for the employment of the artisans in different vocations. Despite this handicap, the artisan class lived a fairly comfortable life. The unskilled labourer could be employed either on daily or monthly basis. The wages had regional variations. Keeping in mind the cheapness of the food stuffs during those days, it is clear that even the unskilled wage-earner lived on easy subsistence and in terms of purchasing power of the money, he was better off than his counterpart in the present times. The disintegration of the Mughal Empire during the course of the 18$^{th}$ century exercised great impact on the politics, agrarian system and commercial life of the country.

# 3

# Amir Khusrau as a Source of Indian Culture

Amir Khusrau occupies a unique position in the cultural history of India. A man of singularly brilliant parts and versatile genius, well versed in the known services of his time and a prolific writer, he has left an indelible mark on the medieval literature and society. As a literary giant, he not only wrote elegant and lovely Persian poetry, but through his wide learning he made reflections on the contemporary thought, the religions, socio-religious ideas, the nature and character of Islam in India, the political ideas, the character of the Turkish rule of the Delhi Sultanate, the warfare, the regional languages, the sciences, climate, fauna and flora, the festivities, the painting and other aspects of the cultural heritage of India. Thus it is not without justification that he is being claimed by different academic disciplines viz., linguistics, literature, art and society as well as history. During the last two years, a number of seminars at international, national and regional levels have been arranged to commemorate the 700$^{th}$ anniversary (in fact a little over 700 years) of Amir Khusrau. As copious literature has been produced on many a facet of Amir Khusrau's literary contribution, apparently it may seem that not much can be added on this subject. All the same, if we were to analyse the traits of Khusrau's character and the cast of his mind evolved through the vicissitudes of his own life as well as the contemporary (13$^{th}$-14th centuries) socio-political set-up in the country, we may appreciate Khusrau's personality, concept of his mind and cultural contribution in a better perspective.

Born in India of an immigrant Central Asian father, Saifuddin Mahmud and an Indian mother, daughter of a noble at Iltutmish's court, he (Abul Hasan Yaminuddin Khusrau) combined in his veins both Central Asian and Indian blood. As his father died when he was just 7 years old, he was brought up by his maternal grandfather, Nawab Imad-ul-Mulk in typical Indian environments. Having been brought up in a small village (Patiala - Distt. Etah, Agra Division) and the cultural atmosphere of Uttar Pradesh, Amir Khusrau imbibed all the qualities of Indianhood of which he felt proud to the last days of his life. By the time he completed his education at twenty years of age, he "talked in verse and pearls fell from his mouth". For his career, he entered the service of Sultan Balban's nephew Katlu Khan, nicknamed Chajju who was a patron of learning. Thereafter, he remained with Bhughre Khan at Samana and then with Prince Muhammad Khan (Khan Shahid) who took him to Multan. As the Prince was killed in a battle against the Mongols, Khusrau was taken a prisoner to Balkh. The hardship and suffering in life as a prisoner left a great mark on his literary bend of mind. After considerable vicissitudes of life, Amir Khusrau entered the service of Jalaluddin Khalji and thereafter made his mark as a court poet under Allauddin Khalji. In fact, he served under seven Sultans and held offices under five of them. At the same time, at heart Amir Khusrau had turned a mystic and became a devout follower of the Chishtia Sufi *Silsilah*. A devotee of Shaikh Farid *Ganj-i-Shakar* (1173-1264), he was greatly attached to the Sheikh Nizamuddin Aulya – his contemporary. Association with the court life and the Chishtia Order was by no means a contradiction with him.

Amir Khusrau was the most prolific of poets and he is said to have left behind him 'some half million of verses'. According to the tradition, by Firishta's time he was credited with having produced 92 works. Even when considerable portion of his works has perished his fame as a poet rests on his available poetical works. His works cover wide range from spiritualism, mundane love to history. As against the other contemporary Indian poets of the Persian language, he mostly adopted Indian life and landscape for his poetical material. His works bear the imprint of his fondness and appreciation for everything that was Indian. Steeped in Indian symbolism and imagery, he wrote in Persian language without the slightest alteration in its idiom and diction which won him a rare distinction during his own life time. His contemporary historian Ziauddin Barani, who was closely associated with him, declared him to be the greatest of all the poets, ancient and modern, for whereas other poets had excelled in one or two forms of verse, Khusrau was pre-eminent in all. Khusrau's fame as a literary genius continued to increase with the passage of time and glowing tributes on his thought and ideas continued to be paid by different sections of the people - the administrators, the intellectuals and the mystics. An inscription on a marble tablet in the gallery of the tomb of Amir Khusrau written by Shihabuddin of Herat who had come to India with the historian Khwandamir in 1528 A.D. and was a contemporary of Babur made an assessment of Khusrau in the following words:

> Mir Khusrau, the *Khusrau* of the kingdom of eloquence,
>
> That ocean of excellence, and sea of Perfection;
>
> His prose is more attractive than flowing water,
>
> His poetry is purer than the most limid streams;
>
> A sweet-singing nightingale without a rival;
>
> Honey-tongued parrot without an equal.

Another inscription on the wall of the outer enclosure of the tomb written at a later stage highlighting the intellect, imagery of mind and thought of Khusrau runs as:

> The prince of the kingdom of speech, Khusrau, the chief and leader of pious men;
>
> His name is (impressed) on the tablet of Time as an engraving on stone.
>
> He (lit. his intellect or mind) composed verse in such an elegant style
>
> That, by the imagery of his mind, he gave adornment to the tablet of thought.
>
> He dived deep in the river of Reflection and through his wide (lit. circumambient) learning,

He brought out pearls of 'Truth' from that river.

The fact is that Khusrau never claimed to be a historian. Nor was he so regarded during the medieval ages. Even though he produced historical works in poetical form, unlike Barani he has no reflections to make on the science of history. At the same time to call Khusrau merely a poet is to detract a great deal from him. His works *Khazain-ul-Futuh* containing an account of the first years of the reign of Sultan Allauddin Khalji from 1296-1310 A.D. ; *Qiran-us-Sadain* describing the meeting of Sultan Keikobad with his father Nasiruddin, Sultan of Bengal, *Ghurrat-ul-Kamal*, *Miftah-ul-Futuh* comprising panegyrics upon Nizamuddin Aulya, Sultan Keikobad and other notables; *Ashika* an epic on the love of Deval Rani and Khizer Khan covering the conquest of Deccan in detail do introduce mode of cultural expression in the form of historiography and provide a mint of information on the contemporary cultural aspects of the Indian society. Khusrau has no didactic approach except to make appeal to the cultural and aesthetic taste of the readers. All the same, Khusrau does realize the concept of change in society and lays emphasis on the political ideas, contemporary sciences, art and literature and other aspects of the Indian culture. Khusrau's authority is great as a narrator of contemporary events which he brilliantly described. In fact, he was participator in many of them and his friend historian, Ziauddin Barani also appeals to him for confirmation of his own assertions. In the social context, Amir Khusrau is the true mirror of his age.

Khusrau is influenced by the contemporary historiography which underlines the Turkish conquest of India as a tussle between 'Islam' and the non-Muslim peoples of different regions of India. All the same, he does not have any vision of the implementation of the ideal Islamic concept of polity as underlined by Barani in *Fatwah-i-Jahandari*. Khusrau is more realistic and pragmatic for the nature of the establishment of the Turkish rule in India. In *Ashika*, he remarks, "Happy Hindustan, the splendor of religion, where the law finds perfect honour and security... The whole country by means of the sword of our holy warriors has become like a forest denuded of its thorns by fire... The strong men of Hind have been trodden under foot and all are ready to pay tribute.

Islam is triumphant, idolatry is subdued. Had not the law granted exemption from death by the payment of *jizya*, the very name of Hind, root and branch, would have been extinguished. From Ghazni to the shore of the Ocean you will see all the domain of Islam..." Even though Khusrau adopts the terminology of the historians of his age and considers the Turkish conquest of India as that of 'Islam', he directly hits at the nature of governess. After voluntary submission or conquest after armed conflict, the Hindu Chiefs (Zamindars) and their non-Muslim population, subject to the payment of *jizya*, were to be regarded as the *Zimmis* and were entitled to protection of life and property by the State. Whether *jizya* was realizable in practice from the vast rural areas settled on *zamindari* basis or the State would be contended to realize merely *peshkash* (tribute) as revenues is a further question to be examined by the historians.

By Khusrau's time, different vernacular dialects were spoken in various parts of India. Sanskrit and *Prakrt* were considered to be literary languages whereas Apabhramsa as a modified or spoiled language of the people had been evolved variently in different regions of north India. The Apabhramsa spoken as different dialects had inconsistent development in various regions. Sanskrit–classical and cultivated language–was confined to the upper and educated classes especially to the Brahmins. The vernacular *Hindawi* language was quite developed as a science of exposition and rhetoric with its grammar and syntax. The growth of the regional languages and literature during the medieval ages was accelerated by the emergence of the Bhakti cult and the Sufi *silsilahas* as a part of the socio-religious movements. The dialogue of the religious thinkers and saints with the common people was possible only in the vernacular languages. They expressed their ideas and philosophy both in verse and prose. Both Fariduddin Masud *Ganj-i-Shakar* and Nizamuddin Aulya talked to the simple folk in the *Hindawi* of their respective regions. In the 13th century in Rajasthan, Gujarat and other northern parts of India, the Jains, Nath Yogis, the Siddhas wrote Hindi poetry in the local Hindi dialects. Even though a brief depiction of the regional languages is available from the early Arab travellers and Al-Biruni, Amir Khusrau gives detailed description. He says that having been born in India, it was his privilege to describe the Indian languages. Every province had its own language with its peculiar idiom for the expression of various thoughts. He counts the major languages as Sindhi, Lahori, Kashmiri, Kannari, Dhur-Samundari, Tilangi, Gujari, Maa-Bari, Gouri, Bengali and Avadhi. In Delhi and its suburbs, the language was *Hindawi* which had been current here with all its forms of speech since olden times. Having been brought up in the atmosphere of Utter Pradesh, Khusrau had perfect hold over the *Hindawi* language. He maintains in his introduction to *Ghurrat-ul-Kamal* that before him only Khwaja Masud Saad Suleman had written *Diwans* in the three languages, i.e. Arabic, Persian and *Hindawi* and thereafter nobody could attempt excepting him who had a perfect hold on these languages. In his *Mathnavi-i-Dewal Rani-Khizir Khan,* he takes pride in the Hindi language which in his view was in no way inferior to that of Persian. Khusrau comments, "… if you ponder the matter well, you will not find Hindi words (language) inferior to the Parsi. It is inferior to the Arabic, which is the chief of all languages. The prevalent languages of Rai and Ram, I know, from reflecting well on the matter, to be inferior to the Hindi... The Parsi is deficient in vocabulary, and cannot be tasted without Arabic condiments, as the latter is pure, and the former mixed, you might say that one was the soul, the other the body... The language of Hind is like the Arabic, in as much as neither admits of combination. If there is grammar and syntax in Arabic, there is no letter less of them in Hindi. If you ask whether there are the sciences of exposition and rhetoric, I answer that the Hindi is in no way deficient in those respects. Whoever possesses these three languages in his store, will know that I speak without error or exaggeration."

It may be appreciated that the *Hindawi* language as described by Amir Khusrau stood in contrast to the Persian and cannot be essentially associated with *Braj bhasa* which mostly developed later on. By Khusrau's time, the *Hindawi* in the Panjab and *Hindawi* as *khari bhaoli* in Delhi was written both in the *Devnagri* and Arabic scripts. The Arabic and more especially the Persian words were also assimilated in the *Hindawi* language. The *Hindawi* language was also used by Amir Khusrau as a poetic medium in *Khaliq-i-Bari*. It is only in the 17$^{th}$ century that the

Deccani poet Wajhi in his prose work *Sab Ras* quoted *doha* from Amir Khusrau's works which runs as:

> Oh Saqi, I have been moving like a hand-fan in my longing for union with you,
>
> I kept on burning slowly like *munj* (coconut straw hair) and you thought that I have been feigning.

However, few linguists have challenged that this is a Hindi verse of the 17th century and could not have been written by Amir Khusrau. All the same, it goes without saying that Khusrau did write poetry in *Hindawi* as is confirmed by Khusrau himself though it is very unfortunate that his *Hindawi Diwan* is no more available.

Khusrau takes pride in the learning and linguistic proficiency of the Indians. He observes that knowledge and learning were common and widespread amongst the Indian people and they could speak all the languages of the world clearly. The learned men came to study in India from all the parts of the world. Khusrau's observations stand in glaring contrast to those made by Al-Biruni in the early 11th century who characterised the Indians more insular in character and suffering from superiority complex. A comparative analysis of the works of Amir Khusrau and Al-Biruni would show that the latter's observations on the Indian society were circumscribed by limited scope in source-material and itinerary. Al-Biruni in his observations on the Indian society is not free from prejudice as his portrayal of the Hindu society is neither confirmed by the earlier Arab travellers nor by Amir Khusrau. In confirmity with the inherited tradition from the earlier Arab accounts, Khusrau states with pride the cultural heritage of India and highlights the then known facts that the science of 'Hindsa' and the numerical system originated in India, *Kalila wa Damna* (*Panchatantra*) was composed in India, the chess game was an Indian invention and that the chess and the *Damna* of Indian origin became popular with all other nations.

Music, dance and singing, feats of strength and endurance, jugglary and the *natt*-art occupied an important part of the cultural life in medieval India. Whereas some of the Arab travellers had given a peace-meal description of the cultural achievements of the Indians especially on the coastal areas and southern India, Amir Khusrau being musicologist of vast accomplishment covers much wider range with thorough technical grasp in technical detail and often compares the inherent Indian contribution to music with that of Khurasan and other parts of central Asia. In his long historical poems (*Mathnavis*), Amir Khusrau speaks of the Indian melodies and musical instruments which placed the Indian music in an enviable position. Imbued with symbolic imagery and metaphor, Khusrau gives a graphic description of the *Jabah*, *Alawan*, *Tala*, *Hindi*, *Mandala*, *Ajab-Rud*, *Chang*, *Rabab*, *Nay*, *Daff*, *Arghanun* and *Kansyatala*. One clearly discerns how the Sultans and the Indian Chiefs (Chief Zamindars) patronised groups of artists (*mandalis*) and held regular musical concerts (*Majlis*) where vocalists and instrumentalists displayed their skill. Amir Khusrau himself recited *ghazals* in tune with the music displayed especially for the occasion. Barani comments, "Amir Khusrau, the Chief Amir (*malikun-nudama*) of the Sultan's (Allauddin Khalji) *majlis* every day brought new *ghazals* in praise of moon-faced young boys and heart-enchanting beauties; these *ghazals* were recited while *saqis* (cup-bearers) invited the audience to drink amidst the music and balandishments of graceful beauties and the dancing of the fair girls... The man who did not feel intoxicated in such a *majlis* where the *huris* sat at the door and fairies (*paris*) swept their skirts along the ground, must have been entirely devoid of feeling - a stony man with a stony heart". In *Qiran-us-Sadain*, Khusrau himself describes the *majlis* where "the boon-companions raise their voice reciting *qasidah*, accompanied by the string-players. On one side the male performers hold their instruments and intoxicate everybody in the *majlis*; on the other side, the female musicians strike the chords touching all hearts in the assembly". The musical halls were specially designed for the artists and the audience where full decorum was observed. Khusrau, being himself a *Sufi*, participated in the mystical music which helped in the creation of *sama* and ecstatic state. The recitors of Quran (*mugriyan*), *qawwals* and the instrumentalists were an integral part of the Sufi *Khanaqahs* of the Chisti order of which Khusrau was a follower. Khusrau gives wonderful description of the Indian music in *Mathnavi-i-Deval Rani-Khizir-Khan, Mathnavi-Nuh-Sipehr, Qiran-us-Sadain* and *Aijaz-i-Khusrawi*. He runs into detail of the various species of instruments of Indian design, all with a low and high pitches arranged in their own ways. Proud of being an Indian and equally proud of the Indian music, in *mathnavi-i-nuh-sipehr*, he takes great pains to prove India's superiority over Khorasan and other countries. He comments, "the Indian music and the fire that burns heart and soul is superior to the music of any other country. Foreigners, even after 30 to 40 years stay in India cannot play single Indian tune correctly. The Indian music charms not only man but beasts also". Khusrau testifies to the test fact that the Indian music had never been in a static state and that assimilation had been its basic characteristic. This accounts for India's superiority over other nations. He states that several experts and masters in the art of song came from different lands to India and brought with them their excellent ways of melody and rhythm (*ravisha-i-niku*). The Indian musicians followed them up. Some of their musical compositions and instruments were adopted and popularised by the Indian themselves. Khusrau makes a direct reference to *Raga Todi* (*Turska Todi*) having traversed from the Chinese, Turkistan, and being adapted in India in a natural form. Many a musician and instrumentalist came to Delhi from Bakharz and Farghana. Khusrau refers to a *sur*-drenched melody of India which hyptonised the animals and drew the deer to the hunter's arrow. In *Aijaz-i-Khusrawi,* Khusrau throws a challenge to the Khurasanis and calls upon the Indian musicians - the nightingales of Delhi to flock around him - the Amir of all singing birds (of Delhi). Amir Khusrau's own contribution to the medieval Indian music was well acknowledged during the 17$^{th}$ century by the great musicologist, Nawab Saif Khan, the author of *Raga Darpan*. He mentions 12 *Ragas* and *Raginis* of Amir Khusrau. He as well attributes the composition of *ragas* to Amir Khusrau and gives their details.

Amir Khusrau gives sensuous description of the dance performance by the female dancers both in the *majils* of the royal court and the common streets. In the *majlis*, dance commenced with vocal accompainment. *Mujra* formed a splashing programme of the *majlis*. In *Rag-su-Sarud*, the female dancers came in *mandali* formation from two sides and were accompanied by the vocal music all through the dance performance. In Khusrau's own words, "the dancing-damsels had bodies built for dance alone, and their musky tresses trained to sweep the earth. When they thumped their feet, they provided a rhythemic lead to the fair boromed Venus, and when they gestured with their two hands, the entire assembly fell under their spell. When they wheeled and whirled, it was as if the time took a turn for the best, and all the formalities were shown the way out." Khusrau gives similar description about the melodies of the Hindu dancing girls in fairy-like Deogri apparent which "baffled Venus (the dancers of the skies), and brow-beat mercury." The *natt*-art had been quite popular in India since time immemorial and for the early medieval ages finds mention in the accounts of the Arab travellers. However, Khusrau's eye-witnessed description is moving and marvelous. He depicts the song, dance feats and spiral movement of the rope dancers on the top of the rope and in the air. The dancers played with the threads of their own lives.

An admirable trait in Amir Khusrau's character is that he had no racial or social prejudices. In an age which was ridden by ideas of high-born and low-born (*sharif* and *razil*) complexes, and when Muslims of Indian origin were looked down upon, Khusrau considered himself an Indian. Unlike Barani, he did not despise the low-born people. In his accounts, except for military and political reasons, he shows no contempt for the non-Muslims (*zimmis*) and their culture. Due to the impact of *Sufism* on his mind, his whole social philosophy is different aiming at sympathy and kindness to the low people. In *Ejaz-i-Khusravi* – an Insha work - Khusrau deals with various topics such as law, exegesis, tradition, morality, logic, philosophy, grammar and lexicography. Though it equally throws significant light on the socio-economic life, administration and institutions of some of the regions of the sultanate, Khusrau's ideas and social concept are clearly marked. He as well makes reflections on number of professions. He shows consideration to the labour class and prefers professions of a petty shopkeeper, a tailor and still more a cobbler to that of the nobility or their attendants attached to the royal court. Only the profession which was a source of the welfare of the majority of the human beings and not a source of harm and anxiety to them was worthwhile. It looks paradoxical that the greatest of the poets of the age advised his son to shun this career. Not that Khusrau had grown senile but it was an expression of the *Sufi* mind which gave vent to these feelings. Khusrau wrote to his son that he had wasted a considerable part of his life in the play of word and devoted himself whole-heartedly to adorn the pride of poetry with gems. He further upheld if at all one had to compose poetry, one should devote his faculty, imagination and genius to *Tawhid* (Unitarianism), praise of God and compose *ghazals* to the same end. Eulogy was of no use as praise of mean and low-natured men was not all rewarding. It was better to have contentment which was no less than kingship. An inscription on the Western Hall of Amir Khusrau's tomb brings out the true Khusrau as a *Sufi* and disciple of Sheik Fariduddin *Ganj-i-Shakar*. It runs:

> O thou, who hast the drink of love in thy cup
>
> And receivest messages from the friend, from moment to moment,
>
> The string (of pearls) of Farid has been arranged by thee,
>
> Hence the title Nizam – the stringer (of pearls),
>
> The humble servant Khusrau has attained eternity,
>
> Since with all his heart he became thy devotee.

# 4

# A Note on Source Material in Persian Language

The source-material in Persian language covering the period from the beginning of the 13th century to the closing years of the 18th century occupies an important place in the medieval Indian historiography. The Indian historical writing in Persian corresponds with the contemporary concept of historiography in the other Asiatic countries extending from India to Asia Minor. The Persian school differed from the concept of the Arab historians mostly in the respect that whereas the latter had covered comprehensive aspects of human society and institutions, the former emphasised the history of the sovereign and the court and viewed the political and socio-economic problems from the foot of the Royal throne.

During the Sultanate period (1195-1526 AD), most of the Persian chroniclers wrote not from the academic angle but from the practical end of either appeasing their religious conviction for winning immortal merit or pleasing the Sultan and the nobles under whose patronage they wrote. Hasan Nizam's *Taj-ul-Masair* deals with the history of the Sultans from Muhammad Ghori to Iltutmish (1191-1217 AD). It is written in verbose literary style as a panegyrist and underlines the Islamic nature of the government established by the Muslim Sultans. *Fakhr-i-Mudabbir*, *Bahr-nl-Ansab* and *Adab-ul-Harb* deal more with the *Ghaznavids* than with the early Delhi Sultans. They are more a record of stories written from the traditional "theologian" angle. Minhaju Siraj's *Tabqat-i-Nasiri* covering the early Sultanate period is written in a simple and factual style. Minhaj, belonging to the aristocratic class, viewed the events as a government servant and a politician belonging to an aristocratic family. Amir Khusrau (1253-1325) was primarily a poet and it was his aesthetic taste, love of religion, art and literature which permeate his poetic and prose literature. However, his five *diwans*, four historical *masnavis* and two prose works do form a part of contemporary historical literature which threw light on the political, topographical, social and cultural aspects of life. Though his works like *Ashiq*, *Nuh Sipihr*, *Qiran-ns-Saadam* and *Risail-i-Jiaz*, *Afazl ul-Fawad* have more cultural importance, his works, especially *Miftah*, *Khazain-ul-Futul* on *Tarikhi Alai* (in prose) and *Tughlaq-Nama* (poetry) contain significant information on the political history of the reigns of Alauddin Khalji and Ghiyas-uddin Tuglaq. Zia-ud-Din Barani's family was well connected with the ruling circles of the Delhi Court. His *Tarikh-i-Firuz Shahi* (written in 1358 AD) continues the work of Minhaj's chronicle and deals with the political history from the reign of Balban to the first six years of Firuz Tughluq. He based his works partly on hearsay statements and partly on personal observations. Barani's concept of history was governed by practical and didatic religious purposes. Though he emphasises truthfulness and honesty as the basis of historical writing, it cannot be denied that his history smacks of sympathies and antipathies based on his personal relations with the Tughluq Sultans. He had also his personal fads and prejudices. He had a fascination for the Turkish terminology used in the Persian literature. All these facts have to be borne in mind while understanding the historical data recorded by Barani. He had an equal interest in politico-religious philosophy of the State which found expression in his work *Fatawa-i-Jahandari*. Fakhr-i-Mudabbir' s *Adabul Harb wa Sh-Shujaah* is equally valuable for the study of the medieval political thought. Isami's *Futuh-ns-Salatin* (written in 1349-50) is an epic comprising the deeds of his Muslim rulers in India from the time of Mahmud of Ghazni to the Tughluq times (1350 AD). His account of the early Turkish rulers was based partly on the stories, legends and reports transmitted to him by his ancestors connected with the administration and partly on personal observances and experiences of his own times. Shams-uddin Siraj Afif 's *Tarikh- Firuz Shahi* (written in the closing years of the 14th century or early 15th century) comprises the biographical sketches and good qualities (*manaqib*) of the Tughluq rulers viz. Giasuddin Muhammad bin Tughluq and Firoz Shah written in an eulogistic style and traces the history down to the sack of Delhi by Timur. His history is based upon information gathered from private sources. Afif wrote history from theological angle and his *manaqib* literature is meant for the edification of the future generations. Yahya bin Ahmad Sirhindi's *Tarikh-i-Mubarak Shahi* (wtitten in 1434-35 AD) records the main military and political events from the early Turkish period to 1435 AD till 1351 AD. He relied on recorded historical versions of Minhaj, Barani and Amir Khusrau and thereafter merely on the evidence of the trustworthy narrators. This forms the main source for the study of the Sultans of the Sayyid dynasty. Yahya bin Ahmed's treatment of history is casual and different. He was a mere chronicler of events in a chronological order and viewed the historical development from the fortunes of Islam in India from the time of the Ghors to his own days.

Ali bin Muhmud al Kirmani (alias Shihab Hakim)'s *Maasir-i-Mahmud Shahi* is a contemporary history of Sultan Mahmud Khalji I (1436-1469 AD) of Malwa. It was an official history based on the official State papers and documents of the reign of Mahmud Shah Khalji. However, it is an important history of Malwa and gives useful clues for the social and political atmosphere.

*Tarikh-i-Nasirshah* (author unknown) covers some facts regarding history of the last years of the reign of Ghiyalh Shah and his opening years of Nasir Shah.

Muhammad Bihamad Khan's *Tarikh-i-Muhammadi* covers his Islamic history from the time of Prophet Muhammad down to 1438-39 AD. It is an important source for the regions of Malwa and Jaunpur.

For the Sultanate period, there is considerable religious literature viz. *tafsir*, *hadis* and *fiqh* which throws light on socio-religious and cultural life of the muslim community in India. The mystic literature comprising *malfuzat* and general works make an equal contribution in this respect. Of the *malfuz* literature, Amir Hasan Sijzi's *Fawaid-ul-Fuad* (1322 AD), Shaikh Hami-ud-din

Nagaur's *Sarur-us-Sadur* (around 1327 AD), Maulana Hamid Qalander's *Khair-ul-Majalis* (1356 AD), Amir Khurd's *Siyar-ul-Auliya* (13th century?) are rather outstanding. It is significant to observe that the above mentioned political chronicles, the literary and the religious works in Persian look upon the historical evolution from the ruling and the Islamic viewpoints and as such fail to take into account the socio-economic and the religious life of the Hindu population in India.

A few important sources, though written during the Mughal age, deal with the Afghan period. Rizd Allah's *Waqiat-i-Mushtaqi* covers by way of narration and anecdotes the Lodhis, early Mughals, the Sur dynasty and some provincial rulers of Malwa and Gujarat. Abd Allah's *Tarikh-i-Daudi* (written in Jahangir's reign) is a very sketchy history of the Lodhi and the Sur dynasties. Hasan Ali Khan's *Tarikh-Daulat-i-Sher Shahi* briefly deals with the Indian history from the establishment of the Muslim rule down to Humayun's and Sher Shah's reigns. It runs into details on the reign and administration of Sher Shah Suri. The author claims to be a contemporary of Sher Shah though authenticity in this respect has yet to be established. Abbas Sarwani's *Tufa-i-Akbar Shahi* (written on Akbar's order) deals in detail with the Sur dynasty. The author did not bank on any official documents but collected information from persons whom he considered to be reliable. Abbas Sarwani wrote about Sher Shah's administration in highly laudatory terms. He is more of a hero worshiper than an analytical historian. Ahmad Yadgar's *Tarikh-i-Salatin-i-Afghana* covers the history of the Lodhi and the Sur dynasties. Though the book was written around 1572-76 AD, some modifications were made later on. Niamat Ullah's *Makhzan-i-Afghana*, written in Jahangir's reign, deals with the history of the Afghans in India.

The historical writings during the Mughal age made a marked improvement on the Sultanate period in various respects. The Mughal historical concept attached less importance to divine causation and didactic approach. It tended to develop a more humanistic tendency underlying the socio-political factors and in some cases even developed secular outlook. The Mughal historical writings abound in political chronicles, biographies, itineraries, epistolary collections, *Dastur ul amls* (administrative manuals), official *Farmans*, orders and correspondence of various categories. Shaikh Zainuddin Khwafi's (alias Waf'ai) *Tarikh-i-Baburi* deals with just a year's (1525-26 AD) activities of Babur. He also translated Babur's memoirs from Chagatai Turkish into Persian under the title of *Waqiat-i-Baburi*. Babur's memoirs were also later on translated into Persian by Abdur Rahim *Khan-i-Khanan*. Mirza Haider Dughlat's (died in 1551) *Tarikh-i-Rashidi* covers the history of the Mongol Khans, the Amirs of Kashgar and some of the events of the reigns of Babur and Humayun. Gulbadan Begum's *Humayun Nama*, while dealing with Humayun's reign, throws light on the social and cultural aspects of the early Mughal rule. Jauhar's *Tazkirat-ul-Waqiat* gives contemporary account of Humayun's reign. Abul Fazl's *Akbar Nama* stands as a monumental study of Akbar's reign. Abul Fazl widened the scope of historical writing. He collected archival data from multifarious sources and recorded facts after critical examination. *Akbar Nama* records not only political history but also deals with the social, economic, administrative and institutional problems of the age. Abul Fazl was the first medieval historian who adopted rational and secular approach to history. The *Akbar Nama* was written in three parts. The first part covers the history of Akbar's ancestors till Humayun's reign. The second part covers the history of Akbar's reign up to the 46th regnal year. The *Ain-i- Akbari*, comprising the third part, covers chapters on the concept of Akbar's state, administration and an account of the Mughal *Subahs*. Later on, Sheikh Munawar, in his *Darj-un-Nafais* (1654 AD), made an excellent abridgement of *Akbar Nama*. *Haft Aqlim* is a geographical, historical and biographical encyclopaedia compiled in 1593 AD. Khawaja Nizam ud-Din Ahmad's *Tabqat-i-Akbari* records the general history of India till 1592-93 AD in a very clear-cut and analytical manner. He also deals with the history of the different provinces in a strict historical sequence. Mulla Abdul Qadir Badauni's *Muntakhabut-i-Tawarikh* is written in a subjective manner. He records the general history of India from the establishment of Delhi to his own times from the well-known sources. Being much less interested in political history, he records selective events and upholds his own concept of the Shariat against the liberal policy and administrative reforms of Akbar. *Haj* Muhammad Arif Qandhari's *Tarikh-i-Akbari* (alias *Tarikh-i-Qandhari*) covers Akbar's reign upto 1580 AD in a very clear and straightforward style. To commemorate the one thousand years after Prophet Muhammad's death, *Tarikh-i-Alfi* was written by a board of scholars, especially Mulla Ahmad Tattawi and Asaf Khan Jaffar Beg, in a simple and easy language. The history was brought down to 1588-89 AD but none of the existing manuscripts cover the period beyond 1588-89 AD. Mir Alauddaula Qazwini's *Nafaisul Maasar* (1573 AD) covers some of the works of the poets, writers and historical personages of Akbar's age. It also briefly covers the Mughal history from Babur's reign down to Akbar's period till 1573 AD. Shah Abdul Haq Muhaddas Dehlvi's *Tarikh-i-Haqq* is a brief general history of India from the Turkish period till 1596 AD. *Tarikh-i-Khandan-i Timariya*, by an unknown author, covers the history of the Mughals from Timur's times down to the 22nd regnal year of Akbar's reign. Muhammad Qasim Hindu Shah Astrabadi (alias Firishta)'s *Tarikh--i-Firishta* (or *Gulshan-i-Ibrahimi*) covers the general history of India till 1606-7 AD. Firishta has given useful information about the provincial kingdoms. As Firishta wrote from Deccan, it is all the more significant for understanding the history and viewpoint of the Deccan kingdoms.

Jahangir's autobiography *Tuzuk-i-Jahangiri*, covering till 19th regnal year of his reign, is extremely useful for understanding his character and the events of his reign. During Jahangir's period, Ala-ud-Din Isfahani (alias Mirza Nathan) wrote his memoirs, *Babaristan-i-Ghaibi*, which throws extremely useful light on the process of Mughal conquest of Bengal and the working of the Mughal administration in this region. Mutamad Khan's *Iqbalnama-i-Jahangiri*, comprising three portions, covers the history of the Mughals, the reigns of Akbar and Jahangir. Though for the earlier portions, it is an abridgement from the known Mughal sources, it is an extremely important contemporary record for Jahangir's reign.

The official historians of Shah Jahan's reign tried to emulate Abul Fazl's way of writing. Muhammad Amir bin Abdul Husain Qazwini (alias *Amina-i-Qazwini*)'s *Padshah Nama* records the early history of Shah Jahan and the first ten years of his reign. As Qazwini could not come up to the mark, the task was assigned to Abdul Hamid Lahori, who in his *Padshah Nama* wrote a detailed history of the first twenty years of the reign. Muhammad Warris continued the work and in his *Padshah Nama* covered ten years' history ($21^{st}$ to $30^{th}$ year).

Of the non-official histories of Shah Jahan's reign, Muhammad Sadiq (alias Sadiq Khan)'s *Tawarikh-i-Shah Jahani*, covering the period 1627-1657 AD, deserves special notice as a reliable account especially by the Deccan administrative problems. Jalal-ud-din Tabatbai's *Padshah Nama* covers first four years' history ($5^{th}$ to $8^{th}$ regnal years) of his reign. Muhammad Sadiq's *Subaha-i-Sadiq* (1638 AD) is a comprehensive historical and geographical work. Inayat Khan's *Shah Nama* (alias *Mulakhas*) is a mere abridgement of Lahori's *Padshah Nama*. Chander Bhan Brahaman's writings make a definite contribution both in the *Insha* and historical literature. His *Munshaat-i-Brahaman* throws light on the activities of the historical personages. The *Guldasta-i-quwaid ul Saltanat* and *Chahar Chaman* serve as an important source for Shah Jahan's daily routine, the working of the Mughal administration and the geographical details of the Mughal *Subahs*. The letters of Sheikh Jalal Hissari and Balkrishan Bahramin included in a manuscript entitled *Maktubat-i-Muzaffar Khan wa Gawalior Nama* (Shah Jahan reign) and Mir Abul Hasan Alamgir's *Muraqqat-i-Hasan* (Aurangzeb's reign) throw significant light on the working of the Mughal administration. Mirza Muhammad Kazim's *Alamgir Nama* (1681 AD) covers the first ten years of Aurangzeb's reign. It is written in a panegyric style. Muhammad Saqi Mustaid Khan's *Alamgir Nama* is an official history of the entire reign of Aurangzeb and was completed in1708-1710 AD. The first ten years are an abridgement of *Alamgir Nama* and the history of the other years is recorded from the State papers and personal recollections Of the non-official histories, Abul Fazl mamuri continued Muhammad Sadiq's work and covered the entire reign of Aurangzeb. Sujan Rai Bhandari's *Khulasatu-t-Tawarikh* is a general history of India and covers Aurangzeb's reign till 1695-96 AD. It is very significant in its account of the Mughal *Subahs* and at times supplies more useful information on the topography and socio-economic life of the various regions than the *Ain-i-Akbari*. Bhaktawar Khan's *Mirat-i-Alm* is a general history of mankind and covers the Mughal history till 1666 AD. Amir Bhakt forms a part of the *Mirat-i-Alm*. Bhim Sen's *Nuskha-i-Dilkusha* is an extremely valuable journal especially for the military activities and the administrative problems of the Deccan during Aurangzeb's reign. Isar Das Nagar's *Futuhat-i-Alamgiri*, Aurangzeb's own correspondence embodied in *Raqaimi-Kariam*, *Kalimat-i-Taiyabati* (collected by Inayatullah Khan), *Ahkam-i-Alamgiri* (*Ibid*), *Ramz o Ishara ha-i Alamgiri* (collected later on) throw a great deal of light on the administrative problems of the reign.

A few good chronicles produced in the Deccan cover the history of the Deccan, especially the Qutab Shahi dynasty of Golkonda. Sayyid A.P. Tabatabai's *Burhan-i-Maasir* (1596 AD) dedicated to Burhan Nizam Shah II (1591-95) deals with the Bahmanis of Gulbarga, Bidar and the Sultans of Ahmadnagar. The author claims to have drawn upon thirty-two works and to have collected first-hand information for the last phase of his account. This is one of the most important chronicles of medieval India for the study of the Adil Shahis, Nizam Shahis and the Qutb Shahis. Mir Rafi-ud-Din's *Tazkirat-ul-Muluk* (1615 AD) provides a good account of the Adil Shahis of Bijapur and the Qutab Shahis though some portions are devoted to the Bahmanis and the Mughals from Timur to Akbar. *Tarikh-i-Qutb Shahi* and *Maasir-i-Qutb Shahi* (1616 AD) give a detailed history of the Qutb Shahi dynasty. Apart from the political facts, it also gives a comprehensive account of the public works and the patronage of literature by Qutb Shahis. Mahmud bin Abdullah Nishapuri brought the narrative of the account of this book till 1629 AD. Mirza Nizamuddin Ahmad's *Haqiqat-u-Salatin* narrates a voluminous history of the first nineteen years of the reign of Abdullah Qutb Shah (1626-72). It is more like a diary of the Qutb Shahi Court and it gives a fairly good account of the social life and the administration of the kingdom. Ali ibn Taiful al-Butami's *Haqaiq-us-Salatin fi Kalami-i-Khawaqin* (1681 AD), though mostly a compendium of Persian poetry, contains letters written by the kings of India and Iran as well as life histories and letters written by certain ministers, judges, *amirs* and learned men from both North India and the Deccan.

Apart from these chronicles, there is an important collection of *Farmans* and letters embodied in *Makatib Sultan Abdullah Qutb Shah ba nam Dara Shikoh Waghariah* (collection up to 1662 AD), *Araiz wa Ittihad Namajat wa Faramin Abdullah Qutb Shah* (collection up to 1662 AD), and *Insha-i-Abdul Ali Khan Taliqani.* The correspondence embodied in these manuscripts throws a flood of light on the relations of the Qutab Shahi rulers of Golkonda with the Bijapur State and the Mughals. The 18th century works viz. Mansa Ram's *Maasar-i-Nizami* and Yusuf Muhammad Khan's *Tarikh-i-Fathiyah* narrate Nizam-ul-Mulk Asaf Jah's relations with the Mughal State and view the events mostly from the angle of Asaf Jah's. A few other provincial histories written during the Mughal age supply very useful information. Abu Turab Wali's *Tarikh-i-Gujrat* gives an authentic account of the Gujarat history from 1536 to 1584 AD. It comprises the author's eyewitness account of the Mughal conquest of Gujarat. Sikander bin Muhammad's *Mirat- i-Sikandari* (compiled in 1617-18) records the history of Gujarat up to 1591 AD. Jahangir bears testimony to the author's thorough acquaintance with the Gujarat history. For Sindh, Mir Muhammad Masum's *Tarikh-i-Sindh* covers up to 1599-1600 AD and Mir Tahir Muhammad Nisyani's *Tarikh-i-Tahiri* brings the narration down till 1609 AD. Yusuf Mirak's *Mahzar-i-Shah Jahani* (1634 AD) gives detailed administrative history of the territories of Sehwan, Bhakkar and Thatta. Shihabuddin Talish's *Fathiya-i-lbriya* gives a detailed account of Mir Jumla's campaign in Assam and Cooch Behar.

During the 18th century, considerable religious literature as commentaries on the Quran, Hadis, jurisprudence and mysticism was produced. However, even though the main interest of the historians remained political in nature, they equally serve an important source for the reconstruction of the socio-economic history of the period. Kamraj's *Azam al harb* (1708) gives a detailed account of Azam Shah's reign. *Bahadur-Shah Nama* is an official history of Bahadur Shah's first two years. Iradat Khan's *Tarikh-i-Iradat Khan* (1714) is a good biography of the seven years (1707-1714 AD). Similarly, Mirza Muhammad has recorded his memoirs and contemporary events from 1705 to 1719 AD. Muhammad Hadi's *Haft Gulshan* is a province-wise general history of India till 1719 AD. Khwafi Khan's *Muntakhab-ul-Lubab* covers the Mughal history from Babur's times to 1731 AD. Khwafi Khan drew heavily upon Muhammad Sadiq Khan and Abul Fazl Mamuri's histories. However, it is very significant for the Mughal-Maratha relations, the early 18th century politics and the problems of the land revenue administration. In his evaluation of data, Khwafi does submit the evidence to thorough enquiry. Muhammad Qasim Ibrat Hussain Lahori's *Ibratnama* (1722-23) creditably records the Mughal history from the death of Aurangzeb to 1721 AD. Another author, also named Muhammad Qasim's *Ahwal-ul-Khawaqin*, traces the history of Aurangzeb's successors till 1739 AD in an analytical manner. It is a good commentary on the political and economic decline of the Mughal Empire. Mir Ashan Ijad's *Farrukh Siyar Nama* narrates the early history of this Emperor whereas his *Tarikh-i-Futuhat-i-Asafi* is in verse and narrates the conquests of Asaf Jah. Muhammad Shafi Warid's *Mirat-i-Waridat* is a narrative story of the Indian Mughal rule till 1733-34 AD. Some of the *Insha* literature of this period is quite informative. Munshi Daya Ram's *Balmukand Nama* comprises important political letters from 1713 to 1720 AD. Anand Ram Mukhlis's *Mirat-ul-Islah* is an excellent dictionary of Persian terms. This dictionary explains the administrative and revenue terminology with interesting historical illustrations. Tazkirah-i-Anand Ram Mukhlis records the war history of Muhammad Shah with Nadir Shah. *Safar Nama-i-Anand Ram Mukhlis* (or *Roznamcha-i-Safar* 1751 AD) and *Manshurat-i-Anand Ram* (1739) throw considerable light on the socio-economic and political activities of the times. Shah Nawaz Khan's *Mirat-i-Aftab Nama* (1765-66 AD) deals with the beginning of the mankind, the Arabs and the general history of India. Ghulam Ali Khan's *Muqaddimah-i-Shah Alam Namah* and Ghulam Husain Chaturman Kaisth Saksena's *Chahar Gulshan* (or *Akhbar al-nawadir*) is a general history of India till 1759-60 AD but it gives detailed topographical account of the *Subahs*. Shah Nawaz Khan's *Maasir ul Umra* gives detailed biographical sketches of the Mughal dignitaries. Kanwar Prem Kishor Firaqi's *Waqai Alm Shahi* (1784 AD) gives an excellent insight into the late 18th century North India politics and its impact on the socio-economic life. Jhan Tabatabai Hasani's *Siyaral-mutakhkhirin* gives a detailed history of the Mughals from Aurangzeb's death (1707) to 1754 and 1781 AD respectively. Lachmi Narain Shafiq's *Haqiqat hai Hindustan* (1789-90) gives an excellent historical and topographical account of India. It also contains detailed statement of the revenues of India.

The 18th century is equally rich in production of provincial histories. The most important work is Ali Muhammad Khan's *Mirat-i-Ahmadi* which traces the history of Gujarat from the earliest times to 1761 AD. The author drew upon not only the well-known chronicles but relied upon the official documents for the Mughal Age, which he has copiously quoted. The *Mirat's* Supplement gives an excellent account of the topography, administrative units and revenues of Gujarat. Aitmad Ali Khan's *Mirat-ul-Haqiqat* is also written on the pattern of *Mirat-i-Ahmadi*. The author has, however, extended the scope as to deal with the economic conditions of the provinces of Gujarat, Delhi, Agra and Allahabad as well as the administrative problems created by the Maratha intrusions in the Mughal territories. Mir Ali Sher Qani Tattawi's *Tuhfat al-Kiram* (1766-67 AD), though mostly a general history of Sindh, also gives a topographical account of the region. Ghulam Husain Salim Zaidpuri's *Riyasal Salatin* (1787-88 AD) is a good general history and geographical account of the territories of Bengal, Bihar and Orissa. Raja Kalyan Singh's *Khulasat-al-tawarikh* comprises a general history of Mughal India along with a detailed account of the regions of Bengal and Orissa from 1760 to 1783 AD.

Apart from these well-known sources, there is an extremely important collection of the Persian manuscripts of the 18th century available at the German libraries viz. *Universitatsbibliothek* (University Libraries) of Bonn, Tubingen, *Bayerische Staatsbibliothek*, Muenchen (Bavarian State Library, Munich), *Westdeutsche Bibliothek*, Marburg and *Staatsbibliothek* (State Library), Berlin (East). Some of the important manuscripts are *Nuskha Hai Bar Kafiat-i-Subah Behar*; *Nuskha Majmuahat*: *Sawalat-i- malik-i-Zamin Kiast az Mister John Shore*; *Dar Bab-r*

*Nuskha Sarusa Hukm*; *Tawarikh-i-Badshan-i-Hind az ibtda-i-Shah Timur Baghayat Shah Alam*; *Majmuha-i-Mutfarika*; *Akhbar ul Sadip dar Kafait Darj Ast*. The real importance of these manuscripts lies in the detailed and well-documented analytical discussion on the 18th century administrative history and land revenue problems of the territories of Bengal, Bihar and Orissa.

The medieval Indian studies may not be confined to the above mentioned chronicles, memoirs, geographical works and epistolary literature alone. There are important *Dasturulamls* (administrative and accountancy manuals) which throw much light on the Mughal administration. Of the many such available manuscripts are *Dasturulaml Navsindagi* (Shah Jahan's reign); *Makhizan-i-Ihetsab maaruf Dasturulaml* (1659-60 AD), *Dasturulaml-i-Alamgiri* (3rd regnal year of Aurangzeb); Jagat Rai Shujai Kayastha Suksena and Udai Chand's *Farang-i-Kardani* written in 1679 and 1699 AD respectively; *Zawabit-i Alamgiri* (post 1691 AD); Munshi Nand Ram's *Siyaq Nama* (1694-96 AD); *Khulasatu-s Siyaq*, (1703 AD); *Dasturul aml-i-Todar Mal Shahjahani* (1708 AD); *Dehi bedehi Subbajat-i Deccan* (alias *Dehighara*) Hidayatullah Bihari's *Hiddayat-alQawaid* AD); Jawahar Nath's *Dasturulaml-i Bekas* (1732 AD); Daulat Rai's *Dasturulaml-i Siyaq* (1769-70 AD); Munshi Thakur Lal's *Dasturulaml-i Shahanshahi* (1771 AD); Munshi Bijai Singh's *Dasturul Insha* (1772-73 AD) and Ghulam Husain's *Dastur Nama* (1791-92 AD).

At present, there is also vast archival source-material in Persian which throws a flood of light on the socio-economic life of the country especially from the 16th to the 18th centuries. Though the Mughal *Farmans*, *Sanads* and *madad-i-maash* (charitable and grants) documents are available at numerous places, the bulk of this valuable collection has been concentrated at three archival centres in India, viz. the Rajasthan State Archives, Bikaner; the Andhra Pradesh Archives, Hyderabad; and the National Archives of India, New Delhi. The Rajasthan Archives has a mine of materials. They comprise various Mughal *Farmans*, *Sanads*, news bulletins of the Mughal Court (*Kagzat-Akhbarat-i Darbar Maula*), *pargana atsatta* documents, miscellaneous correspondence of the provincial and *pargana* officials (*khatut-i*

*Ahalkaran Mutfarik kagzat-i Ahalkaran*) and reports of the *Vakils* of the Maharajas. These documents relate to a number of *Subahs* of North India during the Mughal age. Similarly for the Deccan *subahs*, the Mughal documents (*Daftar-i-Mughaliya*) from the reign of Shah Jahan to the Asafi Jahi regime form an important part of the collection at Hyderabad. Some fragments of the Mughal archives were brought together by the British Indian Government and are now preserved with the so-called Mutiny Papers at the National Archives, New Delhi. The National Archives in its central collection has also preserved the *Akhbarat* (news bulletins) sent by the *Waqai nawis*' of the English East India Company to the Governor General in Council. These documents cover the late 18$^{th}$ and early 19$^{th}$ centuries. They are extremely useful in understanding the socio-economic and political trends of the times. Apart from the miscellaneous collection, the National Archives of India has recently acquired an important Inayat Jang Collection comprising records relating to the Mughal and Asaf Jahi administration of the Deccan (1658-1774 AD).

# 5

# Source Material for the Agrarian History of Mughal India

With an ever-increasing emphasis on the study of the socio-economic structure of the medieval society, it has become imperative to analyse the details of the agrarian policy and land revenue administration under the Mughals. In fact, these two problems have been perennial in the Indian administration and governance as the income from land has been the financial mainstay of the rulers. The stability and solvency of the State has always depended upon the sound and well-balanced land revenue system. Besides, India being mostly an agricultural country in the medieval age, the condition of the overwhelming majority of the masses depended upon the condition of the *Ryots* who formed the backbone of the Indian society. This has continued to be the outstanding feature of the Indian economy until today. Equal in importance is the agrarian administration from the viewpoint of Public Administration which left an important legacy to the later Mughal age and even though modified under the stress of the later Mughal times, it was inherited by the early British government in India.

The early British authorities in India, ever since the time of Warren Hastings, were confronted with the problem of knowing the Mughal agrarian system but they were misguided – partly by the system in existence in the 2nd half of the 18th century and partly by their own way of looking into the problem with some preconceived notions. Moreover, they depended upon only *Ain* and the other few available Persian manuscripts with all their lack of proper knowledge of Persian language. In the first quarter of this century, Moreland, singly and jointly with Ali, examined the system mostly based on *Ain-i-Akbari*, *Akbar Nama* and other chronicles available from the reign of Akbar to Aurangzeb. The accounts of the foreign travellers were also casually referred to by Dr. P. Saran, in his "Provincial Government" and Dr. I. H. Qureshi in his articles mostly treaded, the beaten path differing in the interpretation of the text of the sources utilised by Moreland. Dr. Irfan Habib, in his recent articles on the "Zimmidars" and "The Agrarian causes of the downfall of the Mughal Empire" has, for the first time, extended the scope of source-bibliography by various chronicles recently discovered, Manuscripts of *Insha*, some of the *Dastur ul amls*, accounts of the foreign travellers and the Early Factory Records. I have, myself, written a few articles based on the original documents and *Dastur ul amls* and other recently discovered Persian manuscripts which have been listed below.

I. In the source material, undoubtedly *Ain-i-Akbari*, *Akbar Nama*, Badauni's *Muntkhb-ut-Tawarikh* and other contemporary chronicles from reign of Akbar to Aurangzeb continue with their original importance. But the interpretation of many a technical terms and languages, hitherto wrongly analysed by the previous scholars, has become easier and clearer in the light of the recently discovered *Dastur ul amls* and original documents which explain and exemplify the various terms and vocabulary. To the chronicles already utilised can be added a few more which are quite useful for understanding the agrarian policy. For the early Mughal period, *Tuzuk-i-Baburi*, *Tarikh-i-Baburi* by *Zamiud Din Khawaf* provide us with details of topographical, geographical and various means of irrigation of land. *Tarikh-i-Rashidi* of Mirza Haider gives description of the land of Kashmir. For Akbar's reign, a note may be taken of *Tarikh-i-Arif Qandhari* by Haji Mohammad Arif Qandhari, *Darj-un-Nafais* by Sheikh Munawwar bin Shaikh Abdul Karim Abbas, *Nafais-ul-Moassaf* by Alla-ud-Daula bin Hussaini, *Sawnih-i-Akbari* by Amir Haider Hussaini Wasti Bilgrami and *Tarikh-i-Humayun Shahi* by Alla Dad Faizi-Sir Hindu. For Jahangir's reign, *Iqbal nama-i-Jahangiri* of Muhamad Khan, Jahangir's own Memoirs and Mirza Nathan's *Baharistan-i-Ghiabi* are important. For Shahjahan's reign, apart from the

*Badshah Namahs* of Abdul Hamid Lahori and Muhammad Warris, *Pad Shah Nama* of Mohammad Amin Qazwini, *Tawarik-i-Shah Jahani* by Mohammad Sadiq and *Shah Jahan Namah* by Mohammad Salil *Kamloh* are quite significant. For the reign of Aurangzeb, *Khulas-ul-Tawarikh* by Sujjan Rai Bhandari of Batala, *Lub-twarikh* by Rai Bindra Ban, *Tarikh-i-Abul Fazi Mamuri*, *Tarikh-i-Dilkusha* by Inayat-ullah Kambo Lahori, *Nuskha-i-Dilkusha* by Bhim Sen, *Fateh Ibratyia* by Shahab-ud-din Talish provide with factual condition of the various classes. For later Mughals, *Mantakhali-u-Luliah* by Mohammad Hashmi Khwaji Khan, *Tarikh-i-Chahar Gulshan Mohammad Shal* by Rai Chattar Mal, Kaisth Saxena, *Chahar Gulshan* by Chander Bhan Kaiseth Saxena are valuable. In the provincial histories for Akbar's reign, *Tarikh-i-Sind* by Mohammad Masum and for the later times, *Mirat-i-Ahemedi* by Ali Mohammad Khan are significant.

II. **Insha**: In this category, various letters and correspondence pertaining to the agrarian conditions are recorded. Special note may be taken of

1. *Mukatib-i-Abul Fazl* or *Insha-i-Abul Fazl*
2. *Insha-Harkarn*
3. *Insha-i-Abdul Latif*
4. *Muraqaat-i-Hasan* by Mir Abul Hassan Alamgiri
5. *Majmuaa-i-Munshiat* (No. 211 State Library, Rampur. Important letters written by *Munshies* from Abul Fazl to Aurangzeb)
6. *Muktubat-i-khan Jahan Muzaffar Khan* by Jalal Hissari and Balkrishan Braham (Shabjahan's reign)
7. *Insha-i-Roshan Kulam*
8. *Rakiam Karaim*: Personal letters of Aurangzeb
9. *Kalmiat-i-Taibat*: Letters of Aurangzeb
10. *Ahkam-i-Alamgiri* by Inayat Ullah
11. *Guldasta-i-Sukhn* by Jut Parkash. K.B. Patna
12. *Ruqaat-i-Nawazish Khan* by Nawazigh Khan, Governor of Kashmir from September 1705. Copy of Late Sir J.N. Sarkar

13. *Hafi Anjman*, compiled by Adhiraj Munshi Rustam Hali in 1211 H. These are the letters of Mirza Raja Jai Singh, Sir J. N. Sarkar's copy.
14. *Durr al Ulm*, Bodlein, Oxford.
15. *Nigar Nama Munshi*
16. *Karan Nama* of Chathmal "Hindu"
17. *Riaz ud Wadad*

III. *Dastur ul amls* — now *Dastur ul aml* of Maklizan ul Ibetsab. List attached.

1. The working of the land revenue administration and the agrarian policies can be well noted from the importance of *Dastul ul amls* of the reign of Shah Jahan and Aurangzeb.
2. *Raqba bandi* documents of Akbar's reign – Patna
3. *Deli Jhara* and *Deli Bedebi Sulibajat-i-Deccan*
4. Jaipur Archives – Mine of virgin original material has been thrown open to the scholars.
5. Hyderabad, *Daftar-i-Diwani* documents for the reign of Shahjahan and Aurangzeb.
6. Allahabad Documents
7. Behar Documents at Patna
8. Darga Sharif documents at Ajmer
9. Binai documents
10. Private family documents in District Ajmer concerning Muqaddam's position
11. Original *Farmans*, *Sanads* etc. scattered at different places
12. Abundance of Land Revenue Literature of the early 18$^{th}$ century —Manuscripts on various agrarian and land revenue problems in the Berlin Library. Copies also available in the Museum.
13. Accounts of the foreign travellers, especially Sir Thomas Roe, Pelsaert, Geleynssen Fryer, Dr. John, Fathers St. Monstratte and St. Xavier, Mannique, Manucci, Bernier, Travernier, Peter Mundy, F. Pyrad, and Norris.
14. Early Factory Records of the E.I.Co.

# 6

# Agrarian System of the Punjab during the 18$^{th}$ Century

During the last few decades, the Indian historiography has attached considerable importance to the socio-economic life of the people. For the medieval period, of its manifold aspects, the agrarian system covering the whole of North India or South India or at the regional levels has attracted the attention of the historians who have to underline the current and cross currents of the political, social, economic and geographical factors and formation of institutions which explain the variety of the way of the life of the people within the country, more especially in a period of change. Regional agrarian analysis is a fruitful exercise as it provides opportunity for the exploitation of regional source material of multifarious nature, which has essentially to be linked with the larger landscape at all India level. For the medieval age, worthwhile research has been done covering the agrarian system of the Mughals but it has been by and large confined to the closing years of this 17$^{th}$ and early 18$^{th}$ centuries. The 18$^{th}$ century involving the disintegration of the Mughal Empire has been looked mostly from the political angle and no serious work on the agrarian history has been attempted so far.

The Punjab under Maharaja Ranjit Singh and his successors (1799-1849) attracted great attention on the part of the British and the Indian historians. This is essentially due to the fact that the British took over the territories of the *Dar-ul-Sultanate* of Lahore from the Sikh rulers and were tempted to write past history of the Sikh community. The Settlement Reports of his various districts of the Punjab prepared by the English revenue officers are replete with the revenue practices under the Sikh rulers in the Punjab. Recently too a research-oriented work has been produced on the Agrarian System of the Sikhs (by Indu Banga) covering by and large the above period. However, for the 18th century, a number of writers have laid emphasis only on the political and religious aspects of Punjab whereas the agrarian aspects remain completely neglected so far.

The identity and territorial jurisdiction of the Punjab during the Mughal age as well as under Ranjit Singh is very clear from the contemporary sources. The territorial boundaries of the Punjab extend from river Sutlej in the east to river Indus (Sindh) in the North West and comprised five *doabs*. The earmarked mountainous regions in the north of the *doabs* formed part of the respective *doabs*. Apart from this, some hilly regions to the north of Jalandhar not covered in the *doabs* entitled *Berun-i-Panjnand* also formed part of the Punjab. The Bari *doab* with headquarters at Lahore formed core of the Punjab. During the Mughal age, the territories between the river Jamuna and Sutlej, the Cis-Sutlej regions, the trans-Sutlej territories to the West of Delhi formed parts of the *Sarkars* of Delhi, Hisar Firozah and Sirhand of *Subah* Delhi. Nothwithstanding the fact that during the course of the 18th century, many a sikh *Zamindari*, *misl* and chieftainship were established in the above mentioned territories, they continued to be well within the jurisdiction of *Subhas* Delhi. Under Ranjit Singh too, the Chief of Malwa and Sirhind being under the British protection remained outside the territorial boundaries of the kingdom of Lahore. In fact, considerable change in the territorial concept and traditional boundaries was effected by the British after the occupation at the kingdom of Lahore from 1846 to 1912. In fact, the Punjab as it stood on the eve of the partition of India in 1947 had been formed by the British Indian Government purely due to administrative expediency for the stability of its colonial rule in India.

The 18th century Punjab politics assumed triangular character with three main contestants viz. the Mughals, the Sikh *Misls* and Durranis of Kabul. During the first of the 18th century, the Mughal government had its hold over the administrative pattern and agrarian landed classes. But during the second half of the century, the Mughal Sovereign rights over the Punjab territories had practically vanished and the Durrani rule of Kabul had steeped in. Apart from the occupation of Kashmir and Multan, the Durranis claimed political sovereignty over the Punjab territories and realed *peskash* more or less on the Mughal pattern. However, the Durrani rule was rather intermittent and the *misls* always tried to assert as defacto power. During the last decades of the 18$^{th}$ century, even though the Durranis continued to claim political sovereignty, their affective administration control was minimal. The Durranis continued to claim only *de-jure* political rights.

The 18$^{th}$ century is a crucial period in the agrarian history of the Punjab. The socio-political forces shook the foundation of the Mughal Empire to the point of dismemberment. This had great impact on the regional polity and agrarian set-up with mutual reaction. A comparison of the dominant *Zammidari* clans as known from the *Ain-i-Akbari* (late 16$^{th}$ century) with the dominant clannish order noticeable from the 18$^{th}$ century sources shows considerable change and reshuffling in the dominant and suppressed clannish order in respect of the enjoyment of the surplus produce and land rights. At the same time, the emergence of the Sikh *misls* based on traditional territorial *Zammindari* pattern with landed hierarchy, the suppression of the other landed castes into *khud-kashta riaya* and *muzarian* for the realization of the revenue and extraction of the surplus produce, the inter-*misl* rivalry and mutual welfare that tempt on the part of the powerful *misl* for the establishment of its suzerainty in the name of the *Panth*, the realisation of the *malia* (*mamla*), *nazrana* etc. from the suppressed *misls* and chiefs is a continuous feature till the emergence of the Lahore kingdom under Ranjit Singh by the end of the 19$^{th}$ and early 19$^{th}$ century.

The proposed work would cover in detail the geographical features, the clannish character and the agricultural production of various regions of the Punjab, the varying land revenue practice and classification of lands, the means of irrigation, methods of land revenue assessment, magnitude of the demand on the *riaya* and its impact on the peasantry of various categories, trade in agricultural produce, the landed classes and their mutual relations, the land rights and the concept of the village community; the agrarian administration under the Mughals, Durranis and the Sikh *misldars;* the land revenue assignments-*Jagirdari* system and the relations grants; the *Zamindari* pattern, the relations of the Chieftains in the hilly regions as well plains with the suzerain rulers viz. the Mughal, Durranis and the Misadars respectively, and the emergence of the *misls* into Lahore Kingdom under Ranjit Singh and their mutual landed relations. In the overall analysis, emphasis would be laid on the elements of traditional forms of regional polity, administration and economic system. At the same time, new aspects in these respects would be clearly underlined.

The source material both contemporary as well as covering upto the mid-19$^{th}$ century is of multifarious nature. Apart from the Persian chronicles, *dasturalamls*, (geographical accounts. Travelogues) both in Persian and English, the biographies and memoirs of the officials, there is a vast archival source material in Persian, Rajasthani, Marathi, Hindi and Tankri available at Bhuri Singh Museum, Chamba (Himachal Pradesh); State Archives Patiala (Punjab); Rajasthan State Archives, Bikaner (Rajasthan); Peshwa Daftar, Pune (Maharashtra); Itihas Shshotak Mandal (Pune); National Archives of India, New Delhi; Haryana State Archives, Chandigarh; Punjab Secretariat Library, Chandigarh; Afghanistan State Archives, Kabul; British Museum and Indian Office, Library (UK) and various private collections which cover many aspects of the financial administration and agrarian system of the Punjab. The present writer has already highlighted the importance of the archival source material of the Bhuri Singh Museum, Chamba and published a series of research articles (in the proceedings of the Punjab History conferences which underline the relationship between the Punjab Hill Chiefs (Chamba as a case study) and the Mughal state, the Durranis of Kabul and the Lahore Kingdoms of Ranjit Singh.

As a matter of fact, for the evaluation of the source material for the 18$^{th}$ century Punjab, it has to be essentially borne in mind that Ranjit Singh did not inherit an established State and various regions of the Punjab were conquered by him during the first two decades of the 19th century. As such, the works produced during the Sikh regime–whether commissioned by Lahore Durbar or English East Indian Company or independent writers– provide a detailed description of the various regions in respect of agricultural life and agrarian relations which were in vogue at the time of the incorporation of these territories by the State established by Ranjit Singh. In fact, a number of historical accounts in the Persian language and a few in Gurmukhi were prepared both by the Hindu and Muslim chronicles. The students of the Punjab history are fortunate to have inherited all these sources to which can be added the original archival sources material comprising the *Khalsa Darbar* records, the official documents and correspondence of various categories (in Persian) under the Bhandari collection available at State Archives Patiala give clear insight into the revenue practices inherited by the administration of Ranjit Singh from the erstwhile chieftain and *misl* territories. Similarly, the *Persian Akbharart* addressed by the news writers to the English East Company provide a detailed description on the subject and cover later half of this century and first few decades of the 19th century. The English reports of multifarious nature covering the periods before and after the annexation of the Punjab equally provide a mine of information in this regard. Undeniably, the information available from the English records pertaining to the period after the annexation and the various assessment and settlement reports produced in the second half of the 19th century have to be scrutinized and analysed with a note of caution while clearly underlining the nature of change affected from one phase to another from pre-Ranjit Singh to the period of Ranjit Singh and his successors and finally the post annexation British rule in the Punjab. A professional historian of agrarian history has to be fully conversant with the connotation of the technical revenue terminologies prevalent during these various phases which would go a long way in the proper analysis and understanding of the Agrarian system of the Punjab during the 18th century.

7

# Source Material for the Mughal and $18^{th}$ Century Punjab

The source-material for the Mughal age and $18^{th}$ century Punjab is vast indeed. A political and administrative history can be well constructed on the basis of chronicles and the well-known autobiography of Babar and Jahangir. But for the detailed account of administration and socio-economic life of Punjab, we have to bank on a number of other sources as well. Of course, *Ain-i-Akbari* though a supplement volume to the *Akbarnama* supplies extremely useful material for the *Subah* Lahore as for other provinces. Chandar Bhan Brahman's writings make a definite contribution both in the *Insha* and historical literature. His *Munshaat-i-Brahaman* throws light on the activities of the historical personages. The *Guldasta-i-quwaid-ul-Saltanat* and *Chahar Chaman* serve as an important source for our knowledge of the working of the Mughal administration, and the geographical details of the Mughal *subahs*. Sujan Rai Bhandari's *Khulasat-ul-Tawarikh* is a general history of India and covers Aurangzeb's reign till A.D.1695-96; it is very significant in its account of the Mughal *subahs* and at times supplies more useful information on the topography and socio-economic life of the various regions dealt with in the *Ain-i-Akbari*. Of the *Insha* literature, the letters of Shaikh Jalal Hisar and Balkrishan Brahaman included in a manuscript entitled *Muktubat-i-Muzaffar Khan We Gawaliar Namah* (Shah Jahan's reign) and Mir Abul Hasan Alamgiri's *Muraqqat-i-Hasan* (Aurangzeb's reign) throw significant light on the working of the Mughal administration of the Punjab. *Mahzer-i-Shah Jahani* by Yusuf Mirah, 1634 A.D. (a recently discovered manuscript and published in Karachi, Pakistan) covering the

Indus valley and a portion of Subah Multan; *Tuqat-i-Alamgiri* (Aurangzeb's letters) and *Nigar Nama-i-Munshi* by Malik Zada, 1684 A.D. throw considerable light on the administrative and economic condition of the times.

During the 18th century, considerable progress was made in historical literature. *Bahadus Shah Namah* is an official history of Bahadus Shah's first two years. Iradat Khan's *Tarikh-i-Iradat Khan* (A.D. 1714) is a good biography covering the seven years period (A.D. 1707-14). Muhammad Hadi's *Haft Gulshan* is a province-wise general history of India till A.D. 1719. Khafi Khan's *Muntakhab-ul-Lubab* covers Mughal history from Babur's times to A.D.1713. Khafi Khan drew heavily upon Muhammad Sadiq and Abul Fazl Mamuri's histories; however, his work is very significant for the early 18th century politics and the problems of the land revenue administration. Some of the *Insha* literature of this period is quite informative. The letters of Muheeb Ali (Ms. State Archives, Patiala) gave a detailed account of the local *Zamindari* and *Jagir* problems of the Punjab. Anand Ram Mukhlis's *Mirat-ul-Islah*, an excellent dictionary of Persian problems, explains the administrative and revenue terminology with apt historical illustration. *Tadhkirah-i-Anand Ram Mukhlis* records the war history of Muhammad Shah with Nadir Shah. *Safar Nama-i-Anand Ram* (A.D.1739) throws considerable light on the socio-economic and political activities of the times. Chatarman Kayastha Saksena's *Chahar Gulshan* (or *Akbhar-ul-nawadir*) is a general history of India till A.D.1759-60 and it gives a detailed topographical account of the *Subahs*. Shah Nawaz Khan's *Maathir-ul-Umara* gives full biographical sketches of the Mughal dignitaries. Kanwar Prem Kishore Firaqi's *Waqat Alam Shahi* (A.D.1784) reveals excellent insight into the late 18th century North Indian politics and its impact on the socio-economic life. Ghulam Ali Khan's *Muqaddama-i-Shah Alam Namah* Tabatabai Ghulam Husain's *Siyar-ul-mutaakhkhirin* give a detailed history of the Mughals from Aurangzeb's death (A.D.1707) to A.D. 1754 and 1781 respectively. Lachmi Narayan Shafiq's *Haqiqatha-i-Hindustan* (A.D.1789-90) contains an excellent historical and topographical account of India. It also contains a detailed statement of the revenues of India.

The archival source-material for Persian which enriches knowledge of the socio-economic life of the Punjab especially from the 16th to the 18th centuries is tremendous. Though the Mughal *farmans*, *sanads* and *madad-i-maash* (charitable land) documents are available at numerous places, the bulk of this valuable collection has been concentrated in the State Archives, Bikaner; and National Archives of India, New Delhi. But many of them lie scattered at the State Archives, Patiala and other family depositories in the States of East Punjab, Haryana, Himachal Pradesh and West Punjab. The Rajasthan Archives, Bikaner comprise various Mughal *farmans*, *sanads*, news bulletins of the Mughal court (*Kaghadhat-Akhbarat-i-Darbar-i-Mualla*), pargana *atsatta* documents, miscellaneous correspondence of the provincial and *pargana* officials *Nikhutut-i-Ahlkaran*, *Mutafarriq Kaghadhat-i-Akhlkaran* and reports of the *wakils* of the Maharajas. These documents relate to a number of *Subahs* of North India during the Mughal age and many of them relate to the *Subah* of Lahore. Importance of the *Dastur-ul-amls* (Administration Manuals) of the 17th and the 18th centuries can by no means be underestimated for the administration of *Subah* Lahore. The National Archives in its oriental collection has also preserved the *Akhbarat* (news bulletins) sent by the *Waqai-i-nawis* of the English East India Company to the Governor General in Council. These documents cover the late 18th and early 19th centuries. They are extremely useful in understanding the socio-economic and political trends of the times.

The underlying purpose of the narration of the above mentioned source-material is to draw attention to the fact that where a large number of manuscripts are available, we have essentially to resort to the method of cross-examination. The comparative evaluation and annotation of the published texts or the available manuscripts is rather imperative. The comparative evaluation of the same fact from different sources- Persian or non-Persian (where available) is highly desirable. Some of the manuscripts offer the simplified or abridged version of the chronicles. They give an important clue to the understanding of the higher technical terminology used in the earlier books. The sources in regional languages offer rich material but for the 17th and the 18th centuries the influence of

Persian and Mughal terminology on the Rajasthani and Punjabi is rather marked where incidently documents in the same region are available. A comparison of the 17th and the 18th centuries and their statistical analysis is always worthwhile. The original documents and the *Insha* literature help us considerably in understanding the otherwise general description available in the chronicles and help us equally to interpret the technical terminology used in the chronicles and the Administration *Manwals*. They equally help us to bridge the gap in the analysis of the situation which is otherwise time-gapped.

The accounts of the foreign travellers are extremely useful for the analysis of the socio-economic life during the 17th and 18th centuries. But they too have their own limitations, motives and complexes. The statements about the economic life cannot be accepted at the face value unless authenticated by the contemporary documentary or literary evidence. The description available about the social life has to be equally compared with the picture available on the regional Punjabi literature. However, the detailed description available from the accounts of the foreign travellers of the 18th century, especially in the urban centres and the commercial life, can be well compared with the pithy description available from the chronicles and the geographical *Subah* accounts. This helps us to have more of general understanding and imagination for working on the Persian Chronicles and the archival sources. The historical portions of the earliest district gazetteers, assessment and settlement reports of the early British period are only descriptive and cannot be taken as a part of authentic history. However, the physical, geographical and ethnic descriptions are more useful and the nature of the ethnic settlements and the revenue practices can be well understood in collaboration with the *dastur-amls* and chronicles of the 17th and 18th centuries. There may be continuity in various spheres. The element of continuity and surmises can be framed but it is too risky to accept the 18th and early 19th century description of the people and their habits for the back centuries unless fully supported by the contemporary evidence. It is an intellectual exercise which has to be handled very carefully by a professional historian. In all this the principal of importance of the selection of source-material must be kept in view.

The various accounts of the revenue documents of the 17th and 18th centuries throw considerable light on the concept of ownership of land, nature of land holding on the part of various categories and of the *Zamindari*, *Muqadami*, *Riaya* and *Muzarian* families. Some of the village documents give details of the units of the holdings, the castes of the cultivators and even the agricultural population of the village. The *Ain-i-Akbari* and the contemporary revenue literature also throw light on the nature of the land rights of the tribes and the clans settled in different portions of the Punjab. Similarly, description is available from the account at the *Subah* Lahore from the 18th century sources. The composition of an agricultural population and the nature of land tenures may vary from one group of villages to another or at times from one village to another. During the medieval ages under review, in the course of the historical development the peoples belonging to various tribes, clans and castes imposed and super-imposed their *Zamindari* rights in the settled villages and many a new village were developed by the various cultivating clans and castes in different regions of the Punjab. Under the Mughal rule, the rights of the revenue paying (*raiyati*) land owning, *Zamindari*, *Riaya*, the ordinary present proprietary *Riaya*, the *Muzarain* settled in the villages whether belonging to the same clan or different cultivating clans and castes were confirmed acquiring an element of stability. All the same, a comparison of the clans and castes with *Zamindari* right in the 17th century Punjab and latter half of the 18th century Punjab would show that tremendous changes had occurred in the *Zamindari* title to the ownership of the land in the villages. Thus the social picture on an ethnic plane in the agrarian society is by no means static. The practice of communal *vesh* traceable in many villages in the western Punjab during the second half of the 19th century involved historical redistribution of the land amongst various branches of the clan on inter-village basis or the re-distribution and re-adjustment of the land within a single village or periodical exchange at certain ancestral land within a single family. The ethnology and economic study of these tribes suggests how the joint family proprietary notions of the medieval age descended from the communal rights of the tribes. It is not intended to suggest that this communal order of land ownership had existed in these villages throughout the medieval age for this region had been the scene of political vicissitudes and clannish domination in the 18th century which may have brought about this practice into existence. There were no communal lands owned by the 'village community'. So far as the 16th and 17th century and documents reveal, it is difficult to trace such a concept. In matters relating to the agricultural life, the revenue administration and social behavior, a village society was never a complete socio-economic entity. It was essentially an integral part of large territorial and clannish settlement. The obligation of the maintenance of the irrigation and channels drawn from the lakes, canals, streams and river beds was basically a territorial and clannish concept being the joint responsibility of the *Zamindar* and the *Riaya* even though it ultimately evolved on the village agricultural *Riaya*. During the 18th century in many a region of the Punjab, the nature of *pattidari* and *bhaichara*, land tenures are traceable. The entire concept of the village community in the Punjab has to be recast on the basis of the contemporary documentary evidence available from the 16th to the 18th centuries.

Based on the chronicles and the contemporary documents it can be well maintained that in the Punjab, the Mughal government was keenly interested in the extension of the irrigation facilities to the cultivators for the development of agricultural economy. Though the chronicles attach importance to the construction of a few canals like the East Punjab i.e., West Jamna; the Lahore i.e. Upper Bari; the Delhi canal entitled *Nahr-i-Bihisht*, scattered regional contemporary sources point towards the existence of many a perennial mall canals in either parched area or at places where even constant water was available from the streams and the *nalas*. A number of such canals were constructed both by the Mughal States and the Mughal *Zamindars* for stepping up the agricultural and horticultural production. There were no private canals during the Mughal age. Even when some of the Mughal nobles get a few canals repaired or excavated at their own initiative for the irrigation of their gardens or assigned *Jagir* lands, they could not claim these canals as their private property. In fact, the real basis of irrigation administration was cooperation between the government and the cultivators. The headworks of the canals, the main lines and branches, the distributaries were all constructed and maintained by the State administration but the water course and the field channels were constructed and invariably maintained by the *Riaya*. In regions close to the main rivers or streams, the construction of the canals, the water-course and the *bunds* was the joint responsibility of the State and the *Riaya*. In this respect, the *Riaya* met a part of the maintenance charges on collective basis. Though the British government improved and extended the perennial irrigation system in the Punjab, it has yet to be established whether apparent addition to the irrigated area by the large scale government canals was a net addition to the effectively irrigated acreage. This is because of the fact that the problem of water logging and salinity resulting from the neglect of proper drainage, the new canals often replace the older inundation canals in the Punjab. Thus one may be cautious in interpreting the increase in the apparent area claimed as a net addition to the effective irrigated area.

On the basis of the source material of the various categories mentioned above, it can be well maintained that there was an integrated pattern of commercial life during the 16th-18th centuries. In the developed regions, the concept of village self-sufficiency can no longer be maintained. The regional sources point towards the inter-dependence of groups of adjacent villages on the local *mandis* both for commercial crops and non-agricultural products. Within a *pargana* or a larger territory, a few commercial centres served as links between the villages and the *qasbas*. The *qasba,* apart from serving as the administrative headquarters of the *pargana,* was also the main commercial centre of the rural areas. However hard it is to lay a strict line of demarcation between the rural and the urban areas in the medieval Punjab society, a *qasba* with its jurisdiction over *tappaha*, *mandis* and villages was more a part of the rural society than an urban centre. The names of the 17th century peddling castes with specialisation in certain merchandise commodities as well as the pastoral and animal breeding tribes are available for the Punjab. The internal trade, the local agricultural and industrial products, the export commodities, the river system for transportation, the inland road transportation organisation of the *Banjara* communities, the commercial organisations with Hindi system, the revenues from the commercial items, the commercial organisation in the urban centres, the inter-provincial and foreign trade and the role of the trading castes can be well constructed from the above sources. A clear picture of the inland trade routes and with that of the other provinces and the neighbouring countries can be well drawn. Because of the turbulent conditions of the $18^{th}$ century, a change took place in the commercial set up which equally affected the trade routes.

In the end, I must say that with an objective approach and disciplined methodology of research as outlined above, we can construct a fairly accurate and dependable picture of the social and economic life of the people of the medieval Punjab.

I thank you all for the indulgence and the patience shown to me during the course of my address.

# 8

# In The Enam of God, The Merciful, The Beneficient

*Dasturul-amal* of the Universe is the praise to the Highest King (God), who, through the deputation of his deputies, the prophets (*anbiya'*) and the messengers of God (May the grace of God be with all of them) bestowed upon mankind an ordained arrangement of the means of livelihood and sustenance. Similarly, the praise of the chosen messenger of God is the linking thread of law and order of this terrestrial world which has adorned the propagation of the continuance of this world from the day of Creation to last moments of existence.

Now to begin: the man of low profession, Muhammad Saqib Siddiqi, on the demand of the *Sahib-i-Qadr Bakhsh* (the patron of talents), *Wala Jah* (the exalted) Mr. Francis, may his prestige continue, has written down in this short statement, a few *Sarishtas* of the present which are familiar to the men in services, alongwith their literal and technical meanings for the sake of the knowledge of the Englishman (*Sahibs*) who are beginning to learn Persian, so that it may help them in their understanding.

A few homes of the *raiyat* comprise a *mauza*; a few *mauzas*, a *pargana*; a few *parganas*, a *sarkar;* a few *sarkars*, a *zila;* a few *zilas*; a *suba* and a few *subas* constitute the Empire (*mamalik-i-mahrusa*) of the Emperor.

Q: How many categories of land are there?

A: *Khalisa*[1] and *Khairat*. *Khausa* is that from which the treasure of the *mal-i-wajib*, is entered into the Government

(*Sarkar*). That too is of two type: *Sair* and *mal*[2] is that which is realized from the *zamin-i-raiyati* under cultivation and *jalkar* and *bankar* etc. *Sair*[3] is that which is realized on the grains traded through roads (*rah*), through rivers (*ghats*), in *bazars*, *hat*, *ganj* and *gola* etc.

*Zamin-i-Khairat* is of many types such as *jagirs*, *milk*, *la-kharaj*, *aimma* whose *jama'* is small, *piratar* which, bestowing on saints (*piran*), is given to Muslim: *devatar* which is given to the deities (*devatas*) of the Hindus; *baramotar* which the *Zamindar*s give to the prehimins and *muhitran* which the *Zamindars* give to their select servants (*maukaran-i-umda*) for the sake of (the up keep) of gardens and *havelis*.

*Jagir* is what the kings give to their servants.

*Nankar* which is the ancestral (*ajdad*) right of the *Zamindars* and *Qanungos* (and) is realized alongwith *banth* for the collection of land revenue. All these *zamin-i-khairat* are also called *ba'zi-zamin*.

Q: What are the types of *Jagir* ?

A: It is of three types:

(i) *Jagir-i-mashrut*

(ii) *Jagir-i-bila-mashrut*

(iii) *Jagir-i-al-tamgha*

*Jagir-i-mashrut* continues till one is in service and after one's dismissal is confiscated with the government.

*Jagir-i-bila-mashrut* (or *bila-shart*) continues till the *Jagir* holder is alive. After his death, the *Hakim* (or) *Mukhtar* either confiscates it with the government or he gives it to the heirs of the deceased. This is also called *Jagir-i-zati*.

*Jagirs-i-al-tamgha* is a type of *inaam* which is bestowed by the Imperial court on the princes, sons of *Amirs* and on the exalted families.

Q: What is meant by *Ba'zl-jama'*?

A: *Ba'zl-jama'* is what the Zamindar realizes as fines for the court cases of disputes etc.

Q: What are the types of Zamindars?

A: Although the word Zamindars is a popular one but technically, the big *Malguzar* is called a Zamindar. If he is the *malguzer* of two or three *parganas* or *mauzas*, he is called a *Ta'lluqdar* and *Chaudhuri* in case he possesses that title.

*Ta'lluqdars* are of three types:

(i) *Huzuri*, (ii) *Mazkuri* and (iii) *Pattadar*.

*Huzuri* is one who himself pays the land revenue to the government without any other person's agency.

*Mazkuri* is one whose name is entered in the office of the *Sadr*, but alongwith the big Zamindar, he does the *malguzari*. In the ease of disagreement with the Zamindar, he could drop out. This type of *Talluqdar* is called *Ta'lluqdarn-i-khurdiya*.

*Pattadar* always pays the land revenue alongwith the Zamindar.

Q: What are the types of *Hakim*?

A: If two or three small Kings (*Badshahs*) or the powerful *Rajas* possess a *khazana*, they are called *Shahanshah*; if one is the *malik* of few *subas* or one or two *iqlim*, he is called a *Badshah* and *Sultan*. Princes are also called *Sultan*. If one is appointed by the *Badshah* to two or three *subas* as his deputy and he collects *khazana* from the *Rajas* and Zamindars, he is called *Nawwab-amir*. If, on behalf of the *Nawab*, he goes to one or two Zamindars for the sake of collection of revenues, he is called '*Amil, Sizawal, Karori* and *Tahsildar*. If, on behalf of the *Nawwab*, one goes to two or three *chaklas* for guarding the region or for the sake of justice, he is called a *Faujdar*. If, on behalf of the *Faujdar*, one goes to one or two *parganas*, he is called *Thanedar*. If , on behalf of the *Thanedar*, one goes to city or one or two *parganas*, he is called *Kotwal*. The leader of the *Chaukidar* of the city is called Shah *Kotwal* (the *Kotwal* of the city). And those to go about in the *chaklas* and *kuchas* in the night to guard, are called *Chaukidar* and *Paik*.

Q: What is the *sarishta'i-diwani* and *sarishta'i-'adalat*?

A: *Sarishta'i-diwani* which dispose off cases of fights and it is of two types. (i) *adalat'i-diwani* and (ii) *'adslat'i- faujdari.*

*Diwani adalat* is where the disputes regarding land, lands trade and succession is decided.

*Faujdari 'adalat* is where is decided the cases of theft, robbery by night, shameful acts and physical conflict.

Q: How was the *bandobast* of *ijara* done?

A: The *bandobast* was done on the basis of the *jama'i-sarasari* of the three years which is also called *har hari jama'.*

Q: I don't understand *jama'i-Sarasari.*

A: Whatever *khazana* that was realized during the *khas tahsil* of the previous three years, fixing one third of that as *jama'* the *bandobast* was done. Thus (for example) from one *mahal* in the first year ten thousand, second year eleven thousand and the third year twelve thousand was deposited with the government during to *huzur* (*Khas*) *tahsil.* Thus the total of these came to thirty three. A third part of this no eleven thousand. Such eleven thousand is called the *jama'i-Sarasari* of three years.

Q: What in the difference between *ta'hud* and *ijara*?

A: *Ijaradar* realizes *ijara* on the basis of whatever amount he has given *qabuliyat* for; without *kaifiyat* he deposits it with the government – gain or loss is his responsibility. He is also called *Mustajir.*

*'Uhdadar* for whatever amount he gives contract to the government, gets it from the government. In case the balance remains, he could do *kaifiyat.* He is also called *Muta'hid.*

Q: If the *'Uhdadar* in case of deficiency in produce, puts one amount of the *ta'hud* as *baqi*, what should be done?

A: Taking his *baqi* on the basis of *Wasilat*, whatever is verified is deducted.

Q: What are the *kaghaz-i-Wasilat*?

A: It is a paper from which is known the condition of *jaidad* and the deficiency in produce in detail.

Q: How do *muta'hud* give a *mahal* (on *ijara*)?

A: Whenever a Zamindar makes representation that whatever amount of *jama'* is due to me, at present due to visccitudes and depopulation cannot be realized from *Zamindari*, something from the *jama'* of previous (years) with the deductions for *bandobast* be given to me. It I show to the contrary, my *Zamindari* may be taken to be as one with a fresh *hastobud*. In such a situation, the *mahal* is given on *ta'hud* or *ijara* and the *Zamindars* receive the *mashahira* and *nankar* from the government. If the *Muta'hid* or the *Mustajir*, due to excessive realization from the *riyaya*, desolate the *mahal*, the Zamindars filing the *kaghaz-i-baramad* against them in the government, sue them.

Q: If someone who died leaving behind one hundred rupees in cash or in kind and his debt is five hundred rupees. Thus in what manner will the above mentioned hundred rupees from *Mahajan* will be proportionately taken?

A: One who is the *Mahajan* of two hundred will get forty rupees, one who is the *Mahajan* of three hundred will get sixty rupees. This type of decision is called *damasahi*.

## References

1. *Khalisa Sharffa* means the land and *parganas* and *mauzas* except the *aimma, jagir milk* and *zamin-i-khairat*, whose revenue is deposited with the Imperial treasury. Also it is something which is without partnership.
2. The money that is received on account of the revenue from cultivation It is the opposite of *Sair*: the money which is received on account of trade.
3. Which in realized apart from the land and crops revenue, like revenue from trade *ghat*, *ma'bar*, *rehadari* and *gola*.

# 9

# The Relevance and Importance of the Ottoman Documents to the Study of Agrarian System in Medieval India

The present paper is based upon the study of the archival sources available in Bulgaria (East Europe) which remained under the Ottoman rule for nearly five centuries, i.e. from the closing years of the 14$^{th}$ century to 1878 A.D. The documents of multifarious nature for the above period have been preserved at the Cyril and Methodius National Library (State Library) at Sofia whereas the documents relating to the period after 1878 A.D. covering various political, territorial and administrative issues involved between Bulgaria and Turkey as well as other East European countries are available at the National Archives of Bulgaria, Sofia.

The oriental unit of the Cyril and Methodius National Library, Sofia, has a very rich collection of documents from the 15$^{th}$ century onwards. Apart from political and diplomatic aspects, the vast mine of sources cover the political-cum-territorial organisation, the demographic-cum-ethnic settlements, the institutional set-up, trade and commerce and above all, the working of the agrarian system in Bulgaria. The documents cover both internal and external aspects. Number of *Farmans/Sanads/Mazharnamas* memoranda etc. issued from Istanbul to the regional *Qazis* and administrators forms a part of this valuable repository. A document of the mid-17$^{th}$ century gives a list of the Ottoman *Vilayats,* i.e., 11 in Europe and 29 in Asia and Africa. The list covers some of the territories of Central Asia, viz. Karim, Afluk, Moutova and Evtel, etc. at present forming part of the U.S.S.R. As such, many aspects of political and financial administration relating to Egypt, Cyprus and a few Arab Asian and Central Asian countries are equally covered.

The documents relating to the agrarian system prevalent in the *Vilayats* comprising Bulgaria are of multifarious nature. These are mainly covered under the categories of assignment of *awaras/aulub* (revenues) viz. *khasi (khas) ziamat, timar, almaqutuh* to *Amirs* and the *Mir-i-miran* (Chief *Amirs), timar* holders and their sub-assignees, the collectors of revenues as well as revenue-farmers, establishment of *waqfs* and the *waqf* assignments of varying nature. Apart from it, there are *Farmans,* orders of the *Vakils* at Istanbul, *Tappus/Kadurs,* i.e. *Sanads* issued by the high officials and *Qazis* relating to the revenue assignments, *waqf* and realisation of *jizya* from the non-Muslims. Quite distinctly, there is a separate category of the *jizya* documents. There are also administrative manuals comprising copies of the official orders and documents relating to the *Fatawa* judgments of the *Qazis* in accordance with the *Sharah* and *Quanni-i-Hanifa* for the realisation of the revenue viz. *rasum, ushr* with detailed working, *timar-i-muqatia, imalak* of the *waqf* and the realisation of *jizya.* The judgments/orders were compiled annually by the *Qazis* in respect of various *riyats/madinas/qasbas* and in fact, separately for each *qasba.* The copies of the documents therein throw much light on the administrative pattern of the *vilayats, qiryas, mahals, mauzas* and the institutional relationship both with the non-Muslim and Muslim house-holders.

The *Timari* documents give details not only of the names of the assignees and sub-assignees along with the amount of revenues assigned, at times along with the amount stipulated under *almaqtuh,* the number of revenue paying houses *(khana)* along with the details of the religious communities to which they belong, the revenues realised *(almahsul/hasil)* under different categories viz, specified taxes/crops, *rasum* and usher realised in respect of mentioned crops/horticulture, the *sair* (cesses) along with the incidence of the State demand in respect of each category and crop varying from region to region. It is significant to note that though at times the Muslim houses *(khana)* of a specified region were exempted from the payment of certain taxes in lieu of service, the land revenue system does not make any discrimination between the Muslim and the non-Muslims comprising the Christians and Jews in respect of the incidence and magnitude of State demand imposed on various crops and horticultural produce under the categories of *rasum* and *ushr.* It is still more interesting to note that *ushr* in respect of certain crops/horticulture was realised both from the Muslim and non-Muslim *riaya* and at the same rate.

The judgments of the *Qazis* are stated to be in accordance with the *Sharah Sahrifa.* This gives the apparent impression that the administrative and agrarian pattern was based on the theocratic concept. But at the same time, it is clear that the interpretation of the Islamic law *(Hanifa)* is quite flexible based on pragmatism, expediency and varying customs and practices of the peoples settled in different regions of the *Vilayats.* For the same *Vilayat, Fatwas*/judgments of the *Qazis* were passed at regular intervals regarding the detailed working of the agrarian pattern of the *Vilayat.*

The *Aghnam-i-asas* documents for numerous *qiryas* give details of the taxes *(rasumat)* imposed on the animals *(hiwananak),* i.e. *qayun* (sheep) and *kachi* (goats). For every *qirya,* the names of the persons/owners, the number of *qayun* and *kachi,* the amount *(rasm)* paid for either of the categories, the total amount paid by each owner in the *kharosh* (currency *rasumat-i-aihasaidai khrosh)* are listed. The rate of *rasm* charged from the owners of the sheep and goats is the same–both for the Muslims and non-Muslims – and there is no discrimination on this account.

The *Waqf* documents provide details of the revenues (*aulab*) assigned *malkiyat, inam, wazifah* to different categories of the beneficiaries. The latter comprise the *Qazis,* the mosques, stables and other public buildings, kitchens *mutawallis,* teachers, *naqibs, hafis, katiba, mahmars,* schools, *Khudam, Imams* and others connected with the religious and educational institutions. The names/designations of the persons availing of such grants are also given. The revenue terms, viz. *aulub, mahsul, hasil, mal, malia, tayul, muqatiah, injara, barat* have been used in their proper contexts so as to clarify their respective connotations. Like the

*Timor* documents, some of the *Waqf* documents spell out the details of the sources of the revenues, the varying types of *ushr, rasum and sair,* etc. realised from the *riayat* and the remission given on certain accounts. From the *Waqf* income, further alienations could be made to varying categories as *wazifah* or subsistence on daily/monthly/annual basis. The revenues could be further assigned or farmed out to the *Ijaradars* and *Muqataihs* and grants in terms of *qulbas* forming a part of the *waqf* funds are also on record. The documents also provide details of the income and expenditure of the *waqf* establishments.

The *Jizya* documents are available under various compilations viz. *Jizya Daftar* from the *Qaza, Ajmali Daftar-i-Jizya, Mushaba Jizya, Muhasba Ziadai Jizya, Sanads* and judgments of *Qazis.*

# 10

# Original Records of the Mughal Times

(These original reports of the *Mughal* period have been collected at various places.)

1. Records of the *Daftr-e-Diwani-va-Hazuri*, Jaipur. They can be divided under various categories

a) *Khatut-i-Mutsadian-va-Ahalkaran* (Miscellaneous letters to the land revenue and administrative officers in the *Parganas* of the *Khalsa* land and in the *jagirs*); total 2,641.

b) *Khatut-i-Ahalkaran*. (Correspondence of the land revenue officials in the *parganas* to the *Sirkar* and *Suba* officers.) Total 1,643.

c) *Mutfarik Kagzat-i -Ahalkaran* (correspondence and various other documents bearing on the land revenue system in the *parganas* and the *jagirs*) total 1,097.

d) *Kagzat-i-Mutfarik-Mutalka-Maharaja* (various letters addressed by the State revenue officials to the *Maharaja* in his capacity as Mughal officers); total 3,251.

e) *Vakil* Reports.

These reports were sent by the *Vakils* of the *Maharaja* of Amber stationed at the Mughal Court and deal with the various *jagir* and land revenue and administrative matters of the State. Total is 1,421 up to the reign of Aurangzeb and 1,766 up to Bahadur Shah's reign.

f) *Kagzat-Akhbarat-i-Darbar-i-Maualla*

These are from the original news bulletins of the Mughal

court of the reign of Alamgir. Total 3,022.

g) Original *Farmans* and *Sanads* from the time of Akbar to Aurangzeb.

2. *Atsatta Documents*

Besides these, there are original *pargana* land revenue papers of various categories, both in Hindi and Persian, starting with the year 1069. The Hindi records of the *parganas* are regular from this day year after year, whereas the Persian records are irregular. These are the very original land revenue papers of the *parganas* of the *Suba* Ajmer of the Mughal times and run into thousands of papers and are lying as uncatalogued *bastas*.

3. *Ajmer Papers*

a) Original *Farmans* and *Sanads* from the time of Akbar onwards going to *Dargah Sharif* and to its various *Khadims* lying in the Records Office of the *Dargah Sharif, Dargab Moin-ud-Din Chisti* and its various *Khadims*, Ajmer

b) Personal *jagir* parers of the *Khadims* of the *Dargah Sharif* dating from the time of Akbar.

c) Early records of British times from the year 1818 to 1857, lying in the District Court Records Office, Ajmer.

d) *Caverdish's* enquiries deal with the holdings and land revenue matters compiled in four volumes in Persian.

4. *Original Records of Daftre Diwani, Hyderabad*

a) *Farmans* and *Sanads* of the Mughal times in *Daftre Diwani* Hyderabad -Deccan.

b) Various *pargana* and *jagir* papers, running into thousands, of the days of Shah Jahan and Aurangzeb. Some of these have been or published under the title 'Documents of the Reign of Shah Jahan' and 'Documents of the Reign of Aurangzeb', edited by Dr. Yusuf Hussein, Osmania University, Hyderabad-Deccan.

c) *Dehi Badehi Subajat-i-Deccan* (Dehi Jahda). Ms. No. 1184 *Daftre Diwani*, Hyderabad.

These original papers comprise a detailed list of the villages of the six provinces of the Deccan with their revenue etc. compiled by the government of Aurangzeb in 1669 A.D. This is an original and extremely rare manuscript.

d) *Sanads* and *Farmans*, recording *Madad-i-Maash* and *pattas* ant other religious grants lying with Manuscript Section Library, Muslim University, Aligarh.

e) *Farmans*, *Sanads* and *Pattas*. Manuscript section, Patna University, Patna and Behar Secretariat, Patna.

f) Original *Farmans* and *Sanads* published in Persian and also some of them translated into English in various series of the Indian Historical Records Commission's proceedings at National Archives, New Delhi.

*11*

# Approach to the Writing of Medieval Indian history

A great challenge which faces the Indian historian today is the reconstruction of the Indian history. From the British times, especially the days of James Mill, we have inherited the popular division of Indian history into Hindu, Muslim and British periods. As this division is extremely illogical and arbitrary, we have discarded this version. An attempt has also been made to recast the periodization of Indian history on European model viz. Ancient, Medieval and Modern. Though the centuries and the factors governing the beginning of the medieval and modern phases of European history are quite different from the history of India, we may accept this connotation of ancient, medieval and modern divisions in the Indian history.

The first question that faces us is as to when the medieval phase starts in the history of India. Hitherto, the popular version adopted, so far in the Indian historiography, is the religious factor. It is commonly assumed that with the Muslim inroads and the establishment of the Turkish rule in north India, towards the close of $12^{th}$ and early $13^{th}$ century, India entered the medieval phase and that it lasted till the end of the Muslim rule and the emergence of the British power in India in the $18^{th}$ century. This is basically an incorrect view. In fact, any single historical date or a single factor, like religion, however significant it may be, cannot characterize the beginning or the end of a phase of the civilization of any country. To my mind, the medieval concept of Indian culture comprises the ages from the $7^{th}$ – $8^{th}$ century A.D. to the late $18^{th}$ and first quarter of the 19th century. Where the phase of modem industrialization, mode of thought emerges, we end the medieval ages.

So far, the religious factor, the political and the administrative history have played a dominant role. As the overemphasis of these aspects very much limits our compass of history, it is essential to circumscribe them to their proper place. Our canvass of history is much larger where it comprises the civilization and culture of the Indian people. In this we have also to deal with the social and economic aspects of society at different levels from time to time during the medieval ages. As India is a vast sub-continent, the regional variation is an important factor in the socio-economic and political analysis of the Indian society. Social and political ideas as well as their institutional set up have to be worked out. Art, architecture, music, science, technology, medicine, regional languages and literature, speculative ideas and thoughts as well as historiography of medieval times should find the proper place in the re-writing of history. So far attention has been paid only to the political aspect at the centre and the provinces, the nobility and the urban life. We have to concentrate more on the rural society, the agrarian set up, the role of the caste, the landed intermediaries, the condition of the peasantry, rural trade, new crafts and industries in the rural and the urban society. Even though we have ample of source material in Persian and regional languages supplemented by epigraphic sources, so far we have carried on the tradition inherited from the British times to bank mostly on the Persian chronicles which is an extremely inadequate methodology for the reconstruction of Indian history. Unless we exploit the wide range of source material available to us for different regions of India, we can never reconstruct a proper perspective of the Indian society during the medieval ages. We have to study both at the regional and all India level and the varying and the unifying factors of the Indian culture have to be clearly underlined.

As the medieval factor emerges in the 7th and 8th centuries, the early medieval phase of Indian history lasts till the Turkish conquest by the end of the 12th century. This is the period of regionalization. After the Hun, Gujara invasions, politically speaking regional states dominate the scene. The Rajput hegemony meant the suppression of the non-Rajput and the other castes to the position of petty landed intermediaries and the peasantry. A clear picture of the socio-economic structure based on the landed intermediaries with Rajput chiefs at the apex emerges. On the religious side there is the transformation of Buddhism and increasing hold of neo-Brahmanism and Tantrism. Jainism also asserts itself. There is marked development of art and architecture, languages and literature at the religious level. The Rajput - Brahmanical alliance results in large number of religious grants to the Brahmans. The low caste Hindus have a depressing position in the society. The internal tussle for political influence and economic factor for the enjoyment of surplus produce of the land and its territorial hold between the Rajputs and non-Rajputs clans and castes within a Rajput state is a persisting factor in the social life. The inter-state Rajput conflicts are equally marked by similar motives. All these aspects rather than mere narration of the political and military history of the Rajput kingdoms done hitherto needs to be emphasized for the reconstruction of this phase of history. In the $8^{th}$ century, the territories of Sind were occupied by the Arabs and in the beginning of the $11^{th}$ century as a result of Gaznivides campaigns Punjab was annexed to the Gaznivide empire. The Arabs and the Turks, though both Muslims, had different traits of culture. It is futile to regard them simply as episodes in history. The impact of their respective rules on the social economic and cultural life of these territories has still to be worked out.

With the Turkish conquest of north India and the establishment of Delhi Sultanate, we enter another important and main phase of medieval India. The popular view is to describe it as the establishment of Muslim rule in India. Even though the contemporary Persian chroniclers while describing it as the Turkish conquest and glorify the conquest in the name of Islam, it is inept to put it as the conquest of north India by Islam. The Turkish Sultans and the Rajput Chiefs were more influences by political and economic factors rather than by religious fervour. Throughout the centuries, apart from the independent and the semi-independent Hindu states, the Hindu landed structure of both Rajput and non-Rajput clans played a significant role in the rural society. In the face of the contemporary evidence, it cannot be accepted that the Islamic concept of polity and administration was enforced on the agrarian structure of the society. In concept, it remains pre-Turkish in character. Mere general description would not do. The independent and semi-independent states of north India, the sub-Himalayan states in the Punjab, Kumaon, Tihri and the eastern Himalayan ranges and Assam, Rajasthan and some portions of Gujarat and Orissa remained completely uninfluenced by the Turkish concept of administration. The socio-economic and political character of these territories has still to be analysed on the basis of epigraphic and literary evidence. The character of Islam had itself changed in the Indian milieu and the Turkish rule was governed more by political expediency and political considerations rather than the enforcement of the Islamic social order on the Indian soil. The problem of conversion to Islam has to be explained as much on the social and economic plane as on political basis. Otherwise, the 'en bloc' conversion of the communities rather than the individual conversion remain inexplicable. Rather than merely concentrating on political history, the scope for analysis of culture during this period must be widened as already explained. More emphasis has to be laid on the socio-religious ideas and institutions within Hinduism and Islam. Even though work on Sufism and Bhakti cult has been done, it is not possible to reconstruct the social order unless we were to analyse the reformists and the liberal movements vis-a-vis revivalist forces within Hinduism and Islam. Above all, Hindu Muslim relations at different levels of society and with regional variations have still to be clearly underlined.

With the Mughal age, especially from the time of Akbar onwards, we enter a period of centralization and integration. This is an age of grand vision as well as imperialism. It is during this period that we start getting huge archival source material and documents of the centre as well as different regions which enables us to reconstruct the entire socio-economic and political set-up. Notwithstanding the fact that recently some good works have been done on the Mughal nature of government, nobility, administration and agrarian relations, a considerable field with new avenues of approach in the realm of social structure i.e., rural and urban society as well as foreign trade and commerce awaits a full treatment. With copious source material at hand, it is possible to reconstruct the rural agrarian society, the role of the caste in the agrarian holdings and that of the landed intermediaries. A detailed account of the Hindu-Muslim relations in the rural and urban society is still to be given. The disintegration of the Mughal Empire cannot be explained only on religious factors. The rise of the Marathas, Sikhs, Jats, Gonds and other non-Rajput clans can be explained only against the socio-economic background. This alone can explain the crisis of the medieval order and the stagnation in the Indian scene, decadence of the urban culture, impoverishment of peasantry, decline in crafts and industries, the loss of interest in science and technology, the failure to develop industrial revolution which ultimately paved the way for the foreign domination in India. It is only with this pragmatic approach that we can reconstruct the medieval Indian History.

## 12

# The Role of Political, Diplomatic and Military History versus Social, Economic and Cultural History

We must first discard the idea that a radical change in the subject matter taught would in itself be a sufficient contribution to understand people. A world history can, in fact, be written from a nationalist or imperialist point of view; economic, social and cultural history can provide examples of conflicts as well as demonstrations of collaboration.

The important thing is the spirit which pervades the teachings. This spirit, however, can only make its appearance if the teaching of history is based on a judicious balance among the different fields of activity which are usually distinguished in the past of mankind.

**A) Division of subject matter taught**

1) A very important place must be given in the teaching of history to economic, social, cultural, religious and other similar branches of history.

-because they can supply a satisfactory explanation for the unfolding of events which cannot be found only in diplomatic, political and military history;

-because, while showing the underlying reasons for conflicts and covering the main reasons for the diversities between human groups, they reveal even more sharply the resemblance, the reciprocal influences and the growing interdependence of peoples, and enable us to become aware of mankind's common heritage;

-because they provide the opportunity, in so far as the facts allow, for stressing man's constructive efforts.

2) This should not, however, imply neglect of political, diplomatic or military history, for it would be quite wrong to leave pupils in ignorance of the importance of political evolution, and crises or wars, and to neglect the connection of these with economic or cultural facts, or to paint history in misleading colours.

3) It is desirable that world history should be taught in all countries in a way best adapted to the school system of each country, and that it should be viewed as something other than a mere juxtaposition of national histories.

4) This world history should be a real history of the world, not merely of Europe or the West. Non-European people must be given a place which is in proportion to their world importance or to their contributions to world civilization. This condition, which is valid for the study of all past periods of history, must be respected most particularly when dealing with the present times.

5) More generally, the importance accorded to the different peoples should not depend only on the extent of their territories, their wealth, or the power of their armies, but also on their contribution to the common heritage of mankind.

**B) Connections between the subjects taught**

1) Teaching must show the mutual interaction of the various aspects of a given society at a given time. The essential phenomenan, arbitrarily analysed and classified as economic, social, political, military, cultural, religious and other facts, should be treated as entirely separate subjects. In any case, if one of these aspects is made the centre of interest, the relations between the various aspects should be clearly shown. Only such a study is capable of providing adolescents with that understanding of the conditions of social life which will enable them to become citizens capable of better understanding the problems of their times.

2) National history must be studied as closely as possible with

the world history. As far as the organisations of studies permit, and wherever the past of the country makes this possible, it is desirable that national history should be studied at the same time as world history and within the frame work of the latter. The adolescent will thus see that at all ages, his own country has found its own answers to problems which were not special to that country; he will understand that his country is part of a vast community; and he will learn to reconcile a legitimate attachment to his own country with a much wider feeling and a world view.

**C) The spirit in which these subjects are taught**

1) The teaching of local history should be inspired in a spirit which is capable of developing a feeling of the inter-dependence of mankind, since local can often provide a concrete proof of all those various and distant contributions that are constantly combining to form that which appears as the most particular.

2) World history must not only clear the similarity between men but also their difference, the latter being explained with due regards to the geographical, historical, etc. factors in such a way as to encourage people to consider them as legitimate and worthy of respect in themselves and creating a situation in which there should be no inequality and no obstacle to the joint pursuit of common aims.

3) The civilizations which differ from our own should be shown, not in their external aspect, but with a view to explaining historically their external aspect, and with a view to explaining historically their religions or ideologies, philosophical, moral, political, social systems and ways of life.

This attitude of mankind is necessary:

-for intellectual probe

-to encourage pupils to broaden their normal ways of thinking and to acquire more flexible minds.

The historians must build their work upon one paramount value: the value of truth. The truth must stand above all other things. It is superior to one's own country, church or political party. Coleridge said something like this: "If you start loving

Christianity more than truth, you will go on by loving your special church more than Christianity, and you will end by loving yourself more than your church". For our teaching, the consequences of this all-dominant value–the truth–will be that we keep to the facts and try to be objective. Our duty as teachers may not give the whole truth, because this is not known to any man, but to give as much as possible of the truth, and above all to teach our pupils to seek the truth themselves. What has really happened? What is going on in that which seems to be going on? Why did it happen–what were the causes? Let the pupils think.

The historic development might, of course, be looked upon as the realization of some eschatological idea, e.g., *Civitas Dei* on earth, or the classless society of Marx. But none of these future aims can be scientifically vindicated – they are only expressions for our wishful thinking.

As individuals, we are striving for some ideals – say, brotherhood of mankind. But as teachers, we must take care not to press the facts into any system which was constructed to a *priori*. "Opinion is free, but facts are sacred". (Manchester Guardian's founder).

Our task is to find out and teach the inter-relationship of the things themselves and to explain the historical stream of events with all means at our disposal. That is the reason why we cannot confine ourselves to the political, diplomatic and military history only. This sort of history gives us only the outward side of the events and, if isolated, is unable to explain the underlying streams of the development. We must take also the inner side – the social, economic and cultural history – into consideration. For example:-

a. The beginning of the Renaissance cannot be explained only by saying, as in the older textbooks, that Constantinople was conquered by the Truks in 1453 and the learned Greeks, who fled from their country to Rome, gave a new life to the study of the antiquity. The Renaissance began in Southern Europe long before that year, and among its causes were the European contacts with the Arabian culture in Spain and the revival of the Mediterranean commerce. The Renaissance is reflected not only in the forming of the national states or in the political ideas of Machiavelli, but also the products of the literature, painting, architecture and music.

b. The defeat of the Swedish Baltic power in 1718 cannot be explained only by the Russian victory at Poltava and the death of the Charles XII, nor is the expansion of the Russian imperium the only reason. We must seek the causes also in Sweden at that time–its poverty and its very small population.

c. The first French revolution had not only political causes (e.g. the weakness of the King, or the American war of liberation but also economic (the bad finances of the state), social (the strengthening of the bourgeoisie) and ideological (the enlightenment, the freemasons). The bad social conditions did not automatically provoke the revolution. It was also necessary that some people demonstrated and criticized the conditions, and that these critical men were able to gather groups around them. We must teach our pupils the cost of the court at Versailles, the suppressed position of the French farmer, the influence of World commerce upon the power of the merchants, lawyers and others. But we must give them, in addition, some notice of the ideas of Montesquieu and Rousseau. There is also a connection between the neo-classical influence on costumes, furniture and buildings in the revolutionary period, and the revival of republication thinking.

d. World history of the 19$^{th}$ and 20$^{th}$ centuries is mainly determined by two things: the industrialization and the development of communications. To pass these things in silence would give the pupils a false and superficial picture of the events. You cannot explain the 19$^{th}$ century revolutions in France or the building of the modem large metropolis towns without talking of it as continuation of the industrial revolution. Neither the modern imperialism, the struggle for colonies and the two world wars nor the modern peace movement, the internationalism, League of Nations and United Nations can be explained, if the communications are not brought into the picture. Since Fulton started the first steamer, our world has been steadily shrinking.

e. The development at social legislation is not an exclusively political question - for instance, the conflicts between Tories and the Wigs or the Chartism in Great Britain. You must also take into account the trade unions and the propaganda for social responsibility in the novels of Dickens and Hugo, as well as later on in the pictures of Van Gogh and Kollwitz.

f. To a certain degree, the entrance of Nazism can be explained by referring to the German attitude towards the Treaty of Versailles, or to the policy of the Western powers after 1919, or to inner German traditions - e.g. the anti-Semitism and the expansionist ideas of the Pan-German League (Alldeutsche Verband). But you must also take into consideration the economic world crisis which began in New York in 1929 and which continued the results of the first after-war inflation, making the German, middle-class poorer and thereby driving it to support Hitler.

g. The Second World War did not begin in 1939 but in 1931 - through the Japanese aggression against China in Manchuria. To explain this aggression, you must tell your pupils something of the Japanese tradition: the holy mission given by the Goddess Amaterasu to the Japanese people to conquer the whole world. But you must also tell them about the industrial revolution in Japan and the following struggle for the world markets.

What space should be given to the different branches of history? That depends to a certain degree upon which period you are to treat. The attitude of the teacher is to be balanced by the critical mind of the pupil.

Let us say that in the Greek history the largest space should be given to the social and inner political life, to philosophy, art and literature; because these Greek things have had the greatest influence on the forthcoming development. In the Roman history, more space should be given to the building of the Roman Empire. The main topics of the 19$^{th}$ century are not the Napoleonic wars, as some believe, but the industrialisation, the development of communications, the struggle for democracy, and the international cooperation in commerce and science.

The period 1933-1945, on the other hand, is dominated by dictatorship and war, and so very little space can be given to cultural history at this time.

History tells about wars, but also about the struggle for peace. War is destructive-peace constructive. As far as facts permit, we must give more space to the constructive efforts of mankind. But we must bend our bow to truth, and we have no right to paint the world more beautiful than it really is. Our attitude to world history must not be based on escapism.

**Results**

If we broaden our teaching, combining political, social, economic and cultural history, and trying to use individual and social psychology to explain the material and human factors, we have reason to believe that we are taking some steps nearer to the truth. One hundred and twenty years ago, the Swedish historian Gaijer said that the history of the poor people was almost unwritten, and the same might be said today. The richness and beauty of, let us say, the French cathedrals and castles and the exquisite products from the China factory at Sevres, are only outward sides of history. The poverty of French farmers and workers is as inner, hidden side.

There are other results to be expected. If we give more space to the social history, we might reach things which are common to mankind: the toils, the houses, the methods of transport are the results of a common parallel, although not contemporary development.

The economy might show us the deeper causes of conflicts -about new materials, the markets, the space for growing population and so on. But at the same time, this sort of history cannot but demonstrate the international interdependence which was growing since the end of the 15th century and which is still growing, whether we like or not.

The cultural history might show that our own national culture has been influenced by that of other nations. We have all borrowed art and literature from others, and we have given all to others. The same is true with regard to the sciences and technical research.

The history of religions, of philosophy, of art, and, of literature tells us about the multitude, the differences, and the contrasts. But at the same time, these aspects of history demonstrate, much more strongly and much more evidently than the political and military can do, that all men are dependent or each other.

## Conclusions

If we as historians are eager to seek the whole truth about the causes of evolution, and if we as teachers want to use history teaching as a means of developing international understanding, we ought to treat not only all aspects of history, but to give more importance to social, economic and cultural history.

# 13

# Russian Authors on Indian history

During the course of the 19th century and pre-October revolutionary era, the Russian school of Indology mostly followed the Western school and emphasized the Sanskrit philology and Buddhology. However, the Russian orientalists made a distinct departure from the Hegelian thought which had identified the Indian philosophy merely with the religious concept and had separated it from the world philosophical thought. Professor O. Novitsky of Kiev University (1844) stressed the educational value of the Indian philosophical teachings underlining the gradual separation of philosophy from religion. V.P. Vasilyiv (1857) equally stressed the discrimination between the religious and philosophical aspect of Buddhism. Thus, Ivan Minayeb (1840-90), the founder of the Russian school of Indology, studied Buddhism both in its religious and philosophical aspects. He analysed the social thought enshrined therein as an integral part of the system of socio-political relations and spiritual life of the people as a whole. The great Soviet Indologist, Fydor Shcherpatsky, followed it up and studied Indian philosophy as the reflection of the social movements and social relations, as an ideological and theoretical expression of the peoples' spiritual culture. The October Socialist Revolution ushered in the new era and the scope and horizon of the indologists became very wide so as to underline an integrated approach with the study of philosophy, history, economics, sociology, history of literature, art and linguistics. Shcherbatsky, with scientific interpretation of the documents of Indian philosophical thought made immense contribution to the study of the history of Indian philosophy. His concept of Dharma in Buddhism *(The Central*

*Conception of Buddhism and the Meaning of the word Dharma,* London, 1923, *The Buddhist Logic, 1930-32)* and study of Indian philosophy won him world-wide recognition, and even his tomb carries the epitaph "He explained to his country the mind of ancient Indian thinkers". M.A. Reisner made significant contribution in the study of religion and philosophy of India *(Ideology of the East, Survey of Eastern Theocracy, 1927).*

The recent western studies in historiography (A.D. Momiglian, *Studies in Historiography,* London, 1966) do not show any intimate knowledge of the post-October Revolution Russian historiography. Even though most of them, except H. Butterfield, L.B. Namier, Max Weber and March Bloc, do not concede the point that the Soviet Marxist historiography has definitely more strength and wider scope for the analysis of the society and the universal history which emphatically embraces the East as well. It has been conceded that historical studies had to be within the framework of much larger social process. Above all, the economic factors and the interpretation of history have left an indiscernible mark both in the West and India, as well as on non-Marxist historians despite themselves. The role of the individual within the framework of the social structure, the literary ideas and achievements of human intellect, and cultural phases of society and its achievements equally find place in liberal Marxist interpretation of history. Such a concept of Marxist historical method contains sufficient degree of truth so as to withstand any challenge from the mere traditional or academic approach to history. In the field of ancient history, the archaeological research (Uratu, *Civilization of the Stebbes and Zang-tebe,* District in Central Asia undertaken by L. Albaum and B.Y. Staviski) has conclusively established the antiquity and stability of economic ties between Central Asia and India. G.M. Bongard Levin has ascribed the disappearance of the Harappan civilization to internal factors before penetration of the Aryan tribes into India. He has also drawn parallel between ancient Greek authors (Megasthenes) and the epigraphy of the Ashok period and has given definite meaning to the numerous terms of Indian epigraphy establishing the accuracy of the depiction of India by earlier authors in the ancient period.

A remarkable feature of the Soviet studies of ancient times has been to trace the unifying cultural and economic links between territories stretching from Central Asia down to northern India. The Kushana studies in USSR are a classical illustration of this fact. The Kushana period is an integral part of the history of the people of India (ancient), Afghanistan, Iran and Central Asia. The Kushana phase was the fruition of the long process of development of the peoples of these regions. The literary sources and archaeological evidence testify the economic ties and cultural relations existing in the Achaemenian period amongst the people of the vast area. B. Gafurov in his brilliant analysis of the 'Kushana Civilization and World Culture' has rightly emphasized the co-existence between the various ethnic-cultural traditions and different religious systems and creeds of the Kushana period. The existence of various systems and sects — Buddhism, Jainism, Shivaism, Zorostrianism, existing within the framework of one political organization of the Kushana Empire was a rare thing in the history of world civilization. It was during this period that the people of the East began to appreciate as never before the benefits of the cultural relations and contacts so as to evolve common cultural values and build a community of culture for all the peoples living in the territories of the Empire. All this is governed by the remarkable masterpieces of artistic schools of India as well as those discovered in the Soviet Republics of Central Asia and Afghanistan. It may, however, be borne in mind that the legacy of the Kushana culture was great as it equally influenced the development of the cultures of the regions from Central Asia to India. Despite many vicissitudes, it left an important inheritance for the early medieval ages.

It has been well conceded by the Soviet historical writings (Max Meyhehof, *Transmission of Greek and Indian Science*) that with the rise of Islam in Arabia and the establishment of Abbasit Empire in the middle of the 8th century A.D., the cultural contact between the Arab territories comprising even some portions of Central Asia and India assumed closer cultural ties. The process of exchange was reciprocal and it meant diffusion of maximum amount of knowledge in the sciences and arts, religion and philosophy, and social and cultural ideas. During this period, a number of Indian scholars, scientists and physicians visited the Arab countries and influenced their intellectual and cultural life. Books on medicines, astrology, astronomy, literature and ethics were translated from Sanskrit to Arabic. Besides, many scientific books, the game of chess and Bidpai's celebrated book of Kaliha and Dimna found great popularity amongst the Arabs and Central Asian people.

Professor Guforov's observations on the impact of Sufism on Central Asian society is a challenge to Indian historiography if we test whether this fact is equally true of medieval Indian society. The system of assigning revenue free grants to various Sufi *darghas* and other religious classes had an extremely important bearing on the agrarian relationship and the socio-economic evolution of the rural structure of the Indian society. Many a family holding personal grants lingered till the 19$^{th}$ century whereas many institutions enjoined *waqf* grants, renewed under the Maratha and the British governments have persisted till very recent times or to the present day. The medieval State essentially viewed the issue of providing economic subsistence to various deserving social categories from the spiritual, philanthropic and cultural aspects. It appropriated a share of its revenues for the maintenance grants and formulated regulations for their proper governance. From the agrarian aspect, the fact that the State passed major portions of its waste cultivable land to revenue-free grantees fell in line with the State policy of maximum coverage of lands under tillage. It is quite evident from the contemporary literature that the rent-free grantees fully justified the expectation of the State for the development of agricultural and horticultural lands. The overwhelming majority of the grantees could be grouped with the middle class or the lower middle class of the rural structure leading a fairly comfortable life. Economically, they were better off than the *rayat* who had to pay revenue on the lands and came next to the landlords holding *zamindari* and *taaluqdari* lands. The *Ain-i-Akbari* categorizes grants of unconditional subsistence to those, who, in order to seek the truth, had renounced the world, those who underwent a hardship and suffering in conquering worldly desires. In return, the State equally believed in the efficacy of the prayers of the beneficiaries who remain faithful to the dynasty and pray for its stability and perpetuation. This accounts for the fact that all such socio-religious orders banked on the support of the State, the *Jagirdars* and various categories of the Zamindars and thereby supported the status quo rather than any fundamental institutional change. It also goes without saying that some sections enjoying such revenue-free grants were bound to develop parasitic attitude. Such a baneful effect was inherent in the medieval concept of such grants which meant loss of revenue to the State and led to an idle habits of the assignees preventing them from taking to socially creative professions like craftsmanship, trade and commerce or State service. Some of these institutions did, of course, serve useful purpose and became the repository of culture and served as centres of education and learning.

For the medieval ages and the pre-British era, the Soviet writers have rightly emphasized the identical social values on the part of the Hindu and Muslim communities and have struck down the "two nation theory". The fact that majority of the Muslims were converts to Islam did not detract them from following many of the Hindu practices in the rural society. The Hindus also came to have reverence for the Muslim saints. The Sufis enjoyed special popularity amongst both Muslims and Hindus. They studied the religious and philosophical systems of the Hindus, the epics and the folklore of the country and spoke local dialects like Multani, Sindhi, Punjabi, Hindi, Gujarati and others. According to Professor Guforov, Hinduism and the Vedanta had a great impact on Sufism. The influence of Hinduism is especially noticeable on the Sufi orders of *Chishties.* They came in contact with the *Yogis* and *Sadhus* and borrowed from them the practice of music and singing during prayers. The establishment of Turkish rule in India was by no means the conquest of Islam over Hinduism. The Rajput clans (7$^{th}$ or 8$^{th}$ century –12$^{th}$ century) ruled over the last Hindu State, which ruled before the Turkish onslaughts. The imposition and re-imposition of the intermediary rights of the conquering clans is a recurring phenomenon, which persisted throughout the medieval ages. The ethnic settlements in the rural areas, the relationship of the clannish landed interests with the caste-ridden villages during the early medieval age offer much of an explanation of the State and society during the Turkish rule. A microscopic study based on epigraphy and literary evidence shows that the process of the establishment of the new Rajput States subduing the weaker sections of the Rajputs clans as subordinate chiefs through mutual warfare, at times fighting against the States of Malwa, Gujarat and Delhi Sultanate, the suppression of the lower caste Hindu chiefs as well as Muslim tribal chiefs and communities on the part of the Rajput *Raja* for the sanction of their own state continued throughout the medieval age till the merger of these territories in the Mughal Empire under Akbar. Thus, the social action is essentially political and economic rather than religious. During the Mughal age, the imperialist and secular approach of historiography on the part of Abul Fazl is well known. Akbar did his best to develop mutual understanding and peace amongst the Hindus and Muslims. It equally served the economic and political interests of the Mughal Empire in this relationship.

On the social level, according to Professor Guforov, Nanak initiated free thinking and equally preached Hindu-Muslim understanding. As a matter of fact, Guru Nanak made a severe attack on the social injustice and political corruption of the time. He indicted as much the Afghan regime as the first phase of the Mughal empire. It seems that Nanak's Panth was not sheer religious entity as it equally stood for a socio-political order, which later on brought the *Panth* in conflict with the Mughal Empire.

# 14

# Indo-Soviet Relations-"An Approach to Indian History"

Mr. Chairman, Ladies and Gentlemen,

I regard it a privilege to have been invited here by the Cultural Department of the USSR Embassy to give a talk on "Indo-Soviet Relations – *An Approach to Indian History*". More than anybody else, I am quite aware of my own limitations in comparison to the distinguished scholars who have spoken from this platform. It is only the affection of the members of the Cultural Department which has given me this honour. I am equally conscious of my ignorance of the Russian language which would ordinarily disqualify a professional historian from speaking on a topic like this. However, by this time, there is considerable historical literature which has been translated into English as well as in Indian languages. Apart from reliance on the translated versions of the Soviet historical literature, my understanding of the Persian language has enabled me to understand at least one of the Soviet languages and culture of some of the people of Central Asian region which has attracted the historians of medieval India very greatly. Also, my discussions with various Soviet scholars both at personal and symposia levels have greatly benefitted me in having a perspective and an approach of the Soviet historians to the study of history, more so of Indian history.

It is not my intention to go into the details of the Indo-Soviet relations or the historiography covering Indian history from ancient to the modern times. My more appropriate choice could have been Soviet historiography on the economic aspects of medieval India.

But my general appreciation of the Soviet historiography has tempted me to speak on the approach to Indian history underlining the main trends and the unifying factors in the historical writings. The trends in the historiography may be equally examined in the context of Indo-Soviet relations. I may as well be posing a few problems being faced by the Indian historians in the face of the Soviet historiography.

As close neighbours, the people of India and the regions covered by modern Soviet Union have had intimate cultural and commercial relations over a number of centuries in the past. Fifty years before Vasco da Gama landed on the western coast of India, a Russian traveller, Afanasi Nikitin, had visited India traversing the vast expanse of India in the 15th century. Afanasi, who left a detailed personal account of the conditions in India, has become a legend in Indo-Russian relations. During the second half of the 18th century, another notable Russian traveller, F.S. Yefremov, spent eight years from 1774 to 1782 in India and made reflections on the socio-economic life of the people of India. His sympathetic viewpoint stands in glaring contrast to the other contemporary European travellers and missionaries. A similar friendliness and understanding towards the Indian people runs through the writings of Gerasim Stepanavich Levedev, a musician and dramatist who lived in Bengal for eight years from 1785 to 1793. He greatly appreciated close aspects of affinity between the Russian and the Indian culture. On his return to Russia, Levedev, who is generally known as the father of Russian indology, emphasized the need for a scientific study of Indian society and culture. The latter part of the 18th century and the early 19th century also marked the beginning of a keener Russian interest in the Indian languages and literatures, not only in Sanskrit, but also in Indian regional languages such as Bengali, Marathi, Gujarati and Telugu. The establishment of a chair of Oriental Languages in the Moscow University in 1851 constituted yet another landmark. This was followed by the establishment of the chair of Sanskrit Studies at St. Petersburg University in 1855. Ivan Pavlovich Minaev, Professor of Comparative Grammar at the University of St. Petersburg after his visit to India, produced two Volumes on 'Sketches of Ceylon and India' (1878). His work is considered to be the best appreciation of Indian society which the 19th century produced.

The Russian progressive circles viewed with great sympathy the Indian struggle for independence against the British imperialism. The leader of the Russian revolutionary youth, N.A. Dobrolyubov wrote articles on the uprising of 1857 exposing the predatory nature of the British rule and described the uprising as a turning point in the Indo-British relation. The Indian Nationalist movement stood against imperialism and colonialism of the European powers in Asia. It may be interesting to note that the Russo-Japanese war was viewed in the same context. The victory of Japan against Russia, one of the great powers of Europe, shattered the illusion of European invincibility and helped the East to shake off its feeling of inferiority. It raised the self-confidence of the people of India to fight against British imperialism. The Russian Revolution of 1905-07 helped to forge new bonds between the Indian national liberation movement and the Russian progressive movement against the Czarist autocracy. Even Gandhi, who had not till then joined the politics on the Indian scene and later on a great protagonist of non-violent non-cooperation movement, sympathetically wished for the success of the Russians in their revolutionary struggle.

The success of the great October Socialist Revolution in Russia (1917) exerted a powerful influence on the Indian national liberation movement. The Leninist principles of anti-colonialism, anti-imperialism and implementation of the principle of self-determination in the hitherto oppressed Russian territories left great impact on the minds of the progressive Indians. Lenin, who had actively followed the Indian events, dilated in his works upon the continued problem of the Indian peoples' struggle for freedom and social progress. While he drew up a coordinated programme of liberation and social emancipation of oppressed nations of colonial and dependent countries, he categorically commented that this would have an impact on India and the East at large. Jawaharlal Nehru considered Lenin to be a great thinker who creatively developed Marxism in the new historical conditions. He conceded that "millions have considered him as a saviour and the greatest man of the age" and that he lived "in the hearts of the hundreds of millions of workers." He appreciated Lenin's works and stressed the vast historical importance of Lenin's activities specially in the realm of New Economic Policy and his plans of building socialism in the Soviet Union. In his own concept of personality too, Nehru emphasized the role of masses in the history of the dialectics of the relationship between the individual and society. Nehru appreciated this trait of 'man of the masses' in Mahatma Gandhi and later on himself fully embodied this quality. Nehru equally extended the whole-hearted sympathy to the Soviet Union during her struggle against the fascist forces. Both for the pre-independence and post-independence periods, he may rightly be considered the architect of the Indo-Soviet friendship. The response for friendship on the part of the Soviet people was no less equivocal. It was in this spirit that even before India achieved formal independence, India and the Soviet Union established diplomatic relations at the ambassadorial level on 30th April 1947. Since the 1950's, peoples of India and the Soviet Union have had stable friendship and mutually beneficial economic cooperation based upon the principle of peaceful co-existence. This bond has been further cemented by the Indo-Soviet Treaty in the recent past.

During the course of the 19th century and pre-October revolutionary era, the Russian School of Indology mostly followed the West and emphasized Sanskrit philology and Buddhology. However, the Russian Orientalists made a distinct departure from the Hegelian thought which had identified the Indian philosophy merely with the religious concept and had separated it from the world philosophical thought. Professor O. Novitsky of Kiev University (1844) stressed the educational value of the Indian philosophical teachings underlining the gradual separation of philosophy from religion. V.P .Vasilyiv (1857) equally stressed the discrimination between the religious and philosophical aspects of Buddhism. Thus Ivan Minayeb (1840-90), the founder of the Russian School of Indology, studied Buddhism both in its religious and philosophical aspects. He analysed social thought as an integral part of the system of socio-political relations and spiritual life of the people as a whole. The great Soviet Indologist, Fydor Shcherpatsky, followed it up and studied Indian philosophy as the reflection of the social movements and social relations, as an ideological and theoretical expression of the peoples' spiritual culture. The October Socialist Revolution ushered in a new era and the scope and horizon of the indologists became very wide so as to underline an integrated approach with the study of philosophy, history, economics, sociology, history of literature, art and linguistics. Shcherbatsky, with scientific interpretation of the documents of Indian philosophical thought, made immense contribution to the study of the history of Indian philosophy. His concept *Dharma* in Buddhism (*The Central Conception of Buddhism and the Meaning of the Word Dharma*, London, 1923, *The Buddhist Logic,* 1930-32) and study of Indian philosophy won him world-wide recognition and even his tomb carries the epitaph "He explained to his country the mind of ancient Indian thinkers". M.A. Reisner made significant contribution in the study of religion and philosophy of India (*Ideology of the East, Surveys of Eastern Theocracy*, 1927).

The recent Western studies in historiography (A.D. Momiglian, *Studies in Historiography*, London, 1966) do not show any intimate knowledge of the post-October Revolution Russian historiography. Even though most of them accept H. Butterfield, L.B. Namier, Max Weber and March Bloc, they do concede the point that the Soviet Marxist historiography has definitely more strength and wider scope for the analysis of the society in the universal history which emphatically embraces the East as well. It has been conceded that historical studies had to be within the framework of much larger social processes in which structural analyses, social tensions, the stand of the historian from the viewpoint of the class he belongs and above all of the economic factor and the interpretation of history have left an indiscernable mark both in the West and India even on non-Marxist historians despite themselves. The role of the individual within the framework of the social structure, the literary ideas and achievements of human intellect, and cultural phases of a society and its achievements equally find place in the liberal Marxist interpretation of history. Such a concept of Marxian historical method contains sufficient degree of truth so as to withstand any challenge from the mere traditional or academic approach to history.

In the field of ancient history, the archaeological research (*Urartu, Civilization of the Stebbes and Zang-tebe, District in Central Asia undertaken* by L. Albaum and B.Y. Staviski) has conclusively established the antiquity and stability of economic ties between Central Asia and India. G.M. Bongard Levin has ascribed the disappearance of the Harappan civilization to internal factors before the penetration of the Aryan tribes into India. He has as well drawn parallel between ancient Greek authors (Megasthenes) and the epigraphy of the Asoka period and has given definite meaning to numerous terms of Indian epigraphy establishing the accuracy of the depiction of India by earlier authors in the ancient period.

A remarkable feature of the Soviet studies of ancient times has been to trace the unifying cultural and economic links between the territories stretching from Central Asia down to Northern India. The Kushan studies in USSR are a classical illustration of this fact. The Kushan period is an integral part of the ancient history of the people of India, Afghanistan, Iran and Central Asia. The Kushan phase was the fruition of the long process of development of the peoples of these regions. The literary sources and the archaeological evidence testify to the economic ties and cultural relations existing in the Achaemenian period amongst the people of this vast area. B. Gafurov in his brilliant analyses of the '*Kushan Civilization and World Culture*' has rightly emphasised the co-existence between the various ethnic-cultural traditions and different religious systems and creeds of the Kushan period. The existence of various systems and sects–Buddhism, Jainism, Shaivism, Zoroastrianism existing within the framework of one political organisation of the Kushan Empire was a rare thing in the history of the world civilization. It was during this period that the people of the East began to appreciate as never before the benefits of the cultural relations and contacts so as to evolve common cultural values and build up a community of culture for all the peoples living in the territories of the empire. All this is confirmed by the remarkable masterpieces of artistic schools of India as well as those discovered in the Soviet Republics of Central Asia and Afghanistan. It may, however, be borne in mind that the legacy of the Kushan culture was great as it equally influenced the development of the cultures of the regions from Central Asia to

India. Despite many vicissitudes, it left an important inheritance for the early medieval ages.

It has been well conceded by the Soviet historical writings (Max Meyerhof, *Transmission of Greek and Indian Science*) that with the rise of Islam in Arabia and the establishment of the Abbasid Empire in the middle of the $8^{th}$ century A.D., the cultural contact between the Arab territories comprising even some portions of Central Asia and India assumed close cultural ties. The process of exchange was reciprocal and it meant diffusion of maximum amount of knowledge in the sciences and arts, religion and philosophy and social and cultural ideas. During this period, number of Indian scholars, scientists and physicians visited the Arab countries and influenced their intellectual and cultural life. Books on medicine, astrology, astronomy, literature and ethics were translated from Sanskrit into Arabic. Besides, many scientific books, the game of chess and Bidpai's celebrated book of Kaliha and Dimna found great popularity amongst the Arab and Central Asian people.

The Soviet writings have emphasized the impact on the social and cultural history of medieval India. The concept of Sufism as a social order was equally common to India and the West Asian and the Central Asian cultures. It emphasized the concept of *tauhid* and *vahda-i-vujud* ('He is everywhere and yet hidden') and the associated concept of the exile of the soul and its longing for return.

Having passed through various phases, it had developed into a potent socio-religious order by the $12^{th}$-$13^{th}$ centuries. In its initial stages, it had emerged as a reaction against the worldly ambitions of the dominant political and military sections of the society within the ambit of an Islamic State and had endeavoured to establish itself on the true underlying principles of Islam.

The Sufi mind rebelled against the formalism, hair-splitting Islamic theology, the rigidity of the interpretation of the Muslim jurisprudence. A Sufi had a passion for direct experience with the Supreme Being and the religious truth. Above all, the Sufi experience rebelled against the injustice of the social order which accepted the difference between the theory and practice of the Islamic ideas and principles. It is this trait of Sufism which has been essentially coeval with social concern which needs emphasis. The resentment against the social structure based on marked division between the privileged governing classes and the poor people becomes more pronounced and is a marked feature of Sufism from the 12th -13th centuries onwards.

Islam was a unifying force for a new civilization of the Muslim world. Islam offered the mass of the people release from the conditions of social inferiority. If Islam offered to influence the social and economic institutions, in its own the Islamic theory was modified by the prevalent pre-Islamic social concepts and customs of the conquered territories. The pre-Islamic social order in Persia, Afghanistan and India attached sanctity to family ties, private property and landed estates. There was a marked distinction between the different classes of society. Each class had its own assigned place in the social order. Islam itself recognized the concept of private property and materially affected the development of landed property and land-tenure. In practice, the pre-Islamic landed hierarchy in India was maintained. The social class division was not only recognized but further accentuated by the taxation and administrative policy of the Turkish rulers.

Professor V.G. Gafurov has pointed out the negative impact of Sufism in Central Asia. According to him the Sufi doctrine right from the beginning of its propagation proved to be an obstacle to the development of the profane sciences and blocked the way to economic and cultural progress. He has emphasized that under the Timurids and the Khans of Bukhara, Sufism participated against the liberal thought and resistance movement of the common people against the oppression of the feudal Lords and Khans.

Professor Gufrov's observations on the impact of Sufism on Central Asian Society is a challenge to Indian historiography if we test whether this fact is equally true of medieval Indian society. The system of assigning revenue-free grants to various Sufi *dargahs* and other religious classes had an extremely important bearing on the agrarian relationships and the socio-economic evolution of the rural structure of the Indian society. Many a family holding personal grants lingered till the 19th century whereas many institutions enjoyed *waqf* grants renewed under the Maratha and the British Governments have persisted till very recent times or to the present day. The Medieval State essentially viewed the issue of providing economic subsistence to various deserving social categories from the spiritual, philanthropic and cultural aspects. It appropriated a share of its revenues for the maintenance grants and formulated regulations for their proper governance. From the agrarian aspect, the fact that the State passed major portions of its waste cultivable land to revenue-free grantees fell in line with the State policy of maximum coverage of lands under tillage. It is quite evident from the contemporary literature that the rent-free grantees fully justified the expectation of the State for the development of agricultural and horticultural lands. The overwhelming majority of the grantees could be grouped with the middle class or the lower middle class of the rural structure leading a fairly comfortable life. Economically they were better off than the *rayat*, who had to pay revenue on their lands and came next to the landlords holding *zamindari* and *taaluqdari* lands. The *Ain-i-Akbari* categorises grants of unconditional subsistence to those who in order to seek the truth had renounced the world; those who underwent great hardship and suffering in conquering worldly desires. In return, the State equally believed in the efficacy of the prayers of the beneficiaries who would remain faithful to the dynasty and pray for its stability and perpetuation. This accounts for the fact that all such socio-religious orders banked on the support of the State, the *Jagirdars* and various categories of the Zamindars and thereby supported the status quo rather than any fundamental institutional change. It also goes without saying that some sections enjoying such revenue-free grants were bound to develop parasitic attitude. Such a baneful effect was inherent in the medieval concept of such grants, which meant loss of revenue to the State and led to the idle habits of the assignees preventing them from taking to socially creative professions like craftsmanship, trade and commerce or State service. Some of these institutions did, of course, serve useful purpose and became the repository of culture and served as centres of education and learning.

For the medieval ages and the pre-British era, the Soviet writers have rightly emphasized the identical social values on the part of the Hindu and Muslim communities and have struck down the two-nation theory.

The fact that majority of the Muslims were converts to Islam did not detract them from following many of the Hindu practices in the rural society. The Hindus also came to have reverence for the Muslim saints. The Sufis enjoyed special popularity amongst both Muslims and Hindus. They studied the religious and philosophical systems of the Hindus, the epics and the folklore of the country and spoke local dialects like Multani, Sindhi, Punjabi, Hindi, Gujarati and others.

Hinduism and *Vedanta* had a great impact on Sufism. The influence of Hinduism is specially noticeable on the Sufi order of *Chishties*. They came in contact with the *Yogis* and *Sadhus* and borrowed from them the practice of music and singing during prayers.

This can be further confirmed by the institutional study of the socio-economic structure of the early medieval ages. The establishment of the Turkish rule in India was by no means the conquest of Islam over Hinduism. The Rajput clans ($7^{th}$ or $8^{th}$ century - $12^{th}$ century) ruled over the last Hindu State which fell before the Turkish onslaughts. The imposition and re-imposition of the intermediary rights of the conquering clans is a recurring phenomenon which persisted throughout the medieval ages. The ethnic settlements in the rural areas, the relationship of the clannish landed interests with the cast-ridden villages during the early medieval age offer much of an explanation of the State and society during the $11^{th}$-$12^{th}$ centuries in North India. A microscopic study based on epigraphy and literary evidence shows that the process of the establishment of the Rajput states subduing the weaker sections of the Rajput clans as subordinate chiefs through mutual warfare, the suppression of the lower caste Hindu chiefs as well as other Muslim tribal chiefs and communities on the part of the Rajput *Rajas* for the extension of their own States continued throughout the medieval age. Thus the social action is essentially political and economic rather than religious. During the Mughal age, the imperialist and secular approach of historiography on the part of Abul Fazl is well known. Akbar did his best to develop mutual understanding and peace amongst the Hindus and the Muslims. It equally served the economic and political interests of the Mughal empire in relationship with Hindu Chief Zamindars and other landed intermediaries.

On the social level according to Professor Gufrov, Nanak initiated free thinking and preached Hindu-Muslim understanding. As a matter of fact, Nanak made a severe attack on the social injustice and political corruption of the time. He indicted as much the Afghan regime as the first phase of the Mughal empire. It seems that Nanak's *Panth* was not a sheer religious entity as it equally stood for a socio-political order which later on brought the *Panth* in conflict with the Mughal empire.

It has been well established that the literature of the times is the cultural reflection of the society. Only three writers, namely, Amir Khusrau, Zeb-un-Nissa and Bedil, may be quoted who have left considerable image of the Indian cultural life on Central Asia.

Amir Khusrau, born of Central Asian father (Amir Saifuddin Mahmud) and Indian mother, took pride in being an Indian to the core of the heart. A follower of Nizamuddin Auliya as well a State servant, Khusrau was the foremost Indian poet and thinker. He found many common factors amongst the Hindus and the Muslims and his concern for the friendly relation between the two religious communities permeates his famous poem *'Devalram'* and *'Hizrahan'*. His assessment of the Hindu society imbued with knowledge and education is very sympathetic. Although Khusrau knew Persian and Arabic very well, he had a good command over Sanskrit and some of the local Indian languages. Khusrau's Persian poetry and his writings have equally left an indelible mark on the West and Central Asian literature and thought.

Second half of the 16th century witnessed extensive cultural contact between Mughal India and Central Asia. Many a poet came from Bokhara to India and others went over there. The Indian side of poetry reached Central Asia, specially the cultural centres of Bukhara and Balkh, during the course of the 17th century and as well firmly dominated the work of Tajik writers. The poetess Zebunnissa, daughter of Emperor Aurangzeb, was extremely fond of reading Arabic and Tajik poetry. Under the pseudonym 'Mahfi', she is the author of a *Divan* of nearly seven thousand verses, which contains many progressive ideas, opposing the oppression of the common people, underlining their poverty and starvation as well as condemning the dishonesty of priesthood and the enslavement of women. Her poems have been extremely popular with the Tajik people.

Another poet Mirza Abdul Qadir Bedil, a widely travelled man and well acquainted with Brahman philosophy, wrote in the second half of the 17th and early 18th centuries. He was the product of the North-Indian Tajik Persian literature and was never a court poet. He was extremely popular in Afghanistan and Ma-Vara An Nahr where Bedil cult came into being under the name 'Bedil Khoni'. Shibli Numani is quite critical of Bedil. But a number of studies on his work have been published in the Soviet Union where the Tajik writers for the first time devoted serious attention to this poet. Bedil has been characterized as a great poet. He expressed his ideas on the basic problems of life trying to discover the truth of life through independent thinking. Philosophy also permeates his lyrical poems. He had progressive outlook on life of the world, combining features of both Islam and Hinduism. His sympathy with the common folk and philosophical skepticism marks a progressive feature of his poetry which positively influenced his contemporaries and followers. By the middle of the 18th century, Bedil's works were quite popular in Northern India, Afghanistan and especially Central Asia. In Central Asia, Bedil school continued to influence the writers right till the beginning of the 20th century.

On the economic studies of medieval and pre-British India, much work has been done in the Soviet Union in the post-Revolutionary period. Many important issues have been raised which have generated not only controversy amongst the Soviet historians but amongst the Indian historians as well. Most of the Soviet Works rest on Marx understanding of the Indian society and the historical methods applicable in his writings. At the very outset, I may frankly state that for his reflections on Indian society, Marx banked on the secondary source material and writings of the English administrator – scholars and he himself recorded that his observations on the Indian society were rather inadequate and tentative. We have no objection to the application of the Marxian terminology in the Indian contest provided in matter of detail it is qualified and spelled out in context of the Indian society based on the original archival source material vis-a-vis the European society of which Marx had stupendous and thorough understanding.

In early thirties of the twentieth century, Professor I.M. Reisner gave theoretical substantiation to the concept of medieval India as a feudal society in regard to its socio-economic character. He himself distinguished this from the other feudal societies. He underlined the role of the mass movements (Peoples' Movements in India in the 17$^{th}$- 18$^{th}$ Centuries) and characterized the Sikh, Jat and the Mahratta basically as agrarian mass movements against the Mughal Empire. According to him the agrarian causes/were ultimately responsible for the disintegration of the Mughal Empire as well as the Mahratta confederacy. Much earlier, Bernier, the French traveller, had expounded the fact of economic exploitation by the Mughal State and its *jagirdars* and had predicted that the Mughal Empire would collapse from innate socio-economic and agrarian weaknesses. Professor Reisner's work generated great interest in the Soviet Union and he has been followed more or less in the same direction by K.A. Antonova, K.Z. Ashrafyan and A.M. Osipov. This has generated great interest and controversy in India as well. Professor Irfan Habib has recently toed more or less Professor Reisner's view point, though with much original source material at command and has also ascribed the disintegration of the Mughal Empire to the agrarian factors. A recent microscopic regional-level agrarian study of 17$^{th}$ century North India does not bear out the complete authenticity of the above viewpoint. Much literature has been produced on the rise of the Sikhs as a socio-political movement. The Jat and the Mahratta movements can as well be explained against the socio-economic background of the territory of *Subah* Agra and Maharashtra respectively, primarily as *Zamindari* revolts with political and economic factors at the grass root.

The question of State and private ownership of land is another issue. Here, the Soviet approach has been slightly flexible. Starting with the traditional European concept borrowed from the writings of travellers who visited India vesting the ownership of land with the State, the Soviet scholars K.Z. Ashrafyan (*Agrarian System in North India in 13th- mid-18th centuries*), E.N. Komarov and N.I. Seinyonova on their respective regional studies on Bengal and Punjab have gradually shifted to the viewpoint that in many parts of the country, State ownership gave way to private ownership. This is substantiated by them on the basis of the various mortgage and sale transactions on the part of the landed class and members of the village community. Notwithstanding the appreciable intensity of research being carried out on the problems of land ownership, land tenure and concept of village community, the problem needs further probing on the basis of the contemporary original agrarian source material both in Persian and regional languages. The present speaker has already considered this issue on the basis of his publications (*Nature of Land Rights during the Mughal Age; the "Concept of Village Society in North India during the Mughal Age and pre-British era"*, and *the Nature of Dehat-i-Taaluqa and the Evolution of the Zamindari and Taaluqdari Systems*) published during the last fifteen years. Except for the jungles and the unreclaimed jungle land, the Medieval State did not claim ownership of the cultivated land of the *riaya* which comprised the *zamindari* families of various categories, the peasant proprietor *riaya*. The *Muzarian* (tenants) and *Pahikashtkars* were regulated by different terms of occupancy ranging from occupancy to short tenure basis. The composition of an agricultural population and the value of the land tenures may vary from one group of villages to another and at times from one village to another. The main traits of the agricultural population during medieval ages rested upon the rights and obligations of the cultivating families which in their own term were essentially correlated with the nature of land rights. The nature of their rights has been fully spelled out and it has been difficult to agree with the viewpoint that, except for isolated pockets, there were any communal lands owned by the village community. The concept of 'brotherhood' and the village management was confined to the landed interests of the proprietors (*malikan*) of the agricultural lands and the villages. In general, it also comprised the landed rights and obligations of the *muzarian* and the other non-cultivating professional classes connected with the village. A village was essentially a territorial concept for agriculture and habitation as well as a unit of revenue administration. In fact, the village as a socio-economic unit must be studied in relation to the regional tribal and clannish settlements as well as the *zamindari* rights and jurisdiction of the dominant clans. This is of vital importance. A *zamindari* family may own numerous villages. Its agricultural and pecuniary interests in lieu of the *zamindari* rights were by no means confined to a single village. This may as well be true of the *muqaddami* (headmanship) families in possession of multiple villages. Ordinarily, a *tappa* composed of various villages and forming a fiscal unit of a *pargana* was associated with a clan exercising dominant rights in its jurisdiction. At times, a clannish settlement may cover more than one *tappa* and still more at times of a full *pargana*. The families and clans possessed self-cultivating agricultural lands and would divide the *zamindari* rights and perquisites among themselves. The various categories of the *zamindari* rights have been spelled out. There is a significant trend in the growth of the *taaluqdari* and *zamindari* rights on hierarchical pattern during the 17$^{th}$ and the 18$^{th}$ centuries. During the 18$^{th}$ century in some regions even the religious grantees (*madad-i-maash* assignees) started claiming rights of ownership in land. The *inam* lands given in lieu of the services to the hereditary families started acquiring the same traits. The complexity of the land tenures during the 18$^{th}$ century and pre-British era needs a further probing before any generalization is possible.

Another question which has attracted the Soviet Indologists is the fact of a level of India's development at the time of the establishment of the colonialism. On this, the Soviet scholars are divided. Some are inclined to believe that certain prerequisites of capitalist development had already been taking shape in the economic and political system of pre-colonial India. This process was nipped in the bud by the British colonists in the first half of the 19$^{th}$ century and was re-established in the form of capitalist system in the second half of the century as the result of the transplantation of manufacturing from the metropolis and the new development of petty capitalist crafts and manufactories. This viewpoint has been contended by Antonova who considers the British colonialism as a landmark for the beginning of the disintegration of Indian feudalism and the emergence of the capitalist system. Still others followed by Reisner maintain that the British rule has been unable to destroy the tendency of the local craft industries to develop into higher capitalist form. This tendency has made itself felt in India's industrial development. Thus the crucial point is that of the social processes that were taking place in the pre-British era. Very recently, Professor A.I. Chicherov (*India : Economic Development in the 16th - 18th Centuries: Outline History of Crafts and Trade*, Moscow, 1971) has examined the progress of social division of labour and the economic pattern of crafts and trade in India in the 16th –18th centuries. Covering a number of regions in India, he has utilized the primary sources comprising Persian chronicles, accounts of the travellers, English records and regional translated literature. He has equally laid emphasis on the working of the village community in relation to the introduction and pattern of crafts and trade. His analyses shows that during 16th –18th centuries, the development of the productive forces of the society, notably agriculture and rural handicrafts and on growth of the property differentiation among the village community peasantry, destroyed the traditional community land holding and created new agrarian relationship and community. A special role was assigned to right of private property land holdings and the commodity money relations penetrated ever more deeply into the countryside. All these processes actively undermined and broke off traditional forms of economic organisation of village community handicrafts. At the same time, he believes in traditional forms of combining agriculture and the handicrafts within the framework of the village community which ensured to some extent a subsistence character of economy, its transformation within certain limit to an isolated, self-sufficient whole look on the form of domestic industry in the peasant households and also the form of collective maintenance in the kind of village community artisans to supply the peasants with the products of their labours according to their demands. The handicraft labour found in these two forms in the village community was a requisite of the feudal mode of production, within the framework of which functioned the predominantly natural economy of the village community.

This analysis has generated considerable discussion in India. As to the question of putting out system and its implication for the transition from merchant capital to industrial capital, Professor Irfan Habib has already pointed towards the potentialities of the capital development in India in the pre-British era. Another scholar, A. Jan Qaisar (Aligarh) in her study on the role of brokers in medieval India, has contested Chicherov's viewpoint on the ground that the penetration of merchant capital into the existing artisan-level mode of production could occur through the putting out system (*dadni*) which seems to have been quite an established practice, though on a small scale even prior to the 17th century. She has also contested the viewpoint of Chicherov in terms of 'economic bondage', 'economic dependence', 'physical coercion' and 'merchant monopoly' with regard to the relation between the merchant and the producer during the 17th century. The artisan had not been alienated from the ownership of raw material and tools of production for according to the Jan Qaisar, there is any evidence for creation of surplus value through 'depression of wages' during the 17th century. The present speaker has also already approached this problem in his paper on *'An Integrated Pattern of Commercial Life in the Rural Society of North India during the 17th -18th Centuries'*. The concept of village self-sufficiency, at least in the developed territories of India, has been well exploded for the 17th and 18th centuries. The rural mentality was to export commodity to the main *qasba* and the city through well-established rural and *qasba mandis*. The role of the cash-nexus, both in the agricultural economy and rural commercial life, is marked during these centuries. The putting out system, the role of the brokers (*dalals*), and the commercial class had sown seeds for the growth of the middle class and rise of capitalism. However, the process was put in the reverse gear with the establishment of the British colonial rule.

During the medieval ages and pre-British era, India had very intimate commercial relations with the Central Asian territories as well as Russia which now form a part of the Soviet Union. Number of routes connected Agra and Delhi with Qabul, Qandhar,

Bokhara and Balkh. Though the discovery of the Cape Comorin route diverted a considerable portion of the Indian trade to the Western Coast, the trade with the Central Asian countries was by no means affected. The strategic commercial importance of Qandhar is quite well known to the students of economic history. The Agra-Qandhar route via Delhi, Lahore, Peshawar and Qabul was the most common and beaten route. It took about seventy days journey for the merchants. The alternative route via Multan was shorter by ten days journey but was less popular due to desert and shortage of water on the way. The third route from Delhi to Kashmir via Nahan and Jammu and then to Bokhara was also common in the later half of 16$^{th}$ century due to disturbed conditions in North India. The travellers give vivid accounts of various kinds of merchandise imported and exported. In most important cities of Asia, the Indian merchants had taken permanent abode. During the 18$^{th}$ century, in Qandhar itself there were many Hindu families chiefly from Multan and Rajasthan who had settled there and acquired good deal of wealth through trade. The detail of the commercial life, tarrif rates, local cesses imposed by various regional chiefs, the insurance and the banking (*hundi*) system need still to be worked out and require more attention on the part of the Soviet and Indian economic historians than has been paid hitherto.

Even for the analysis of institutional and agrarian structure, there are vast archival sources preserved both in the Soviet Union and India. The study of the Mughal documents in India in coordination with the documents in the Soviet Union would throw much fresh light on the similarities and dissimilarities as well as the analyses of the institutional set-up both on political and economic plane during the Mughal age. It may be stressed that the proper interpretation of the written tests is possible only in coordination with the archival source material.

For the British colonial period, the Soviet historians have concentrated on agrarian relationship and India's struggle for national independence. In an excellent collection of essays in 'Tilak and the Struggle for Indian Freedom' (edited by I.M. Reisner and N.M. Goldberg, New Delhi, 1966), the authors have given an analysis of the national and anti-feudal movement in

Maharashtra in the seventies, the national liberation movement in Bengal and the nation-wide upsurge of the liberation movement in 1905-08, of the role played by the working class and the activities and outlook of B.G. Tilak. Professor Kotovsky has rightly contended that the British policy deliberately converted the erstwhile *inam* territories into private ownership of the *inam* holders. The British ruling class deliberately followed a policy of strengthening the alliance with the rulers and feudal landlords and finally making them the social support at British colonial rule in India. Levkovsky has analytically examined the labour movement and development of freedom struggle with the conclusion that the working people were the motive force of the national liberation movement, that the people's struggle against feudal exploitation and colonial oppression determined the outlook of Tilak and his followers.

Lastly, I would refer only to Gankovsky and Gordon–Polonskayas, reflections on the partition of India in their work on '*A History of Pakistan, 1947-1958*'. While tracing the history of the Muslim community in India, the authors have dubbed the two-nation theory merely as an ideological basis for India's division which had been absolutely incompatible with the social outlook of the Muslim community during the 19$^{th}$ or early 20$^{th}$ century. They have ascribed it to vested economic interests on the part of the Muslim League, especially in Sind and Punjab where the landlords wanted to expand the scope of their commercial and banking activities. The Muslim League bourgeoisie and the bourgeois Muslim intellectuals in the Punjab chauvinistically supported the creation of Pakistan to expand their business not only in the Punjab alone but also in the adjacent Muslim areas. Though similar and other vested interests were at stake in Bengal, as an eye witness to the events in the Punjab, I can vouch for their authenticity. The British colonial policy of 'Divide and Rule' and playing off different religions and castes against each other had ultimately succeeded in destroying the cultural, economic and political integrity of India.

I thank you all for the indulgence and the patience shown to me during the course of my talk.

# 15

# Contribution of History towards Nation Building with special reference to India

***Rashtra Nirman Me Itihas Ka 'Yogdan' Visheskar Bharatiya Sandarbh Mein***

'A'

I. In the evolution and march of human civilisation, the historical forces have had great impact on the formation of social structure of the people of any territory or country. In this regard, the role of history in welding together the tribal and socio-political orders unto nationhood has been a no less marked. However, its proper appraisal depends upon our understanding of the concept of *Itihas* (history) as well as that of *Rashtra* (Nation).

In the recent times, there has been considerable development in the field of historiography. Both the Western and the Indian scholars accept the fact that the scope of history is by no means confined to the narration of the military and political aspects of a country. The most significant aspect in history is the approach to the study of the culture of the people. In the recent years, the canvas and scope of history has been so much widened as to encompass more or less all the facts of culture of mankind. An historian has to underline the currents and cross-currents of political, social, economic, religious, regional end geographical factors which adequately explain the variety in the way of life of the people within and outside the country. He equally aims at covering comparative study of social formations and institutions more especially with the neighbouring countries and the outside world. An Indian historian may as well emphasise the study of such problems which emphasise Indian contact through the ages underlining mutual influences on the life of the people and totality of culture. The entire approach has to be scientific and objective so far as possible. The historical processes which have determined the history of mankind are immensely complex and an explanation of any historical situation in the history of a people without reference and analysis of the accumulative social, economic and ideological urges of the society at large becomes rather an over-simplification of the historical situation in a period of change.

Historiographic trends have undergone changes from time to time. The writing and reinterpretation of history has been going on from one age to another. It is written afresh not only because new facts and data have been discovered but because the life and culture of the people has to be looked at from new aspects than done in the past. Today, historiography is passing through a crucial stage. It is well accepted that historical facts of the past cannot be changed. All the same, there is a danger that a historian inspired by political, regional, communal or ideological considerations may attempt to alter the past picture through distortions. There is every danger of making history as an instrument of propaganda for vested ideologies and groups in a community in the name of nation. *"Five Thousand Years of Pakistan"* is a glaring example in this regard.

The understanding of the concept of culture for a proper scientific study of mankind is essential as culture exists within the society and not outside it. The present day developed means of communication and smallness of the world have left a great impact on human thought. Even science and technology would not have much relevance without humanistic studies and historical insight. The changing values of mankind and reciprocal appreciation of cultural heritage of different peoples of the world are bound to affect the character of human thinking and the concept of history. All the same, elements of continuity and change in the socio-economic formation from one phase to another may be equally discerned. With all the desirability for giving a comprehensive account, any historian with imagination has to prescribe limits for himself for investigation of particular aspects and problems of history in this regard. The methodology of research needs more of coordination on the part of historians and scholars of other disciplines in the social sciences for analysing the cultural and institutional aspects of the people.

II. (a) In the field of historiography, some of the European countries evolved art and pattern of historical writing which emphasised the narration of the dynastic military and political history in a chronological manner. During the medieval age, in Asia, the Arab and the Persian writers produced geographical and historical works from one period to another. They specialised in the writing of the Chronicles which mostly narrated the dynastic military and political exploits of the past rulers, more especially since the rise of Islam. They had essentially a didactic approach either for the glorification of Islam or deriving lessons from history to be learnt by the monarchs for the perpetuation of their respective dynasties. As these chronicles are mostly deficient in cultural history, a modern historian has to glean through the texts for shifting the relevant passages and references for the construction of the cultural history of the people of a particular period or phase.

During the 19th century, keen on understanding the past civilisation and history of India, the British Imperial administrators and scholars guided by the Christian or European concept of historiography, with some rare exceptions, failed to trace such historical writings in Ancient India and formed the opinion that the Indians during the ancient period had no historical sense. To their mind, regular historical writing according to their concept started only with Arab/Turkish rulers during the medieval age. When confronted with *Kalhana's Rajatarangini* in Sanskrit (mid-12th century), a regional history of Kashmir, it was considered that Kalhana, while writing about the history of Kashmir in a dynastic and chronological manner, might have been influenced by the Arab/ Turkish/Central Asian/Chinese concept of historiography. This is, notwithstanding the fact, that Kalhana as poet–historian claims to have gleaned facts from the previous chronicles and historical literature so as to have given connected and sustained account out of the past fragmentary narrations. He also claims to have made an objective study of the past with full historical awareness and made observations on the court rivalries, the character and activities of the past rulers with a special eye on the declining concept of the morality of the age.

The ancient Indian historical writings were covered under the category and nomenclature of *Itihasa*. Kautilya, in *Arthasastra* (3rd century B.C.) puts *Itihasa* – Veda as one of the Vedas. It defines and covers *Itihasa* with much wider scope than envisaged by the European or Arab concept of historiographies. *Itihasa* is defined as "*Purana* (old tales and anecdotes), *Itivrtta* (history comprising traditional account of occurrences), *Akhyavika* (anecdotes and stories/account of divine and human beings), *Udaharana* (examples referring to particular stories and biographies), *Dharmsastra* (Social Code of Conduct for *Dharama* and morality) and *Arthasastra* (economy and polity).

Thus Kautilya'a concept of *Itihasa* is very comprehensive and inter-disciplinary in approach. It comprises various aspects relating to socio-economic and political matters of man's life in relation to society. It covers not only the historical accounts but also authentic traditions, biographies, political life, theoretical aspects of morality, social order, economy, legal usages and institutions as well as the latter's application in practical life as the *Sastras* dealt with only the secular life of society.

The emphasis of *Itihasa* was on the inherited cultural history of the people. As such, not only the *Puranas* but the great epics i.e., The *Ramayana* and *Mahabharata* formed an integral part of *Itihasa*. In fact, the very propose of the narration of *Itihasa* by the seers was to apprise the people of the ancient cultural heritage in its manifold aspect. This accounts for the fact that not much importance was attached to chronology by the *Puranas* and *Akhyavika*. If the narration of the tales and anecdotes embodied in the latter cannot be accommodated in the concept of modern historiography, their cultural contribution is undeniable. Even the authenticity of the contents could be examined by the comparative evaluation with the other branches of *Itihasa*. The epics of *Ramayana* and *Mahabharata*, once treated as legends have been shown as historical facts by the archaeological excavations conducted by Prof. B.B. Lal and Dr. S.R. Rao.

In comparison to *Ramayana* and *Mahabharata*, the authenticity of the Jain and Buddhist literature incorporating as well *Mahavamsa*, the Ceylone Chronicle depicting the ancient Indian history and culture has never been doubted and yet it is not chronological in order. The viewpoint about the date of Lord Buddha's *Nirvana* varies from 5$^{th}$ century B.C. to 11$^{th}$ century B.C. in different countries. The first convention of the Buddhists which collected the teachings of Lord Buddha took place in the year of his *Nirvava*. Even when the year of *Nirvava* is not known, Buddha's teachings have been well accepted as a part of historical l iterature. It is also well known that the second convention took place in Ashoka's reign and even then the date of Buddha's *Nirvana* was not recorded. Of the numerous inscriptions available for the reign of Ashoka, the date of his coronation is not recorded in any of these inscriptions. All the same, the historicity of Ashoka's reign is well accepted. As such, the lack of chronological pattern in the ancient Indian historical literature does not by any means cast doubt on its authenticity and importance in the cultural history of India. Historically speaking, the Buddhist tradition is more reliable than *Puranic*, though both supplement each other as constituents of *Itihasa*. Similarly, even though the *Prakrit* inscriptions of the second century have been considered to be more accurate than the later Sanskritic inscription of the Pali literature, both need comparative evaluation.

The comprehensive concept of *Itihasa* of the ancient period, as outlined above, persisted right till the early medieval age. This is well borne out by Jinasena's *Jaina Adi Purana* (9$^{th}$ century A.D.) who, like Kautilya, spells out *Itihasa* incorporating tradition i.e. "which relates what actually happened", also described as *itivrtta, aitihya* and *amnaya* (authentic tradition) as well as *Sukta* (pleasant instruction) and *Dharmasastra* (advocating moral principles). However, in due course of time, the connotation of *Itihasa* underwent a great change. Its scope became much limited as the erstwhile significant constituent aspect like the *Puranas*, *Dharmsastra* and *Arthsastra* came to be treated as distinct full-fledged subjects for study. The understanding of *Itihasa* came to be confined to the narration of past events accompanied by *katha-vyuktam* i.e. didactic stories imparting values in *dharma* (morality), *artha* (economy), *kama* (sensual desire) and *moksa* (salvation). This was a typically medieval concept of history in which many of the Persian historical writings could as well be placed. However, the recently developed concept of historiography, as outlined at the very outset, falls more in line with the ancient Indian concept of *Itihasa*.

(b) As the roots at the Indian nationalism lie in the ancient Indian culture, it is imperative to remove some distortions which have crept in the Indian historiography. In the last couple of decades, in order to determine the chronological order and to fill up gaps in the understanding of the pattern of ancient civilization, the archaeologists and the social scientists, both Indian and foreigners, have brought out revealing facts. Their methodological research involves even the marine archaeology, the land survey as well as satellite study of the ancient landscapes. In this regard, the contribution towards historical research made by B.B. Lal, S.R. Rao, N. S. Raja Ram, L.S. Wakankar (all Indians), David Frawley, H. Weiss and A. Seidenberg (U.S.A.) and M.A. Court (France) is indeed, laudable. As a result thereof, a number of distortions in ancient Indian history and culture stand exposed.

The greatest wrong done to the ancient Indian culture by the British imperialist historiography followed by the German and French Scholarship of the 19$^{th}$ century is the 'Aryan' invasion and racial theory which, in fact, is a complete myth and is not at all supported by archaeology and the past Indian records. For the pre-colonial, there is no reference to the 'Aryan' invasion or migration of the tribes named 'Aryan' from abroad in any of the Sanskrit or Persian literature of the ancient and the medieval ages. In fact, the word 'Arya' as an adjective stood for 'cultured', 'respectable'/'venerable' etc. and thereby connoted qualitative rather than racial or linguistic concert.

In the Vedic and post-Vedic Brahmanical, Jaina and Buddhist literature in Sanskrit and Prakrit, the word 'Arya' was never used in the racial sense. This word finds expression not only in the

Vedic but the Buddhist and Jaina literature as well. Some of the Jaina works cover members of all the traditional four *Varnas* as *arya jatis* and mention the foreigners like Sakas, Yavanas, Barbars and Murundas as *anariya jatis*.

Based on scientific investigation, the refutation of the 'Aryan' migration anti racial theory would also imply the collapse of the other myths, i.e. the racial origin of the caste system, the Brahmins being the direct descendants of the 'Aryans' , the 'Aryavarta' lying between the Himalayas and the Vindya mountains as the holy land of the Brahmins, the South Indian as belonging to the Dravidian race of non-Aryan origin, the Aryan Dravidian Conflict, and above all the speculation about the incursion of the nomadic 'Aryan' tribes being responsible for the break-up of the Harappan civilisation. The latest data from the two major archaeological and satellite studies conducted by the above mentioned American and French scholars show that it was ecological change (around pre-2000 B.C.- 1900 B.C.) that ended the Harappan civilisation not only in India but a vast belt stretching from Aegean Sea in East Europe, Egypt, Mesopotamia to India. The studies of David Frawley and Raja Ram also show that the Rig Vedic river Saraswati dried up or stopped being a perennial river long before 3000 B.C. The Vedic mathematical texts *Sulba-sutras* which served as a source not only for the Harappan archaeology and geometrical town planning but also as mathematics, especially geometry, of Egypt and Old Babylonia as well. The French satellite study has shown that the geography of North India belonged to a period long before 3000 B.C., whereas the statements made in the Rig Veda can be archaeologically placed around 6500 to 7000 B.C.

Briefly speaking, the latest studies on the Vedic Age, both by the Indian and foreign scholars as well as the marine excavations at Dwarka in Gujarat (by S.R. Rao) dismantle the colonial concept at the so-called 'Aryan race' and its immigration to India. The archaeological findings well establish the fact that the Indus Valley/Harappan culture (late 3$^{rd}$ millennium B.C.) followed the Vedic Age rather than preceding it. In fact, it coincided with the last phase of the Vedic Age, being its integral part. Unless this is accepted, one could not explain the identical nature of the Vedic ideas about science, mathematics and engineering with those of the ancient Egypt and West Asia which is well corroborated by the archaeological findings over there.

Both the terms, Hindu and Indi (Indian) are of foreign origin, the former used by the Iranian and the West Asian Arabs (6$^{th}$ century B.C. onwards) and the latter used by the Greeks (5$^{th}$ century B.C. onwards). Initially, the Arabs called the land of the Hindus as Hind, which later on was termed as Hindustan. However, in the course of history, the connotation of the territorial extent of Hind/ Hindustan continued to change. Initially, the term 'Hind' stood for Northern India from the east of river Indus to West of Bengal, and thereafter the word 'Hind' also put as Hindustan, covered the whole of North India as distinct from Deccan and Southern India and finally by the 16$^{th}$-17$^{th}$ centuries, invariably it covered the whole of India.

During the ancient age in India, the connotation at the indigenous terms such as *Aryravarta*, *Jambudvipa*, *Bharat-mata*, *Bharata-Lakshmi* and *Bharata-Varsh* underwent change from time to time. *Aryavarta* stretching from *Hima* mountains (Himalayas) to the Vindhya or to the north of the river Narmada vis-a-vis *Dakshinpatha* stood for the North and the South in the geographical and cultural sense. *Jambudvipa* under Asoka (3$^{rd}$ century B.C.) stood for the territorial extent of his Empire. The Roman art of the early Christian era puts India as *Bharata-mata* or *Bharata-Lakshmi*. The Chinese traveller, Yuan Chwang (early 7$^{th}$ century A.D.) describes India as *Jambu-dvipa*. As the Indian culture spread abroad, the term *Bharta-varsha* earlier denoting proper India came to be used for much wider than the Indian territories and comprised the other neighbouring territorial divisions as well where the *Bharatya* culture spread. However, the present Constitution of India (1950) in Part I, the Union and its Territory, vide clause 1 (1) puts India and *Bharat* as co-terminous. It states, "India, that is *Bharat*, shall be a Union of States". In the context of the past Indian culture, it could have been, better, put as "*Bharat*, that is India…'s.

(c) During the ancient period, the term Hindu was basically geographical and cultural in connotation. This name was given by the ancient Iranians for the people of this sub-continent to the east of the river, Sindh. According to the Achaemeind inscriptions, the Iranian monarch Darius I (C.522-486 B.C.) during the 6th and 5th Century B.C. extended his empire not only towards a part of Central Asia inhabited by the Skuthai (Scythians) including the people named Sakas but towards the east as well comprising this sub-continent territories of North-West, Western Punjab as well as Sindh, to the West of the river Sindh. Even the Greek writer Herodotus (484-431 B.C.) speaks of this part of Indi (India) being the remotest provinces of the Persian Empire towards the East which constituted the twentieth strappy of the Emperor Darius. As the Iranians pronounced the vowel 'S' as 'H', they called the people of Sindh and beyond as the Hindus. As such, during the ancient period as well as early medieval and pre-Islamic era, a person from this subcontinent (Indi/India) belonging to any tribal social order or any religious sect, i.e. Brahmanical, Buddhism, Jainism, Shivaite and Vaishnavite etc. was termed as Hindu. Apart from it, during the ancient and early medieval periods, many a tribe viz *Jats* (Zotts'), *Meds*, *Gujars* and *Rajputs* etc. along with their branches from Sindh, Punjab and Western India migrated to the Arab countries, they were all named '*Zotts*' and described as Hindus. By the early Christian era, even the Sanskrit language was termed as *Hindwani*. It also seems that the Sanskrit literature had also picked up the term Hindu as a Sanskrit manuscript quoted by the later Arab/Persian sources states, "By the Arab, the Hindus are called *Zatt*". Interestingly, during the medieval age, in due course of time, even after conversion to Islam, these immigrants continued to be named as *Zatt*/Hindus.

As such, during the ancient period, the Hindu culture comprised all faiths viz. the Brahmanical, Buddhism, Jainism, Vaishnavite and Shivaite etc. and all their literature affords information for an analysis of the ancient Indian society. Even during the medieval age and pre-colonial era (8th-18th centuries), the term 'Hindu' was never used in the strict religious sense. As a matter of fact, right from the 8th century onwards, the Muslim writers used the term Hindus (*Hanud*) in India in contrast to the followers of Islam (*Musalmin*). In the early medieval age, even though Buddhism was well established in Sind, Multan and other parts of the West

Punjab, despite social tension between the Buddhists and the Brahmans, the Arab accounts insist on covering both as a part of the Hindu society. From 13th century onwards, the Persian sources maintain this concept of the Hindus and Muslims and consider all religious sects in Hindustan which were outside the Islamic religion and its people (*Musalmin*) as the Hindu people (*Hanud*), though of course, both were divided into various clannish social groups (*firqas*).

Like Buddhists and Jains, the *Nank Panth* (16th century) in the Punjab and North India was essentially a part of the Hindu community and culture. Both Guru Nanak Dev, the first Sikh Guru and Guru Gobind Singh, the 10th Guru, as exponents of Hindu culture were great liberal thinkers and preceptors. In the Punjab, Guru Nanak (15th-16th centuries) also took inspiration from the *Sant Panth*. However, Nanak's approach to monotheistic religion based on experience was clearer, more consistent and comprehensive. Nanak's thought revolves as much around God as man and the social order. Apart from Nanak's own composed sayings, the *Adi Granth* compiled in the early 17th century comprises verses from the teachings of many a *bhagat* (devotees). Nanak's own language is basically Punjabi (Hindavi spoken in the Punjab) but he freely uses nouns and words from *Brajbhasha*, *Khari boli*, Persian and Arabic. In Nanak's eyes, in the contemporary society, the *Pandits*, *Jogis*, *Bairagis*, *Shaikhs*, *Qazis* and *Mullas* laying emphasis on scriptures and ritual prayers were not 'true' Hindus or Muslims.

Guru Nanak was, par excellence a humanist, a liberal thinker and a fervent believer in the composite culture. Nanak's liberal thought finds echo in Akbar's liberal thinking as outlined by Abul Fazl in the *Sulha-i-Kul* policy, thoughts recorded for an inscription for a temple in Kashmir and in Dara Shikoh's *Majma us Bahrain*. This is equally true of the writings of Guru Gobind Singh as cited below.

"Many have become shaven-headed *sanyasis* (recluses), many have become *jogis* (ascetics),

Many have taken to *brahmacharia* (celibacy), many have become *jatis* (with long twisted hair),

Many are Hindus, Turks, other Rafiji, Imam and Shafi.

But reckon all human beings of one race."

"He (God named) as *Karta* (Doer), *Karim* (Kind-bestower), as well as *Raziq* (Sustainer) and *Rahim* (Merciful) is the same. They are all basically one and that is Brahma incarnate. (Do not make any basic difference amongst them)."

"We should serve only one (Supreme God) and all human beings have the same *Guru Dev* (Preceptor).

They (different names of God) have all the same form and we should acknowledge one Light (Joti-God)."

"They are neither Hindav (Hindus) nor Turka (Muslims).

Different peoples have started different *mat* (faiths).

But every individual cannot succeed in propagating his own (separate) *panth* (religious order).

As such, one's concept becomes contradictory."

The gradual transformation of the socio-religious character of the *Nanak-Panth* into a socio-religious-cum-political aspect of the Sikh community comprising followers from various clans (*aqwam*) and castes (*jatis*) during the course of the 17th and 18th centuries is a significant feature of the social change. It may be reiterated emphatically that right from the 16th century down to at least the mid19th century, the *Nanak Panth* was regarded as an integral part of the Hindu society. Even though distinct from the other Hindu faiths viz., the Brahmanical order, Vaishnavism, Shivaism, other *Bhakti* cults and the socio-religious orders like the Jains, *Jogis* (*Faqirs*, i.e. *Kanphattas* and *Augars*, etc) it remained within the Hindu socio-religious structure. It is clear from the hymns of Guru Nanak and the writings of Guru Gobind Singh that when they appeal for social cohesion and composite human culture, they only mention the Hindus and the Muslims as the two main religious classes in Hindustan and regard their own socio- religious order as a part of the larger Hindu society with multifarious sects.

It is evident from the 18th century documents that gradually the term *Khalsaji* or the *Panth* comprised all the Sikhs (*Singhan*) divided for political purposes unto various ethnic, tribal and clannish groups (*qabial or qabalian or qabilas*) under the *Sardars* (*Sardaran-i-Khalsa*) with their respective *dals* and territorial *Zamindari* and *Taaulqadari jurisdictions* (*makanat*) all over the Punjab, cis-Sutlej territories and other regions of *Subah* Delhi. As before, the distinction between the *firqas* of *ahl-i-Islam* and the Hindu *aqwam* (*qaums*) is maintained with the Sikh *aqwam* (*qaums*) as a part of the latter. At the close of the 18th and the early 19th century, Mirza Qatil, a converted Muslim in *Haft Tamasha* while giving an account of the creeds, traditions and sects of the Hindus, and of the *Musalmans* of India regarded "the Sikh disciples of Peshwa Nanak Shah Punjabi" as part of the Hindus of the Punjab. This concept is maintained both by the Hindu and Muslim writers in the reigns of Maharaja Ranjit Singh and his successors. It is only after the annexation of the Punjab that the British administrators while writing their memoranda and reports in the English language that they gave connotations to the existing technical aspects of the socio-religious orders so as to make Sikhism as distinct from Hinduism. Even as late as 1881-83, when the Report on the Census (1881) was compiled as the first experiment in the Punjab, the English administrator responsible for carrying out the Census conceded the fact that it was based on "the initial experience", "infinite diversity of the material to be dealt with" and their own i.e., the English, "infinite ignorance of the material" as well as "ignorance of the customs and the beliefs of the people." It was meant not only for the guidance of the British Indian officials but it also aimed to feed "European science" about "the social and religious phenomena" of the Punjab. All the same, in many a region, of the peoples of various castes and clans professing the same religious faith, some got themselves recorded as Hindus while others as Sikhs.

As a matter of fact, it was only during the British rule in the Punjab, towards the closing decades of the 19th century, that under the impact of the *Singh Sabha* Movement, some politically motivated sections of the Sikh Community in the Punjab, asserted that they were not Hindus (*Ham Hindu Nahin Hain*). During the 20th century, before Independence, (1947), the evolution of the Punjab policy under the colonial rule led to the emergence of the

Sikhs as a separate religious and political entity but never as a nation. Despite the emergence of the distinct Sikh religious and political entity, the concept of the Sikhs as a nationality or nation cannot be accepted. Such a version is historically neither viable nor correct. Of course, the Sikhs constitute a religious cultural minority within the Indian pluralistic society and nation.

The *Shiromani Akali Dal* in its Resolutions of "the New Policy Programme" at Sri Anandpur Sahib, adopted on 28th August, 1977, while endorsing "the principle of state autonomy in keeping with the concept of Federalism," urged the Janta Government to 'recast the constitutional structure of the country on real and meaningful federal principles to obviate the possibility of any danger to national unity and integrity of the country..." As such, the *Shiromani Akali Dal* at Anandpur Sahib put forward 12 demands to be met by the Government of India within the framework of an amended Indian Constitution based on federal structure. There is no mention of the words i.e., Khalistan or Sikh home land in any of the resolutions. All the same, the Anandpur Sahib New Policy Programme adopted in the Punjabi language asserts the supremacy of the *Khalsa Panth* (*Khalsa Panth ka bol bala*) as well as the strengthening of the Sikh *qaum*. Even though the term *quam*, unlike the word *milat*, does not connote a nation, the published English version of the educational programme aimed at grooming the Sikhs into a strong and sturdy nation and talks about its "educationists, scientists, philosophers, poets, writers and artists of the Sikh nation as its most prized assest". The assertion in the Anandpur Sahib Resolutions of the Sikhs being a nation within the framework of the proposed amended Indian Constitution and Indian nation-state is basically contradictory in character. Here, the authors of the Resolutions either tried to follow the U.S.S.R. Constitution, now defunct, which gave the constituent units, within the framework of federal structure, the status of nationalities or it tried to imitate the pre-partition Indian Muslim League which at the Lahore Resolution (1940) declared the Indian Muslims as a nation and then strove for a separate independent Islamic State which was realised with the creation of Pakistan (1947). It is much less realised that in the pre-1947 era, the British Government had a determining hand in shaping the

Indian policy, a position which exists no more. Moreover, since the Anandpur Sahib Resolution (1977) and the ill-conceived Blue Star Operation (1984), much water has flown down the Punjab rivers whereby the overwhelming majority of the Sikhs in the Punjab are neither inclined towards the creation of Khalistan as a nation-state nor do they favour the Pakistani inspired terrorism in Punjab which is fast fading out.

It is only during the course of the British rule in India, especially in the 19th and early 20th centuries that the term 'Hinduism' was coined. It was made co-terminous simply with the religion and way of life of a particular Hindu community, i.e. the Brahmanical order with belief in the ancient Vedic religious rites as well as the *Varna* social system. It broadly covered a *Virashaiva,* a *Lingayat* or a follower of *Brahmo, Prathana* or Arya Samaj. It was rendered distinct from the religious faiths and tenets of the Buddhists, Jains and the Sikhs. Notwithstanding all such distinctions and connotations effected during the British Raj, the present Constitution of India adopted in 1949-50 (November 26, 1949 and January, 26, 1950) in Part III – Fundamental Rights, vide Article 25, relating to Right to Freedom of Religion and in sub-clause (b) of clause (2) of Explanation II categorically states that the reference to Hindus shall be construed as including a reference to persons professing the Sikh, Jaina or Buddhist religion, and the reference to Hindu religious institutions shall be construed accordingly. Similarly, the Hindu Marriage Act (1955), in the Preliminary Section, in clause 2 (a-b) of the Act, even though the Hindus, Buddhists, Jainas or Sikhs are mentioned with separate religions, the Explanation (3) clarifies that the expression Hindu in any portion of this Act shall be construed as if it included a person who, though not a Hindu by religion, is nevertheless a person to whom this Act applies by virtue of the provisions contained in this section.

The recently coined term '*Hindutavata*', in fact, stands for the Hindu culture and nationalism in the pre-colonial sense but has been dubbed by certain sections with ideological and vested interests as the Hindu religious fundamentalism and fanaticism. Such is the distortion which has emerged in the present socio-political phenomenon of the country.

'B'

In Europe as well as in India, the evolution of a State in the ancient, medieval and modern times has been quite distinct from the rise of nationalism and the making of a nation-state. A State is not essentially a nation-state. The sociologists and the political scientists have already theorised on the kin-articulation of primitive society leading to the union of the matriarchal families unto exogamous clan and further union of the clans unto phratry tribes and the ultimate formation of the Council of the Chiefs of the tribe. The further combination or subordination of Chieftainships or the smaller units like the village communities or city-states led to the emergence of the State with all its constituents like the geographical territories, customs, codification of the customary laws, the emergence of citizenship, the formation of the country state from the feudal order and above all, the emergence of the State as a legal or sovereign entity.

In Europe, the phenomenon conducive to the growth of nationality emerged during the closing years of the medieval ages. The common elements of culture, manifested in religion, a new sense of community leading to the fatherhood and unity of the country became quite marked. The community feeling, identical customs and traditions, the rise of vernacular languages, coupled with loyalty to the territorial concept of the State rather than any allegiance to the racial concept were reinforced by the Renaissance and the Reformation movements of the $15^{th}$-$16^{th}$ centuries and gradually led to the emergence of nationalities. The socio-political interests were strengthened by the economic factors, which found expression in mercantilism, fortified in the background by the zeal of nationalism. In Western Europe, some of the homogeneous and independent states like England, France, Spain, Portugal and Denmark became nation-states. The concept of nationalism was reinforced by the rise of the bourgeoisie which claimed share or full power in the State. Emphasis was laid on common interests and heritage, common territory and Government as the basis of nationalism.

The 19$^{th}$ Century saw the emergence of the modern form of nationalism which formed the basis of building up of many a nation-state in Europe. The French Revolution and the Napoleonic Wars (1789-1815) ignited the spirit of nationalism not only in France itself but in the neighbouring countries of Italy, Germany, Russia and East European territories under the Ottoman–Turkish rule. During the Napoleonic regime, the people of Italy, Prussia (Germany) and Russia had undergone great suffering and hardships which awakened them to national spirit and desire of national unity and independence of their respective countries and their formation as nation-states. By 1830, Belgium broke away from the Dutch dominion and became an independent nation–state. For Italy, which in the words of Metternich (the Austrian Chancellor) was merely a geographical expression, Mazzini, the prophet of Italian nationalism, appealed (1845) to the same name comprising the people of Italy, natural geographical limits from sea to the mountains, same language modified by dialects with pride in the noblest tradition in politics, science and art, and having twice given to humanity tie, a watchward of unity under the Roman Empire and the Roman Popes. And yet, Italy lacked commercial and administrative cohesion, liberty of press or united action as it was dominated by the foreign rule. Many an idea of Mazzini very much impressed and influenced the Indian nationalist thought during the early 20$^{th}$ century.

The flare of a nationalism kindled by Mazzini was carried forward by Garibaldi and Cavour who through military and diplomatic manouvers brought about the unification of Italy (1871). Similarly, in Germany, the fervent desire of the people for national unity found expression at the Frankfort Assembly (1848) where the "fundamental rights" of the German nation were discussed with great eloquence. Even though the Frankfort Assembly failed in its mission, the ultimate national unity of the German Empire was destined to be effected in 1871 A.D. by Bismarck, the Iron Chancellor through his policy of "blood and iron". As such, the special characteristic of the European nation-state was that the institution of State represented the nationalistic forces and aspirations of the people in a centeralised form.

The nationalist forces shook up the territories of the Ottoman–Turkish Empire in East Europe as well. Gradually, the Greeks (1821), the Serbs, Rumanians, Montenegrin and the Bulgarians (1878, 1908) attained the autonomous character and independence so as to become nation-states. During the 19th century, on many an aspect of nationalism and liberation from the foreign yoke, the speeches and writings of Mazzini in Italy as well as Georgi Sava Rakovski and Vassil Levski of Bulgaria are remarkable in character.

During the 20th century, the First World War (1914-19) broke up the Habsburg Austro-Hungarian Empire as well as the remaining portions of the Ottoman–Turkish Empire. At the Treaty of Versailles (1919), the application of the principle of self-determination and nationalism advocated by Woodrow Wilson, the President of U.S.A., resulted in the formation of several new nation-states in Europe, viz. Poland, Czechoslovakia, Albania and Yugoslavia. In the recent years, the breakup of the U.S.S.R. has led to the emergence of new Islamic nation-states in Central Asia, viz. Uzbekistan, Kazakhstan, Kirghizstan, Turkmenistan and Tajikistan. For the last nearly half a decade, some disquieting features of regional chauvinism and religious fundamentalism in East Europe has led to the breakup of the erstwhile national-states into independent entities as states. The nation-state of Czechoslovakia, created (1919) after the First World War, has split unto the two separate states of the Czechs and the Slovaks. Similarly, Yugoslavia which was formed as a nation-state in 1919 with the union of the constituent States has been again split into six small States i.e. Macedonia, Serbia, Montenegro, Croatia, Slavonia and Bosnia-Herzegovina. Even though the peoples of all these States are Slave and have an identical history of struggle for liberation from the Turkish yoke during the 19th and early 20th century, they are, of course, divided on religious ground. The over-whelming majority of the Macedonians, Serbians, Montonigrins belong to the Greek Orthodox Church and use the Slavic script whereas the Croats are Roman Catholics and use the Latin script. Bosnia-Herzegovina, where the civil war is still rampant and peace is being enforced through the good offices of N.A.T.O. and U.N.O., has a mixed population of the Muslims, Serbs, Croats and others constituting 45%, 32%, 17% and 6% respectively of the total population. The Government has been formed through the coalition of the Muslims and the Croats with 62% of the population. The State of Bosnia-Herzegovina has been formed only because the Muslims constitute the majority therein. Bosnia-Herzegovina is not at all a nation-state.

'C'

There are two-fold views about the rise of nationalism in India. Firstly, it has been maintained that the genesis of Indian nationalism with all its social, religious, economic, political and cultural attributes can be traced to the historical process which developed during the 19th century British rule in India. Secondly, an alternative viewpoint put forward by the other school of thought is that the roots and many a trait of nationalism in India can be traced back to the ancient Indian culture and society and that the ancient Hindu (in the pre-colonial sense) culture forms the very basis of nationalism.

(i) The protagonists of the first school of thought who consider that the foundation of the Indian nationalism was laid during the 19th century British *Raj* look towards the West European model of the rise of nationalism and the formation of a nation-state. The awakening and social consciousness instilled by Raja Ram Mohan Roy, the foundation of the Brahmo Samaj (1828), Rama Krishna Brotherhood, a rationalist product of indigenous culture and spiritual traditions of India, the *Parathana Samaj*, Swami Daya Nand Saraswati's (1824-83) *Arya Samaj* Movement, Sir Syed Alimed's Aligarh Movement for awakening the Muslim masses, all served as the bed-rock of the Indian renaissance as precursor to nationalism. The modern transport, industrialisation, the rise of the modern middle class, economic transformation of the Indian society, the spread of education and the role of the press and national leaders for winning freedom from the foreign rule and consequently the fulfillment of the aspiration for the establishment of free and democratic institutions in India, further fostered the growth of nationalism during the 19th-20th centuries. The late 19th and early 20th century political leaders like Surendranath Banerji referred to India as *A Nation in the Making* while some others talked about it as making of a new nation. Ever since the inception of the Indian National Congress (1885), all through the Freedom Struggle, the role of the political leaders and freedom-fighters, from one phase to another, despite all ideological differences made significant contribution towards the cementing of the fabrics of Indian nationalism. In this regard, during the Gandhian phase, the technique and weapon of the direct involvement of the Indian masses in the non-violent struggle for freedom envisaged in the Satyagraha (1919), Civil Disobedience (1930-34) Movements and Quit India Movement (1942) rendered the Indian people as a full-fledged nation in the modern sense. It is only after Independence (1947) that India has emerged to be nation-state.

Even though much historical literature has been produced on the 'Two Nation Theory' of Mohammad Ali Jinnah, the founder of Pakistan, it is worthwhile pondering over whether the pre-1947 Muslims and Hindus, despite different religions, had "different and distinct social orders" so as not to evolve common nationality? Whether despite some differences in "religious philosophies, social customs and literatures", they belonged to "two different civilisations ... based mainly on conflicting ideas and conceptions" deriving "their inspiration from different sources of history", resulting in the conception that the Hindus and Muslims in India were two separate nations? If so, whether the Indian Muslims, who with identical culture and history, did not migrate to Pakistan and preferred to live as an Indian minority do constitute a similar nationality? If religion can predominantly from the basis of a nation, then how did Bangladesh come into being (1972), especially when both Pakistan and Bangladesh have proclaimed themselves to be Islamic states? Can Pakistan with an Islamic bond but with all its ethnic, linguistic and regional differences amongst the people be called a nation-state based on composite culture? Do the people of Bangladesh, excepting the religious aspect, with identical cultural traits with the people of West Bengal, constitute a nation-state? All these are only some of the questions relating to nationalism and making of the nation-states which await the verdict of history.

An alternative viewpoint put forward by the second school of thought is that the roots and many a trait of nationalism in India can be well traced to the ancient Indian culture and society. As a territorial concept, the boundaries of India (i.e. *Bharata*) have been approximately the same as known from the Epic of *Mahabharata*. During the ancient period, the Indian civilisation spread abroad and some tribes from Punjab, Sindh and Western India known as the Medes along with their branches i.e. Kerk/Kurks etc. as well as the Jats (*Zathus*) had settled in the Mediterranean region around the Euxine, the Black sea and in East Europe even beyond the river Danube. Their presence was noted by Herodotus (5$^{th}$ century B.C.), equally supported by Hesychius who considered that Sindi of the Euxine were in reality Indians and calls the Kerkatae of the Black sea also "an Indian nation". Herodotus and Strabo comment that the Medes who were of Indian origin, also called themselves Ari (the term used for respectable and honoured class rather than in any racial context). In many sources, the Indians during the medieval and early modem age, continued to be referred to as a 'nation'. The European ethnologists and orientalists of even the early 19$^{th}$ century who propounded the fallacious theory of the 'Aryan' race on linguistic basis called the peoples from Europe to India, who spoke languages off cognate origin, as the 'Indo-European nations'.

According to this school of thought, unlike the West European concept, the ancient Hindu culture forms the very basis of nationalism. Notwithstanding the fact that during the ancient period, barring very few occasions (e.g. The Mauryan and the Gupta Empires), politically speaking, India remained divided into several independent states, there was the spiritual and cultural nationalism, supported by the more or less uniform concept of *Dharma*, which sustained the social order. As such, the Vedic and the *Epic* literatures, the *Upanishads*, the *Puranas*, the *Smritis* and the *Dharamasastras* served the connecting bond for the peoples spread all over India. Even during the 19$^{th}$ and early 20$^{th}$ century, many a national leader, with a view to inculcate modern concept of nationalism amongst the people, appealed to the ancient Hindu culture. The most striking feature of the ancient Indian nationalism embodied the plurality of thought, religious and secular which rejected Semitic intolerance and exclusivism. Swami Vivekananda (1863-1901), who has been acclaimed as "the real father of Indian nationalism," considered the *Upanishadas* and the *Gita* as containing the noblest and highest philosophy. The concept of equal respect for all religions (*Sarva Pantha Samabhava*) is rooted in the Vedic assertion '*Ekam Sad viprah bahudavadanti*' i.e., truth is one's sages, describes it differently.

Swami Vivekananda was proud of the glory, rich tradition and heritage of Hinduism (in the pre-colonial sense) as it basically accented an individual's right to perfect freedom of thought and belief. In this regard, for the medieval period, he had the highest admiration for Guru Nanak and Guru Gobind Singh's glorious heroism and universal outlook. He described India as "a veritable ethnological museum". For a true picture of Indian history, culture and civilisation, his focus was on misconstrued Hinduism, which had been much maligned in the Western world for centuries.

Even though much criticized by the Western and the Leftist schools of thought in India, the fact is that the media for nation-building in modern India from the late 19th century onwards was simplicity. Hindu in character as it argued that nationalism in India was essentially rooted in Hindu concept and philosophy. Such a concept of nationalism falls more in line with the 19th century German philosopher and social-scientist Spengler, who observed that 'Nations' are 'neither linguistic nor biological, but spiritual (*seelische*) unities' and that the solidarity of a nation rests more on the 'soul unity' than any other factor. Bal Gangadhar Tilak stressed devotion to the Motherland built around Ganpati festival, Bankin Chandra gave to the nation the chant of *Vande Mataram* and Shri Aurobindo described the spirit of *Sanatana Dharma* as the soul and nationalism of India.

Mahatma Gandhi's concept of *Rama Rajya* and *Swaraj* were identical. He wrote, "in my opinion *Swaraj* and *Ramrajya* are one and the same thing... The concept of *Swaraj* is not ordinary one, it means *Ramrajya*... We call a state *Ramrajya* when both the ruler and his subjects are straightforward, when both are pure in heart, when both are inclined towards self-sacrifice... This is the true meaning of democracy... The democracy I believe is described with *Ramayana* in the essence that is derived from my simple and straightforward reading of it. What was the manner in which Ham Chandra ruled?..." (*The collected works of Mahatma Gandhi*, vol. XXXV, pp. 489-90). There is no denying the fact that Mahatma Gandhi's concept of *Ramrajya* and *Swaraj* stood for moral and ethical values tor the establishment of the type of an ideal State proposed to be set-up after winning independence. Such a concept of State with spiritual and moral values of democracy cannot be described as a theocratic one. For mobilising the nubile opinion and involvement of the masses in the freedom struggle, Mahatma Gandhi made an appeal to the values of life in the ancient Indian Hindu culture as embodied in the *Ramayana* and which having permeated all over India had persisted through the ages. At spiritual and cultural level, cutting across all geo-political barriers and varying faiths, languages and castes etc., it served as a common bond amongst the Indian people ever since the ancient times. This is well confirmed by the inherited historical literature from the ancient period to the 20$^{th}$ century. For determining the fact, whether India had been a nation (*Rashtra*) during the ancient period, much would depend upon the attributes of a *Rashtra*, which may, by no means be defined in a rigid manner so as to fall in line only with a particular school of thought.

The protagonists of this school of thought served a pragmatic purpose of further strengthening the concept of nationalism in India. They instilled among the people a feeling of self-respect and self-confidence for achieving freedom based on their strength rather than merely looking to the British for political freedom as envisaged by the Liberals amongst the Indian National Congress leaders. It was a concrete achievement for the national cause and by no means weakened the secular character of the social structure as considered by some sections.

In this regard, a parallel example could also be afforded from some of the East European countries, especially Bulgaria, wherein during the liberation struggle from the Ottoman-Turkish rule, the 19$^{th}$ century freedom fighters made an appeal to the unifying spiritual and cultural bonds of the people ever since the ancient times when both the Thracians (3$^{rd}$ millennium B.C. in the Balkans) and the Indians (Indi), as later noted by Herodotus ($5^{th}$ century B.C.), dominated the world civilisation. Herodotus considered the Thracians as "the second biggest people after the Indians". As is clear from his writings, Herodotus considered both the Thracian and the Indian peoples as 'nations'. The $19^{th}$ century Bulgarian leaders (e.g. the poet Hristo Botev, Georgi Rakovski and Vasil Levski) considered themselves as a nation since the Thracian times which had been struggling against the Ottoman-Turkish domination for the last five hundred years. Even after attainment of Independence, their national anthem proclaims: "Flows the Danube blue and tame/Over Thrace the sun is shining".

In the final analysis, it may be well argued that in the modem age, the very concept of nationalism is of evolutionary character. Its parameters are by no means circumscribed by the $19^{th}$ and early $20^{th}$ century European thought and practice. However, this is not to deny the importance of the $19^{th}$- $20^{th}$ centuries historical forces and contributory factors, as already outlined, under the British colonial rule, which accelerated the growth of modern nationalism and the making of India as a nation-state. But in a changing social and political world order, there cannot be any fixed connotation or yard-stick for the making of a modern nation.

As a matter of fact, since the $19^{th}$ century phases of Mazzini and Rakovaki or even the early $20^{th}$ century political ideology, there has been considerable change in the concept of a nation-state, which has come to be based on fellow feeling, with allegiance only to the State rather than to any group. The Indian experience inherited since ancient times has given a new dimension of the multi-religious and multi-ethnic character to the modem pluralistic social structure and making of the nation-state. In the latest and modern concept of State and nationalism, people even with diverse languages, dialects, religious faiths and customs etc. can form a nation-state. A single language or identical customs or a unitary religion is by no means the criteria of a modern nation-state, which despite all diversity in these respects may command allegiance from all individuals or groups belonging to any religious sect or speaking any dialect or language. The instances of Switzerland with two languages of the people, Canada with two languages and religions, or even the present day India with multiple languages and religions of the people can be well quoted in this regard.

Thus the Indian concept of a Nation (*Rashtra*) is not based merely on expediency and pragmatism but on the ancient cultural heritage as well. This is *Bhartiya* contribution to the science of polity and World Civilisation.

## 16

# Modern Writers on the Mughal Land Revenue Administration

*(From Philip Francis to Moreland)*

The origins of the historical writings on land revenue problems of Mughal India (1556-1707) lie in the official Memoranda and Minutes of the British revenue experts and administrator-scholars. A thorough study of the modern writings on the Mughal land revenue administration is possible only when the official reports of the administrators on regional land revenue problems as well as the works of the professional historians are taken into consideration. Realising the importance of the land revenue as the major item of income in an Indian State, right from the inception of the British rule in Bengal, the English administrators showed a keen interest in the historical aspects of the land revenue administration. The agrarian problems were highlighted by the British administrators when confronted with the entrenched position of the *Zamindars* and the various other classes of assignees after the assumption of the *Diwani* rights in Bengal in 1765. In their well-known controversy over the rights of the State versus the *Zamindars* and other assignees, extremely divergent views were expressed by Warren Hastings, Philip Francis, James Grant, Sir John Shore and Lord Cornwallis before the introduction of the Permanent Settlement in Bengal in 1793.

In support of their contention, each one of the above participants in the controversy tried to base his conclusions on the working of the land revenue system during the Mughal period from the reign of Akbar down to the later Mughals. Much less known hitherto, though extremely controversial, a huge analytical revenue literature in Persian was prepared by the expert Indian *Munshis* and revenue officials to provide background material for the above mentioned discussion. Equally important commentaries in Persian on the working of the land system during the Mughal age were written by independent revenue experts. Most of this material produced by the Indian writers, previously well preserved by the *Staatsbibliothek*, Berlin, is now scattered in the two libraries of Germany, namely, University Library, Tuebingen and *Westdeutscbe Bibliothek*, Marburg,[1] and only a few copies are available in the British Museum.

Its importance is twofold: first, as a contemporary evidence on the agrarian problems of the 18th century, and secondly as a detailed historical analysis of the land revenue problems since Akbar's reign. As a contemporary evidence, it is as important as the Minutes of the Governor-General's Council in Bengal and the other contemporary writings included in the Firminger's *Fifth Report* and its Introduction[2]. For the 18th century, it quotes various Mughal *Farmans* and the revenue regulations enforced in the later Mughal period. But the historical portion dealing with the late 16th and 17th centuries cannot be taken at its face value. All the same, when taken in collaboration with the contemporary 17th century source-material, it is likely to yield very important information.

The English administrators employed the most intelligent method of seeking expert advice from the revenue experts on Persian revenue terminology and the land revenue system prevalent during the Mughal age. Such source-material was translated into English with the help of the translators. In this respect, Sir John Shore was well equipped with the knowledge of the indigenous revenue system with Sayyid Gulam Husain as his revenue consultant[3]. Much revenue literature was compiled for the assistance of Sir John Shore–a fact winch finds clear mention in the manuscripts available in the German Libraries. A minute comparison of the 'Minutes of Sir John Shore' and the contemporary revenue literature in Persian compiled for him shows remarkable similarity in ideas.

Philip Francis, James Grant and Sir John Shore made

an historical approach in understanding the pre-British land revenue administration in Bengal. Philip Francis[4] advocated his conception of Akbar's policy as the model which should be adopted by the English in Bengal. He considered that during the Mughal age, the land revenue was a moderately fixed tribute paid by the *Zamindars* who were the ancient proprietors of the soil with rights of alienation. The Mughal government, even though despotic in nature, was based on justice and was not oppressive to the mass of the conquered people. As such, it did not interfere with the ancient land revenue structure of the territories of the *Zamindars* of Hindustan who continued with full legal possession of their lands on the condition of payment to the government of a moderate permanent '*Jumma* or quit-rent' (i.e. land revenue) . Francis also contended that with regard to the assessment practice, valuation by *hast-wa-bud* was unknown to the Mughal practice. Francis had the least idea of the Indian or Mughal concept of land revenue which was a share in the produce of land rather than a fixed 'tribute' or 'quit-rent' to be paid by the *Zamindars*. Nor did Francis realise the native of the *zamindari* rights of the varying categories of the *Zamindars* and their relationship with the Mughal State. His consideration of the concept of justice and benevolence on the part of the Mughal government towards the people was not based on any detailed analysis of the Mughal land revenue system as in his erroneous belief of the Mughal policy of non-interference into the territorial rights of the *Zamindars* who were required to pay merely a moderate quit-rent (or land revenue).

James Grant[5] wrote detailed retorts on the revenues of Northern Circars and the finances of Bengal. Grant claimed to have analysed his ideas on the Mughal land administration on the basis of the *Ain-i-Akbari* and twenty other Persian manuscripts which were later on lost. Grant asserted that the same principle of land ownership operated in India as in other Asiatic countries where the sovereign claimed the land ownership. In this context, the *Zamindars* of Bengal did not have any right, in form or fact, nor the smallest pretentions to any territorial property beyond their *saverum* (perquisites) amounting scarcely to one-twentieth part of the local civil jurisdiction committed to their management by the sovereign proprietary government. Thus Grant assorted the sovereign's claim to the landholder's share of yearly territorial produce. He maintained that the *Zamindari* rights were based on Royal *sanads* and the *Zamindars* during the Mughal period acted as mere agents of the State. They were official tax-gatherers to realise the stipulated 'rent' (i.e. revenue) from the peasantry. They, of course, enjoyed certain privileges of having hereditary title, developing of waste land, granting of *pattas* to peasants, *moffusil serinjamy* disbursements, distribution of *abwab* (cesses), paying his rents (i.e. before provincial or local Mughal officers) personally or through a deputy on his behalf or his *ryots* subordinate to his authority. As regards the assessment rate, Grant maintained that it stood at 1/4 of the gross produce during Akbar's reign. However, it had increased in the course of the last two centuries due to two-fold factors. Firstly, the discovery of the mines of America affected the entire commercial world. It nearly doubled the circulation of the quantity of coin and reduced the relative value of the precious metals at least by one-half. In other words, it led to depreciation of money value and relative inflation. Secondly, with the rise of the Marathas (in the 17$^{th}$ and 18$^{th}$ centuries) on the Malabar coast, the trade in the manufactures declined in the latter region and led to a vigorous rise in trade, commerce and prosperity in Bengal. Under these circumstances, the raising of State demand was justified, though it never amounted to rack-renting under the Mughal administration. The revenues of Bengal (*Jumma Toomary*) were not permanently fixed upon the *Zamindars* since Todar Mal's settlement, but were repeatedly enlarged and corrected, and a practical scheme of the finances was improved at various periods by actual surveys or particular local investigations in the course of period since Akbar's reign.

It is worthwhile making some reflections on Grant's thesis of the Mughal land revenue administration in Bengal. It has often been regretted that Grant's source-material of twenty Persian manuscripts (apart from the *Ain-i-Akbari*) has been lost to posterity which has handicapped the scholars to properly evaluate his conclusions. Though it is difficult to identify the unnamed Persian manuscripts utilised by Grant, it seems that at present they form a part of the aforementioned vast revenue literature preserved in the German libraries. On the problem of land ownership, Grant suffered from an erroneous generalised European concept that in all Asiatic countries the agricultural land belonged to the State. This, by itself, was s legacy from the European travellers who visited India during the Mughal age[6]. Grant assumed that the entire *zamindari* class of his days owed its title to the Royal *sanads* issued during the viceroyalty of Murshid Quli Khan in the 18th century. This may be correct but Grant did not realise a that the *zamindari* titles were regarded as hereditary and were invariably renewed from one administration to another. As such, many a 16th-17th century *Zamindari* continued right till the 18th century and were confirmed under Murshid Quli Khan. Grant rightly emphasised the role of the *Zamindars* as official tax-gatherers, though he inaccurately took an extreme position which did not recognise the ownership of the *Zamindars* over their self-developed lands. Grant did not understand the varying charaterisation of the *riaya* in Bengal. Grant's notion of assessment rate at ½ of the gross produce under Akbar as a uniform rate in all the regions of the Subah of Bengal could be contested as it was based on wrong reading of a technical passage narrated by the *Ain-i-Akbari* in its chapter on classification of agrarian land[7]. Grant's assumption that in the 16th-17th centuries the influx of silver and gold from the Americas in Europe and from there through either direct trade or through the Middle-Eastern Asian countries to India served as one of the determining factors for the increase in the incidence of State demand seems quite plausible. However, the problem requires a further probe by comparing the volume of bullion imported in Europe and India at phased periods and consequently by analysing the effect on the movement of prices of the agricultural commodities both for inland and overseas trade. Despite the paucity of any comprehensive contemporary data relating to the exact quantity of gold and silver imported in India and the price trends of the food-grains and other commercial commodities, the sporadic 16-17th centuries regional source-material available in these respects points towards the correctness of Grant's general view. However, it would be improper to assume that the incidence of State demand shot up to the flat ½ of the gross produce in the course of the 17th century. The State share was always governed by detailed classification of agricultural land and for assessment purposes, a distinction was made between the grain and the cash crops (*Jins-i-kamil*). In this respect, Sir John Shore had a better judgement than James Grant. But Grant's main thesis that periodical assessments were made after actual surveys and *hast-wa-bud* accounts or particular local investigations is undeniable. Moreland's[8] view that the *Zamindars* paid fixed lump sum unassessed amount to the State identifying them with revenue-farmers paying fixed sums by way of demand is not correct and his criticism of Grant is unjustified.

In his memoranda over the controversy of the enforcement of Permanent Settlement in Bengal, Sir John Shore[9] attempted an inquisitional historical analysis of the land revenue administration in Bengal since Akbar's reign. By this time, British historiography responded to the problems of the British Empire. Major Davy had translated the Memoirs and Institutes of Timur.[10] This shows the keen interest of the English scholars in the political concepts and Institutes of the Timuride family. Shore tried to understand the political institutes of the Mughal Empire from the *Malfuzat-i-Timuri* and the *Ain-i-Akbari*. For the *Zamindari* and various agrarian problems, Shore banked on the historical revenue literature provided to him by Sayyid Gulam Husain. Shore made a comparative study of the Bengal land revenue problems in the 16th-17th centuries and the 18th century especially since the viceroyalty of Jafar Khan (Murshid Quli Khan) as two distinct phases. He contended that the main considerations for comparison of the two periods were the population, the cultivation of the country, the relative value of money specie, commerce, the taxes (land revenue) imposed and the extra demands (*sayer*) annually levied. He maintained that during the Mughal age, the incidence of State demand and the cesses being moderate, were based on regular principles of revenue administration which took into consideration the State of cultivation and the above mentioned factors. The increase in the revenues of Bengal from Akbar's reign to the end of the viceroyalty of Jafar Khan (1727 A.D.) could be explained on account of annexation of new territories, expansion of trade and commerce and the agricultural development. But from Jafar Khan's period, the imposition of heavy incidence of extra cesses (*abwab*) and the exaction of increased revenues from the *Zamindari* class subjected the latter to harsh treatment. The

*Zamindars,* in their own turn, extracted inordinate revenues from the *Ryots*. This meant improvishment of the both *Zamindari* class and the *Ryots* and it was certainly an unwise measure on the part of the Bengal administration. This aspect of Shore's analysis has been confirmed by recent research in the history of Bengal. Firminger, in his introduction to the *Fifth Report,* has criticised Sir John Shore's minutes for his views on the Mughal revenue system and the varying assessment rates fixed at ½, 1/3, 2/5, ¼, of the gross produce for the grain crops and the applications of the sliding scale going as low as 1/8th for certain cash crops. A scrutiny of the Bihar and Rajasthan Archives of the 2nd half of the 17th century covering the territories in the *Subahs* of Bihar, Delhi, Ajmer, Malwa and Agra shows that the views of Sayyid Gulam Husain and Sir John Shore on the Mughal revenue assessment rates were perfectly correct and that Firminger's criticism is unjustified. The above mentioned revenue literature in Persian also reveals the limitations of the English administrators to understand various intricate and technical aspects of the Mughal revenue system. Sir John Shore thought that his main achievement lay in the fact of getting the recognition of the proprietorship of the *Zamindars*.[11] Sayyid Gulam Husain is quite clear in his analysis of the meaning of the term *Malik*. When the latter term was associated with a *Zamindar*, it would not mean an absolute proprietor of the agricultural land. As *Malik*, the *Zamindar* was responsible for the realisation of the revenues of his *zamindari* village and enjoyed perquisites (*haquq* and *rasum*) in lieu thereof. [12] The right of revenue collection on behalf of the State and the entitlement to perquisites was considered a hereditary claim based on the idea of ownership (*malkiyat*). A *Zamindar* could be divested of this right of ownership of a village only on grounds of gross negligence or recalcitrance. A primary *Zamindar* may be proprietor to the lands in the self-developed villages.[13] The English administrators could understand the meaning of the ownership of *zamindari* only in the English concept of the rights in property and essentially associated the hereditary ownership of the *zamindari* with proprietary rights in the lands therein.

Even Sir John Shore, who was considered to be an expert on the Mughal land revenue system in Bengal, found the situation singularly confused. Taking the *malkiyat* rights of the *Zamindars* into consideration and with an instinctive insight into the virtual ownership land rights of the *riaya,* he found the situation by no means compatible. So he tried to strike a 'via media' between the land rights of the *Zamindars* and the *Riaya*. He commented, "that the relation of a *Zamindars* to Government and of a *raiyat* to a *Zamindar* was neither that of a proprietor nor of a vassal, but compound of both the former performed acts of authority unconnected with proprietary right, the latter had rights without real property, that the property of one and the rights of the other were in great measure held at discretion that such was the system we found and were under the necessity of adopting for that present that much time must elapse before a system perfectly consistent in all its parts could be established, and that the compound relation of the *Zamindar* to government and *riayat* to *Zamindar* be reduced to the simple principles of landlord and tenant.[10] At the same time, Sir John Shore added that he for his part was not ashamed to distrust his own knowledge as he had frequent proofs that new enquiries led to new information. Sayyid Gulam Hussain, the revenue consultant of Sir John Shore, is very clear on the comparative position of the land rights of the *Zamindars* and the *Riaya*. Despite this, Sir John Shore could not easily shake off the impact of English concept of the proprietary rights and found the situation a little confused. He wanted to keep his mind open for a further probe into the land rights of the *Riaya* before covering the relationship of the *Zamindar* and the *Riaya* into that of a landlord and tenant in the pure and simple English sense on permanent basis. In fact, under the Mughal administration, the comparative land rights of the *Zamindars* and the *Riaya* were neither vague nor inconsistent in lacking definition and precision.

Whereas some of the Indian *Munshis* could well appreciate the main points of difference between the Bengal revenue practices and other portions of North India, the 18th century English administrators were much circumscribed in their concept in this respect. During the 17th-18th centuries, Bengal had known both the *Zamindars* and the *Taaluqdars.*[15] Apart from the Chiefs (*Rajas*), other big landed-intermediaries were also known as *Zamindars*. The act of *zamindari* lay in the payment of revenues (*malguzari*) to the State; a *Zamindar* was always confirmed by a Royal *sanad* and paid nominal *peshkash* to the State. A *Taaluqdar* with a large *taaluqa* would assume the role of a *Zamindar* when he paid the revenues of his territory directly to the State but, by and large, the petty *Taaluqdars* paid the revenue of their *taaluqas* through a superior *Zamindars*-cum-*Chaudhari* who acted as the representative. Such a *Zamindar* paid the revenues not only of his own *zamindari* but even of the petty *taaluqas* of the *Taaluqdars* under his jurisdiction. His *zamindari* was reckoned to cover both his personal *zamindari* and the petty *taaluqas*. Except in case of the *taaluqa* villages colonized and developed by the *Taaluqdar* himself, a *Taaluqdar* was not the owner of the agricultural lands of the *Riaya* and his proprietary rights in a *taaluqa* were exactly of the same nature as the *Zamindar*'s rights over his *zamindari*. Ordinarily, a *Taaluqdar* did not have an ancient claim to the *taaluqa* and the majority of the *taaluqas* were established after they were purchased from the original *Zamindars* or *Taaluqdars*. The extensive sale transactions of the 17th and 18th centuries established a large class of petty *Taaluqdars*. A *Taaluqdar* of a few villages, unless confirmed by a Royal *sanad* in the *zamindari* rights, could not be designated as a *Zamindar*. A *Chaudhari* family owning *zamindari* villages also belonged to a petty *zamindari* class. In line with the 17th century practice, the 18th century documents insist on distinguishing the *Riaya* from the *zamindari* and the *taaluqdari* classes in Bengal. The petty *zamindari* and the *taaluqdari* families were self-cultivating and they also rented out their personal lands to the *Riaya*. The *Mandals*, *Muqaddams* and the *Paramaniks* were not considered to be *zamindari* families but were regarded as the principal *Riaya*.[16] They could claim ownership in land. The other categories of agriculturists comprising *Riaya* were the *Khudkasht* who would cultivate their own lands or were resident occupancy cultivators; and the *Paikashtkars* who were non-occupancy and non-resident cultivators.[17] The *Muzarian* were occupancy or lease holding cultivators. Like the *Khudkashta Riaya*, the *Muqarari Riaya* may denote both self-cultivating peasant-proprietors and occupancy cultivators. However, the difference in the two lay in the fact that whereas the *Khukashta Riaya* paid land revenue according to the actual land under plough, the *Muqarari Riaya* held perpetual *pattas* for specified holdings and fixed rates of revenue.[18] It is not intended to give here details of the Bengal land revenue system except to point out the limitations of the 18th century British Indian administrators to understand the technical details of the land rights of the varying categories of cultivators constituting *Riaya*. Nor did they spell out details about the methods of assessment and incidence of State demand based upon classification of agrarian land. Even though lot of discussion took place on the position of the *Zamindars*, they could not properly appreciate the varying degrees of the *zamindari* class and the extent to which the Bengal territories were subjected to the Mughal land revenue practices. The position of the 17th century *Zamindars* and the nature of the Mughal revenue practices introduced in their territories can be well analysed from Mirza Nathan's *Baharistan-i-Ghaibi*, *Murraqat-i-Hasan* by Mir Abul Hasan Alamgiri and *Fathiya-i-Ibriya* by Shihabu-ddin Talish.[19] Murshid Quli Khan's revenue reforms in Bengal marked the culmination in the process of integration with the Mughal concept of administration. The comparative evaluation of the above mentioned 17th and 18th century source-material would help considerably in the construction of a co-ordinated picture of the agrarian set-up in Bengal during the Mughal age.

The translation of the *Ain-i-Akbari* by Francis Gladwin[20] was an important step in an attempt to understand the Mughal land revenue administration, but the translation suffered from various limitations. Not only that the best manuscripts of the *Ain* with authentic version of the various technical revenue terms were not available, but their rendering in the English language was not correct. In both these respects, even Blochmann's recension at the *Ain*, translated by H. S. Jarrett and J. N. Sarkar,[21] is not free from blemishes and errors. The passages covering revenue terminology included in the third *Daftar* of Abul Fazl's *Ain-i-Akbari* are mostly inaccurately translated. This has consequently given rise to various controversies and imaginary surmises reflected in the modern historical writings. For the proper understanding of the Mughal land revenue administration, translated version of the *Ain-i-Akbari* is not a safe landing and can be used mostly for its narrative portions rather than for the revenue sentences put by Abul

Fazl in a terse and technical language in the original Persian text. The technique of the comparative study of the Persian manuscripts of the *Ain* and their annotation had not developed so far. Thus in various respects, the views of the British administrators and the Indian *Munshis* were bound to be based on surmises which in certain respects have turned out to be correct and in others erroneous. The Indian revenue experts, serving as advisers to the English administrators, were quite conscious of noting the changes in the land rights, agrarian practices and revenue administration that crept in the Mughal administration in the 18th century on the disintegration of the Mughal Empire, but for want of adequate contemporary source-material, they could not afford a very comprehensive picture of the 16-17th centuries Mughal India. Of course, they were successful in giving a reliable and detailed picture of the 18th century revenue history of the Bengal. This is true not only of the original commentaries on the land revenue system by the Indian revenue experts but of Sayyid Gulam Hussain's *Siyar-ul-mutahkirin* dedicated to Warren Hastings[22] and Gulam Husain Salim Zaidpuri's *Riyaz-us-Salatin* written during the same period.[23] The latter affords typical examples of the attempt at the narration of general provincial history and the revenue practices in Bengal during the Mughal age.

Before James Mill published *The History of British India*,[24] a regular school of thought showing sympathy with the land rights of the *Riaya* was developing. During the debates of last three decades of the 18th century, the main issue involved in controversy mostly hinged on the concept of land proprietorship on the part of *Zamindars* versus the State and the position of the land rights of the varying classes of the *Riaya* was mostly ignored. It was only in the course of 19th century when the British revenue administrators gathered more experience of nature of the land rights of the agricultural classes in the ceded and conquered provinces that the judiciousness of the Permanent Settlement of Bengal was challenged and a keen academic interest was taken to review the position of the land rights of the *Zamindars* versus *Riaya* prevalent in India before the inception of the British rule. A.D. Campbell[25] wrote a very valuable paper on the land revenue of India. Though his chief object was to bring out the main effects of the Permanent

Settlement in Bengal, he also dwelt upon the pre-British concept of proprietary rights in land and the relationship between the *Zamindars* and the cultivators. He pointed out that in a country like India, there were minor regional land tenure diversities which could not be fitted in the general description of the whole. He divided the *Ryots* into three classes viz. the *Khudkasht*, hereditary occupancy and non-occupancy. The *Khudkasht Ryots* were universally considered the descendants of the aboriginal settlers of the village. Campbell held that in Bengal the occupancy *Riaya* with residence in the village of its holdings could also be termed as *Khudkasht*.[26] Campbell also maintained that under the Mughal Government, the *Zamindar* possessed no right whatsoever in the soil itself though it cannot be denied that nearly all the *Zamindars* from the highest to the lowest, were themselves cultivators to a greater or lesser extent. A primary village *Zamindar* was himself in the greatest degree cultivator in his own neighborhood. He enjoyed *malikana* rights (10 to 15% of the collected revenues) and had a hereditary office. He was the owner of only his own fields and the great mass of the hereditary peasantry were their own cultivators. This is a correct version but it may be asserted that many *Zamindari* families owned self-developed villages of which they were the *Maliks* as revenue collectors and owners of land as well.[27]

An attempt was also made to understand the land revenue administration under the Hindu system of government in ancient India. It was also believed that with the exception of the variation in the incidence of State demand, most of these characteristics continued to operate in the Hindu dominated regions throughout the medieval age. Sir William Jones had brought out the main characteristics of the Hindu civilisation as the product of the Hindu peoples and the concept of the continuation of the Hindu agrarian system throughout the medieval age reflected this approach in the study of Indian civilisation. The Committee of the House of Commons which enquired into East India Affairs in 1810 drew a general picture of ancient Indian revenue practices.[28] It emphasised the role of 'the village community' as a 'corporation, or township' and that the inhabitants of India continued to live under 'this simple form of municipal government' or 'a small republic' throughout the ages till the 19th century. As regards the assessment rates, the Report of the Committee put the custom of the Hindu government at 1/3rd of gross produce in respect of crops irrigated through artificial means and ½ of gross produce in respect of crops dependent upon pure rainfall. The State charged the revenues both in kind and cash. The changes brought about by the Muslim conquest reduced the share of the cultivators to 1/6th or 1/5th of the gross produce. The system of giving *pattas* to the *Ryots* by the *Zamindars* and the sub-renting of lands by the latter to the revenue farmers, the impoverishment of the peasantry and indebtedness to the money lenders were the resultant abuses of the Muslim rule. This Report of the House of Commons influenced many a writer in the course of the 19th century. The concept of 'village community' had great advocates in Charles Metcalfe, James Mill, Elphinstone, John Malcolm and Sir Henry Maine. The problem of incidence of State share under the 'Hindu' and the 'Mohomeden' rulers was incorrectly analysed but later on it affected Ephinstone's mode of thinking. The other abuses associated with the 'Mohomedan' rule in fact reflected the deterioration of the Mughal practices during the course of the 19th century.

For an analysis of pre-British taxation system in India, James Mill believed that the 'Hindu' methods of taxation continued to prevail in India all through the ages. So he attempted a detailed description of the laws and revenue practices underlined by Menu. In economic concept, James Mill belonged to the English utilitarian school of thought.[29] In general thought, he was influenced by the English philosophical radicals. Thu English Utilitarians and Evangelicals did not find anything commendable in the Indian societies. With its past unmitigated suffering, India's future depended on the British Empire. So James Mill maintained that in India, the rights and privileges of property were not so extensive and secure as in England. The main feature of 'Hindu ruled state of society' continued to persist. Starting with a communal concept of property, the *Riaya* under the 'Hindu' system of government gradually developed occupancy rights in land–a position which continued to prevail all through the medieval age. Both under the 'Hindu' and 'Muhammadan' periods of Indian History, the land belonged to the 'Sovereign' (i.e. State). The *Riaya* class comprised the husbandmen and the immediate cultivators of the soil. The *Zamindars* were middlemen between the cultivators who raised the crop and the king who received the greater part of the net produce. Thus the *Zamindars* were merely 'collectors of the revenue' entitled to some portion of the produce in lieu of their remunerations. They had, of course, the right to use military force. Like James Grant, Mill also thought that like all Asiatic countries under 'despotic' governments, the ownership of land in India lay with the King. As an economist, James Mill was a follower of Adam Smith and Ricardo.[30] The latter advocated the theory of State landlordship and the perpetual hereditary land rights on the part of the *Riaya*. Ricardo was equally against the Permanent Settlement which recognised the *Zamindars* as the landlords and which in the ordinary course of progress of a society increased their wealth at the cost of the State and the *Ryots*. It was from this angle that James Mill looked at the position of the *Zamindars*. James Hill believed that during the ancient and medieval periods, the *Ryots* developed perpetual, heritable and even transferable rights in land which were not incompatible with the concept of land ownership on the part of the Sovereign. The latter claimed a right to as much of the produce as he pleased, and seldom left to the *Ryots* more then a scanty reward for their labour. The cultivators were left with a bare compensation for the labour and the cost of cultivation and the benefit of land went to the king. He confirmed his belief in the concept of the 'village community' as a 'Corporation.' James's concept of State ownership, the nature of the land rights of the *Zamindars* and the *Ryots*, the arbitrary incidence of State demand, the condition of the *Ryots* consequent on his theoretical economic concept cannot be accepted for the 'Mohomedan' government in general or Mughal India. However, one observation of James Mill that there was no conclusive proof to the effect that the incidence of State demand was higher during the 'Mohomedan' period than during the 'Hindu' government in ancient India needs further probing. It is not because, James Mill bore more sympathy with the 'Mohomedan' government then with the 'Hindu' system of government that he made this suggestion. He suggested that in practice, the State share amounted to higher rate than a simple theoretical enunciation made by Manu.

There is much of validity in this assertion when the principles of assessment underlined by *Arthashastra* are borne in mind. At the same time in a large country like India, there could be no uniformity of State demand which may have varied from region to region depending up the nature of soil, means of irrigation and labour necessary for cultivation.

W.W. Hunter in a '*Brief history of the Indian people*' asserted that Akbar's system was based on the ancient Hindu customs and survived to the day of his writings. Of course, Akbar resorted to regular survey and measurement of land, determination of the produce of each 'acre of land' and that the State demand was fixed at 1/3rd of the gross produce. This could be commuted into cash money. Instead of practicing annual land settlements, Akbar effected settlement for ten years. Hunter evidently picked the main points of the *Ain-i-Akbari* and did not attempt any deep analysis of these features. His reading of '*Ain-i Deh Sala*' as 'settlement for ten years' as against the previous practice of yearly settlements is rather inaccurate. Hunter had a superiority complex for the British revenue system and commented that allowing for the difference in area and purchasing power of silver, Akbar's tax was about three times the amount which the British took. This is a questionable hypothesis. Even though Hunter believed in the concept of continued system of revenue administration from ancient times to the 19th century, in his specialised study of Orissa,[32] he pointed towards the absence of the landlordism (*Zamindari*) and 'the village community' system. Here in Orissa, 'a village lacked the corporate character and was merely a collection of families.' This is a valuable piece of information which cast doubt on the concept of the village community' with 'corporate' life supposed to have existed throughout the ages in India.

Mountstuart Elphinstone[33] was basically a revenue administrator and unlike James Mill, his approach for the study of agrarian system of medieval India was not influenced by purely theoretical economic concept. In outlook, both Hunter and Elphinstone had much in common with each other. Elphinstone had not given any comprehensive description of the Mughal administration as he claimed to have given only 'a slight view' of the internal 'Mahomedan Empire in India.' As regards the revenue system, he asserted that it was the same under the Mughal Empire as it existed 'under the Hindus' in ancient India. The alterations attempted by Sher Shah and later accomplished by Akbar, were not designed to change the system but to render it more perfect. In this respect, Elphinstone regarded the fundamental features of the land revenue system being predominantly 'Hindu' having continued from ancient period to the pre-British era of the 19th century (excepting Bengal which came under the British influence of land settlement after 1765). The only exception he pointed out was with regard to incidence of State demand which having been put at 1/6th of gross produce by Manu had been raised in the course of centuries to ½ of the gross produce by the 19th century. For his sources, Elphinstone banked on Manu, the enquiries made by the early 19th century British revenue administrators on ancient India, whose memoranda were embodied in the Reports of Select Committees of House of Commons (1812 and 1831-32) and other detailed regional enquiries of English revenue experts on the pre-British 19th century revenue practices. Elphinstone was quite adept in the technique of sifting 19th century contemporary sources tempered by regional variations for arriving at conclusions. In line with the early 19th century analysis by Charles Metcalfe and other British administrators, Elphinstone agreed with the theory of the concept of 'village community' having persisted from ancient times till the 19th century. Elphinstone believed that during the 'Mohomedan' period, ordinarily 'the municipal institutions of villages' with some local jurisdiction acted as a deterrent against the imposition of the theory of the 'Mohomedan law' upon the Indian life. He surmised that the general state of the country must, no doubt, have been flourishing. While granting that the 19th century revenue units viz. the village and the *pargana* were a legacy from ancient India, he considered that the *pargana* had throughout ages represented as a uniformly defined circle comprising a set number of villages. He held that the nature of proprietary rights in land may vary from one type of village to another. There were villages wherein land was owned by village land owners designated variantly in different parts of India (i.e. *Zamindars*, *Biswadars*, *Maliks*, *Patels*, *Mirassis* and *Mirasdars*). They possessed hereditary transferable proprietary rights. The right to transfer was conditioned by the law of pre-emption. The land belonged to a family rather than an individual and in making a partition of land, the land owners were taken by families. In some villages, the rights of the landholders were held in common, the whole working for the land and sharing the net produce after satisfying the claim of the government. In some they divided the cultivated lands with mutual responsibility for the dues of the government. In many villages, the practice of exchange of holdings determined by the nature of soil was practiced. The landholders were entitled to perquisites (*malikana* or *zamindari rasum* in 'Hindustan' and designated as *tunduwarum* or *swamibhogam* in Tamil). A landholder may enjoy the office of the *muqaddam* but the nature of the two was different, the former being proprietary right arising from an interest in the soil and the other a mere remuneration for service which was also transferable at the pleasure of the State. The *Ryot* class (also known as *Khudkashta*) constituting the husbandmen were the *assamies* of the landholders. They were the tenants of the landholders and had hereditary rights of occupancy. They did not possess the rights to sell, give away or mortgage their rights. The landholders extorted as much from the *Ryots* as the latter could afford to pay. The permanent *Ryots* were of two categories i.e. *Ryots* who rented the lands of the landlords and those settled in such villages where there were no intermediaries between them and the State. In the latter case, the ownership was vested in the State and the cultivators were simply permanent tenants. The ownership was not vested with the permanent *Ryots* of either of the categories, nor were they tenants at will. In fact, Elphinstone did not believe in the idea of absolute and perfect property. The proprietorship on the part of the State meant its claim on the share in produce which also conceded the occupancy rights on the part of the permanent *Ryots*. Such rights were of value when the State demand was fixed and of no value when the public assessment became arbitrary. It was also possible that the permanent tenants were the erstwhile land owners and were suppressed by the new conquerors from time to time. The temporary tenants held annual leases written or understood.

The continuation of the ancient or medieval revenue system in toto till the 19th century is rather doubtful. It is true that many of the Hindu land revenue practices continued throughout the medieval age during the Muslim rule. During the Sultanate period, the role of the State was mostly confined to the collection of land revenue and the indigenous methods of assessment continued. They found equal acceptance during the Mughal age but fundamental changes were brought in respect of measurement of land, detailed principles of assessment of revenue based on classification of land, some methods of assessment, the role of money economy for payment of land revenue, and the machinery for collection of revenues. The proprietary rights of the *Riaya* (agriculturists) were not tempered with by the State in medieval India but the political factor of conquest by the superior tribes and other socio-economic factors continued to affect the course of their development. Conversely speaking, the main features of the revenue system known to Elphinstone from the 19th century practices were not wholly applicable to the 16th-17th centuries in India. It is true that during the Mughal age, there were landlord's (*zamindari*) villages owned by them but a *zamindari* village would not always carry with it exclusive rights of land ownership.[34] A *Zamindar* also acted as tax-gatherer for such villages in his jurisdiction of which he was not the owner of lands therein. At the same time, Elphinstone's concept of State ownership of non-*zamindari* villages with permanent tenants (*Ryots*) is not acceptable for the Mughal age. It seems that the *Khudkashta Riaya* in the non-*zamindari* villages possessed proprietary rights in land. The right of transfer of land was mostly governed by pre-emption rules and also the fact whether the agricultural land did possess saleable value. It is also doubtful if the *pargana* during medieval age did comprise defined number of villages. In line with Hunter, Elphinstone agrees that the true concept of 'village community' depended upon land tenures like the *bhaichara* or *pattidari*. Where such concept of 'village community' prevailed, the 'municipal' concept of village governance did not exist. He as well recognizes the fact that the autonomous character was not uniformly applicable to all the villages. It may also be wondered if the concept of 'village community' based on land tenure as explained by Elphinstone did ever prevail during the Mughal age.

The main features of the concept 'village community' described by the early 19$^{th}$ century British administration were the 'corporate' character of village managing its own internal affairs with the help of the village functionaries, self sufficiency of the village and the land tenures covering communal *zamindari* estates, *pattidari* and *bhaichara* basis. One or the other aspect of the 'village community' had been underlined by the administrators. This resulted in the formulation of a regular theory about the 'village communities' by Sir Henry Maine, the great jurist and the sociologist.[35] So far as the 16$^{th}$- 17$^{th}$ century documents reveal, it is difficult to trace such a concept of 'village community'. Under the Mughal revenue regulations, cultivating families, whether in the co-sharing *zamindari* or other villages, were reckoned as *asamian* and the assessment on the holdings of the land-owning *zamindari* or *riaya* families as well as their *muzarian* was done directly by the *Amin* and his staff. In the co-sharing *zamindari* villages, the payment of land revenue may be made by the representative *Zamindar* or *Muqaddam* but in case of arrears of revenue, in the eyes of Mughal law, every co-sharer was held responsible for the payment of his share of revenue. At times, if not contrary to the mutual understanding of the land-owning *zamindari* family and its *muzarian*, the latter were equally held responsible of the payment of land revenue. There is no documentary evidence to show that during the 16$^{th}$-17$^{th}$ centuries, distribution of assessment over the various holdings and mutual adjustment amongst the co-sharing land owning families on account of arrears of revenues was ever left to 'village communities'. Of course, the possibility of such a practice cannot be ruled out for such villages which were farmed out to the *Mustajirs* or in the *gair-amil* areas which paid fixed revenues and were not subjected to the Mughal land revenue regulations.

For the 16$^{th}$-17$^{th}$ centuries, no 'corporate' regulations or 'autonomous' and 'self-sufficient' characteristics can be attributed to the 'village communities'. To assert that such unchanging traits lay rooted in 'the archaic institution' of the 'village communities' notwithstanding any change in the ruling dynasties or political revolutions is a sheer historical anachronism. During the Mughal age, the concept of the village society depended upon the nature of prevalent land tenures and the relationship between the agricultural and non-agricultural population residing in a village. The villages of the *zamindari* and *muqaddami* families were owned on co-sharing basis. The holding of each family was reckoned in accordance with the regional method. The agricultural lands were always owned on joint family basis. The operation of the laws of inheritance and the mutations of various *zamindari* and *muqaddami* shares resulted in the division and sub-division of the *zamindari* shares even in such villages which were owned exclusively by one or a few families. This was a continuous process till the 17th and 18th centuries. Thus the villages with multiple shares owned on co-sharing basis by the *zamindari* and *muqaddmi* families (termed *Riaya*), ordinary peasant-proprietor *Riaya* who had also settled both occupancy and non-occupancy cultivating families on their respective lands came to constitute what was termed as 'the village communities' in the early 19th century. Of course, the *Muqaddam* as the headman of the village constituting the principal *Riaya* of the village formed a link between the State and the 'village community'. Similarly, on a large scale, in a *zamindari* village the agricultural interests of the *Zamindar* and the other cultivating families were considered to be integral and corporate in nature. The *Mandals*, *Kalantars*, the *Chaudharis*, *Sardars*, *Arbaban* etc. were equally considered to be guardians of the agricultural interests of the other *Riaya* families especially those of the *Muzarian* (*Raiyat-i-raiza*). It is evident from the 16-17th century documents that without the central control over them, in matters of assessment and distribution of revenues, they were more liable to act in self-interest to him deteriment of the ordinary cultivating families. As a safeguard against it, the Mughal State stressed the assessment work and the inspection of the holdings under actual tilage to be undertaken by the *Amin* and the *Shiqdar* in collaboration with the local semi-government revenue staff. The *Zamindars*, *Muqaddams*, land-owning *Riaya* and the *Muzarian* were all governed by the customary regulations of the village of the *pargana*.

A more serious school of thought for analysing the Mughal institutions in their judicial and revenue aspects was developed by Col. Galloway.[36] This was the first serious attempt to describe the Mughal land revenue system in the background of the Muslim jurisprudence of the middle Eastern Asian countries and the impact of the indigenous Indian land revenue notions prevalent during the medieval age. Col. Galloway made an intelligent use of the *Ain-i-Akbari* and some of the *Farmans* of Aurangzeb to substantiate his conclusions on the legal aspects of the Mughal institutions. Galloway definitely made considerable progress in breaking new ground in the analysis of the land problems during the Mughal age. But he had mostly a legalist approach and could cover the economic background of the agrarian situation in a rudimentary manner.

Col. James Tod was the first English administrator to deal with the regional history of the Rajasthan in a comprehensive manner. In his '*Annals and Antiquities of Rajasthan*',[37] he made use of some epigraphic sources for the early Rajput settlements on clannish basis in Rajasthan but for the Mughal portions, he relied mostly on the local traditions and the *Khyats* of the bards. Tod had a romantic historical approach and his enthusiasm for the past glories of the Rajput dynasties. He could not visualise the true nature or political and administrative relationship between the Mughal State and the Rajput Chiefs. Much less could he realise the administrative limitations placed by the Mughal State upon the Rajput Chieftainships and the extent to which the Mughal land revenue system operated in the Rajasthan territories of the Mughal Empire. Tod's empirical approach for the acceptance of feudalism in Rajasthan and the attempt to find exact parallels of European feudalism and the adoption of European feudal terminology for the Rajasthan political setup and agrarian structure is completely erroneous.[38] There are essential differences between the interior economy of a complete Rajput family based on clannish structure and *zamindari* principles on the one hand and the European feudalism on the other.

However, Tod's excellent account of the geographical and economic condition of the early 19th century Rajasthan based on personal observations is reminiscent of Babur's memoirs covering some portions of Rajasthan. His analysis of the existing position of the land rights and the land revenue practices is a remarkable contribution to the economic history of Modern India. Of course, many of the land revenue practices could be traced to the Mughal age but the exact nature of their prevalence in the 16th-17th centuries and the extent to which they underwent change in 18th century can be known only from the contemporary documentary sources which were not available to Tod.

Kaviraj Shymaldas in 'Vir Vinod'[39] has given detailed description of the political history of the Rajasthan and has also quoted copiously the original Persian and Rajasthani documents comprising the correspondence between the Mughal State and the Rajasthan Chiefs. But it is clear from Kaviraj's narrative details that, like Tod, his vision was coloured by the Rajput spirit of independence. He could not understand the technical aspects and the revenue terminology of the documents that he had himself quoted. As such, he was not in a position to realise the fundamental basis of relationship between the Mughal state and the Rajput Chiefs and the revenue regulations which governed the *Jagir* system during the Mughal age. This verdict is equally true about Gouri Shanker Ohja and the other Hindi writers on Rajasthan history.[40] C.U. Will's[41] analysis of the historical development of the Jaipur state in the 18-19th centuries is mostly based on contemporary documentary evidence and correctly points out various errors committed by Tod in understanding the character of the Mughal revenue institutions and the extent to which latter were enforced in the Rajasthan territories.

C.A. Elliot[42] dealt with the important aspects of the land revenue administration on a detailed regional basis. In his '*Chronicles of Oonao*' he emphasised the ethnic role in the *zamindari* and agrarian settlements during the Medieval Age. He was the first scholar to scrutinise the available family archives, a few regional accounts of the 17th-18th centuries and the local traditions. He offered an adequate historical treatment of the territory of Awadh. Though the importance or the description of the clannish settlement on ethnic basis is undeniable, for the brief description of the Mughal land revenue system, he stood on better footing for the 18th century than for the 16th-17th centuries. In his analysis of the land-rights of the various classes, especially the *Zamindars* and *Taaluqdars* and the concept of 'village community', he was considerably influenced and deceived by the theoretical enunciation of Sir Henry Maine and could not see the land-rights of various classes in their true historical perspective.

W.C. Bennet[43] carried further Elliot's work and his historical introduction to '*The Oudh Gazetteer*' is a masterly treatment giving an insight into the socio-economic, religious and sociological factors which governed the history of the Rajput chieftainships in Awadh. In line with Elliot's methodology, Bennett also stressed the ethnic role of the *zamindari* settlements, more especially in his book on *Clans of Roy Bareilly District*. For the Mughal period, both Elliot and Bennet could see that the Rajput Chiefs did not enjoy any independence and got *jagirs* from the Mughal State which gave nearly a century and a half's comparatively peaceful, stable and prosperous period to the territories of Awadh. But for want of any original contemporary evidence, they could not analyse the true basis of the political structure and the working of the land revenue administration in Awadh during the Mughal age. However, both Elliot and Bennet stood on surer grounds for their analysis of the late 18th and 19th centuries than for the Mughal period.

John Malcolm's[44] '*Historical survey of Central India and the adjoining provinces*' is mostly of a political nature. However, his minute description of the character, habits and practices of the various tribes and peoples inhabiting those regions give a clear idea of the socio-political forces which influenced the nature of the local administration and the revenue problems that above region faced through the centuries. Malcolm's reflections on the prevailing revenue practices having been inherited from the past, especially since the Mughal age, are really commendable. Malcolm is himself very much conscious of making a pragmatic rather than theoretical approach for studying the land problems. His analysis of the land rights of the varying cultivating classes, the units of local administration, the methods of land revenue assessment and the position of the various categories of the local and the *Zamindars* prevalent during the Mughal age bears strong identity with the actual position as discernable from the Mughal documents. It is only in his understanding of the 'village community' and the

Panchayat System that he showed preconceived notions relating to "those ancient institutions which render every village in India an independence and distinct community, ruled by its own officers within its own limits" despite "the bigotry of the Mohomedans, and the rapacity of the Mahrattas." Malcolm's descriptions about the actual state of affairs in early 19th century may be correct but he was not able to see the evolution of the concept of the village society at various historical stages from the past 17th century and since then to the early 19th century.

C.D. Field[45] asserted that the complexity of land tenures in India was inherent in the diverse historical circumstances of different parts of the country. Thus due to regional variations, the growth of institutions in some parts of India became perfect while in others, it remained imperfect. Field dealt with the problem of evolution of land tenures in India from the ancient period to the 19th century in a general manner. For the Mughal period, he briefly analysed the land tenures, the nature of *jagir* assignments, farming system and the role of the landed aristocracy. In this respect, he was mostly influenced by Elphinstone and his analysis suffered from limitations as already commented for the latter. Field equally adhered to the concept of 'village community' with its inherent vitality as a "little republic having its own territory and its own municipal government under a headman." Here too, he was influenced by the earlier writers and his contemporary, Sir Henry Maine. Though like Elphinstone he considered that the *khudkashta riaya* as the permanent tenants of the land owner (village *zamindars*) did not possess hereditary proprietary rights, he was inclined to agree with Carnegy's analysis of land tenures[46] that the saleable rights of the *khudkashta* cultivators, far from being inherent, were based on custom. But Field did not clarify as to when this customary practice had sprung up. Field also considered the primary *zamindari* families as an integral part of the 'village community'. Only if Field had further scrutinised the territorial jurisdictions of the village *zamindaries* based on clannish structure with inherent corporate spirit, he would have realized that the concept of 'village community' as a 'little republic' and the existence of such *zamindari* villages (cultivated exclusively by *zamindari* families or both by *zamindari* families and other *riaya*) were irreconcilable and that the village as a closed society was a historical myth.

Sir Alfred Lyall[47] made a good sociological analysis of Central India and Rajasthan territories. He held that the land tenures in these regions had since ages been governed by the tribal and clannish structure of the society which had continued to preserve some 'archaic' aspects. In Central India, the combination and the crossing of kinship and religion lay at the basis of the clannish structure. There were villages in union and the multitude of people were tightly bound together as brethren by the tradition of lineage. The villages were settled on clannish basis and the lands of the surrounding villages as composite blocks were possessed by the families of the clan inheriting similar socio-religious and political characteristics of common ancestorhood. The tribal migrations and conquests had also led to the emergence of the dominant clans with stock groups that organised and maintained themselves. A graduated social order with aboriginal horde (like *Bheels* and *Meenas,* etc.) at the bottom end culminating with pure clans at the top existed throughout the medieval age. Similarly for Rajasthan, Alfred Lyall equally took into consideration the clannish and geographical factors. He assailed Tod's theory of feudalism and correctly analysed the chief characteristics of the Rajput tenures. The contribution of Alfred Lyall's study of agrarian society and sociological terms is undeniable and it is in this light that the subject of land tenures during the Mughal age may be looked into. Notwithstanding its importance, Lyall's study remains merely suggestive. For Central India, he could not underline the economic factor (i.e.) pertaining to surplus produce and the share of the landed intermediaries therein) for the establishment of the *zamindari* rights and the clannish conflicts amongst the dominant vis-a-vis suppressed or low caste clans or clans professing different religious faiths. Neither the society was stagnant nor was its evolution from the early medieval ages to the 19th century based upon any uniform pattern. Lyall did not appreciate the process of socio-economic transformation and the extent to which the land tenures were affected by the element of political stability during the Mughal age. Lyall could not understand the true basis of relationship in economic and revenue terms involved between the Mughal State and the Rajput Chiefs as he had the least idea of the claim of the Mughal State upon the revenues of the Rajput Chieftainships (*zamindaries*), the way the revenues were assessed and even appropriated to the Chieftains in lieu of their *tankhwah* (salary) and *watan jagirs*. Lyall's description that the Rajput Chiefs and their kindred families were 'lords of the soil' is too general. He did not penetrate into the interior village agrarian relationship which should have given him on idea of the land rights of the cultivators of varying categories (*riaya*) and the landed intermediaries, who, no doubt, were the scions of the dominant clan ruling over a chieftainship.

H.G. Keene[48] in his historical sketch of India during the Muslim rule assumed sympathetic approach to the Mughal land revenue administration, though, keeping in view the limited character of contemporary evidence at his command, his technique of research could not be of high order. In his mind, he was rather conscious of his own superiority over Elphinstone's work. He considered that after the publication of excerpts from the Persian chronicles by Elliot and Dowson and the new recension of *Ain-i-Akbari* (Vol.I) by H. Blochmann, he was better equipped to properly analyse Mughal India. He made an intelligent use of the accounts of some of the foreign travellers. His description of the main features of Mughal land revenue administration is known mostly from the *Ain*. His emphasis that the Mughal land revenue administration was not based on theoretical Islamic principles and that in the incidence of state demand upon the agriculturists no distinctions, whatsoever, was made between the Muslims and non-Muslims. He also underlined the elements of continuity from Sher Shah's administration to that of Akbar when the preparation of record of rights became an essential feature of Todar Mal's administration. The concept with both Sher Shah and Akbar was to keep a margin for the agriculturists between the State's demand and the expenses of cultivation. Akbar's revenue settlement was benevolent for the determination of this margin securing the rights of the agriculturists for its enjoyment. Keene also attempted to review the revenue administration against the political background. He was highly critical of Bernier's object of deliberately presenting an unfavourable picture of administration and social life under Aurangzeb. He was the first writer to suggest that the accounts of the foreign travellers should not be accepted unless corroborated by internal evidence. He pointed out that Bernier tried to humour the French ministry for the existence of good administration in France when compared to the life in Asian countries. He also stressed that Bernier contented to uphold his thesis that the assertion of State ownership in land was adverse to the progress of society. However, of his own, Keene conceded the rights of ownership of soil with agriculturists though he did not spell out the different agricultural classes. Moreover, despite his endeavor for a rudimentary ethnological attempt for analysing rural India, Keene could not go beyond Elphinstone's and Henry Maine concepts of 'the village communities.'

A few of the Settlement Reports written in the 19th century give an excellent description of the ethnic settlements since the medieval age and the prevalent land tenures with sketchy historical background. Most of the Settlements Reports were based on the late 18th and 19th centuries family documents of the *Zamindars* and for the Mughal period often refer to the *Ain-i-Akbari*, a few chronicles and the accounts of the foreign travellers. The Mughal period is dealt with in an extremely sketchy manner. Though many of the agrarian practices which find detailed description in the Settlement Reports could be traced to the Mughal age, the exact nature of their prevalence during the latter period can be determined only on the basis of the contemporary evidence so as to preclude generalisation. Baden Powell's[49] excellent account of land systems of British India is primarily a work on the revenue settlements effected during the British Rule and is based on the Settlement Reports. As such, for the Mughal age, he makes only brief general statements drawing from the Settlement Reports and the observations made by the English revenue officers in their officials minutes and memoranda.

In the beginning of the 20th century, Sir J.N. Sarkar[50] assiduously devoted himself to the Mughal age and produced monumental works on the political history of the period. Sarkar also showed interest in the administrative structure of the Mughal Empire but in this respect, his achievement is rather limited. On the revenue side, he banked on the *Ain-i-Akbari*, *Mirat-i-Ahmadi*, a few *Dasturulamals* and chronicles of the late 17th and 18th centuries. Even on the basis of this material, he could not properly analyse the Mughal land revenue terminology embodied in the Persian texts. Of the two *Farmans* of Aurangzeb he discovered from the Berlin Library and published in the Journal of the Royal Asiatic Society and later on in his book on the Mughal administration, Aurangzeb's *Farman* to Muhammad Hashim had already been rightly used by Col. Galloway,[51] a fact not known to Sir J.N. Sarkar. The Persian texts of the *Farmans* and more especially the commentaries thereupon are extremely unreliable. It has already been observed that the late 18th century revenue literature available from the Berlin Library, though extremely useful for the 18th century History of Bengal and Bihar, cannot be accepted for the 16th-17th centuries without further scrutiny. Moreover, the differences in the revenue practices in Bengal and other regions of North India have to be clearly emphasized. Even though the late 18th century Indian revenue experts in Bengal did have an access to some of the *Farmans* and *Dasturulamals* of the Mughal age, not all the commentaries written by them provide a correct analysis of the revenue practices of the Mughal age. Some of the commentaries were written to suit the firm notions and predilections of the British revenue administrators who were participants to the great controversy over the land rights of the State vs. *Zamindars* prevalent in Bengal before the enforcement of the Permanent Settlement. Having laid his hand first on the two widely publicised documents of Aurangzeb's reign and being completely ignorant of the other revenue literature lying in the Berlin Library, Sarkar could not go into the background of the commentaries written in late 18th century Bengal and was not in a position to arrive at any conclusive truth. Notwithstanding all this, Sarkar's translation and published commentaries on the *Farmans* have been accepted by the later scholars without any further screening of the problem. Vincent Smith's[52] description of Akbar's land revenue administration was mainly based on Jarrett's translated version of the *Ain-i-Akbari* and did nothing to break a new ground in this field.

In fact, Moreland[53] was the first scholar to undertake an

intensive study of the Mughal agrarian system and his pioneer works have laid the students of economic history under lasting gratitude for having shown considerable enthusiasm for providing an overall picture of the Mughal age. However, Moreland's verdict is not final. Having been a keen student of economics and a trained English civil servant, posted in United Provinces in India, in his early work on *The Revenue Administration of the United Provinces*, he made a genuine attempt to trace the legacy of the Indian land revenue system since the earliest times and its evolution under the British rule in the 19th and early 20th centuries. Moreland's approach was essentially didactic. This general historical sketch served the purpose of showing some continuity of the agrarian problems inherited from earliest times. Apart from it, the technique of comparing the land system during the medieval age with the British land revenue system in India and the emphasis on the improvement brought by the British administration upon the indigenous system of revenue administration in various respects with historical illustrations was motivated by the keen desire to show the superiority of the British revenue administration over the past Indian revenue administration in the country. It was also intended to serve as a handbook guide for the English revenue officials in dealing with the 20th century agrarian problems relating to the landlords and the cultivators when visualised in historical perspective. However, it is doubtful if Moreland at this stage could clearly comprehend the clear-cut changes which had worked during the course of the 18th century chaotic period and had sufficiently blurred the main features of the Mughal land revenue administration. However, despite all his short-comings in the proper analysis of the 16th-17th centuries Mughal revenue administration, Moreland cut the gordian knot by undermining the mere narration of the political-military history of India and emphasised the primary role of economic forces with agriculture forming the main source of revenue of an Indian State as well as a determinate economic factor in the past Indian society. This emphasis even permeates all his subsequent writings.

The evolution of Moreland from the role of an administrator to that of an economic historian is a gradual one. By the time Moreland and Yusuf Ali published their joint paper on 'Akbar's land revenue system on the basis of the *Ain-i-Akbari*, Moreland had developed a genuine interest in the Mughal land revenue administration. As a follow up, his works '*India at the Death of Akbar*', '*India from Akbar to Aurangzeb*' and '*The Agrarian System of Moslem India*' were essentially based on historical research. He gradually discarded the moral tone comparisons of the condition of the peasantry during the British rule with the Mughal age. He ultimately developed a technique of historical research but even to the last he never shook off his leaning for looking for only such source-material which he could interpret to suit his predilections and imperialist outlook. As an expert revenue officer, Moreland possessed considerable practical knowledge to steer through the difficult aspects of the problems in hand. Apart from it, he took to the comparative study of the different texts of *Ain-i-Akbari* available to him, contemporary chronicles, accounts of the foreign travellers, a few Mughal *Farmans* and *Dasturulamls*. All the same, Moreland's technique of historical research was circumscribed by his narrow concept of interpretation. The reading of the technical passages of the *Ain-i-Akbari* is by no means an easy one. There is no denying the fact that when Moreland wrote, practically no archival revenue source-material of the $17^{th}$ century was available and it is both very difficult and risky to formulate theories without understanding the correct meaning of the revenue terminology. In the absence of contemporary documents, a technical historian is obliged to be less rigid in his interpretation of ambiguous passages as he was greatly tempted to rely on imagination. This can be well illustrated with a few examples. While interpreting '*Jama Deh Sala*' (Ten Year Settlement), Moreland considers that the word '*Jama*' in the passage does not stand for assessed demand but refers only to the problem of fixation of new valuation. When the tables of cash schedule rates (*dasturs*) immediately follow the description of '*Jama Deh Sala*', Moreland gets involved in a difficulty. He finds that the passage starting with the problems of price communication further narrates the procedure of fixation of valuation and surprisingly ends with the tables of cash schedule rates. Moreland does not consider the possibility of reading *Jama* both as valuation and assessed demand (through assessment schedule rates) to be interpreted in the context of the passage and still insists that the text of the passage stands for valuation. He gets disgusted with Abul Fazl and wriggles out with the solution that the *Ain* is defective and the text must be corrupt. Here is an example of an over confidence on the part of a revenue expert who takes liberty with the technique of historical research. As regards the incidence of State demand under Aurangzeb, the '*Royal Farman to Rasik Das Karori*' (of Bihar) underlines the assessment to be enforced at the varying rates of ½, 1/3 and 2/5 (of gross produce) according to the situation (dependent on classification of land). Moreland contends that the aforesaid *Farman* made only a theoretical enunciation of the variation in the assessment rates whereas the actual demand was made nearer the maximum than the minimum. Even though Moreland had no contemporary documentary evidence to reject the statement made in the *Farmans*, he did so relying purely on his revenue experience for looking after the revenues from the State's viewpoint. The original *pargana* documents now available at Rajasthan Archives, Bikaner, putting the above mentioned variation in State demand show Moreland was completely wrong in his presumption. Moreland's analysis of the methods of assessment of *zabti* and *nasq* based on the reading of the *Ain* are far from accurate. Moreland has wrongly defined the *nasq* as 'group assesment' or 'lump sum' assessment on the village or a *pargana* by agreement with the headmen while leaving to the latter the distribution of assessment on the holdings of the peasants. He also takes a very rigid view about the scope and extent of the prevalence of the above mentioned methods of assessment. He thinks that the most favoured method of assessment under Akbar was *zabti* and that *nasq* comprising village group assessments and annual summary assessments had become the working rule under Aurangzeb. The two fixed poles for his study are *Ain-i-Akbari* and Aurangzeb's '*Farman to Rasik Das Karori*'. He forgets that revenue practices do not disappear in such a sudden manner at the discretion of the monarchs. The *zabti* methods continued to operate throughout the Mughal rule and it co-existed with other methods of assessment. Moreland's reliance on the testimony of the foreign travellers for an account on the life of the peasantry is partial. The foreign travellers did not understand the concept of land ownership in India and found institutional differences from their own countries. They asserted that unless the land ownership is vested in the hands of the nobility, the agrarian evils were bound to occur. They suffered from European complexes and made contradictory remarks about the people of India. Bernier's account of the hardship and the widespread flight of the peasantry is definitely exaggerated and even motivated to present a deliberate inaccurate picture. Unless the accounts of the travellers are subjected to scrutiny on the basis of their motivations and their limitations to understand the Indian way of agrarian life are borne in mind, a reliance upon them for the analysis of Mughal India is extremely risky. This was Moreland's greatest shortcoming. Moreland did not try to understand the ethnic and sociological background of medieval India. He has not dealt with the *zamindari* settlement based on tribal and clannish structure – a fact which gives a real clue to the understanding of the rural society and agrarian history of Mughal India. Moreland did not try to go beneath the *pargana* level. Even his account at machinery of revenue collection is too sketchy. He made no attempt to analyse the socio-economic factors which affected the life of the people in the villages and *qasbas* which in many a region came to be vitally connected with the cities. The spread of trade and commerce had tremendous effect upon the cultivation of cash crops and role of money-economy in the agrarian life. Moreland's main merit was that he explained the revenue development under Akbar in the background of the ancient and medieval periods of Indian history so as to give a coordinated picture of the agrarian life. But he failed to realize the momentum of the socio-economic forces at work during the 17th century. Many a view and conclusions of Moreland on the agrarian problems need radical modification.

## References

1. Some of the important Mss. of the *Staatsbibiothek* Berlin (East) are: *Nuskha Hai Bar Kafiat-in Subah Behar*; *Nuskha Majmauhat*; *Sawalat-i-Malik-i Zamin Kiast az Mister John Shore*; *Dar Bab-i-Nuskha Sarusa Hukm, Tawarikh-i-Badhsahan-i Hind az ibtda-i-Shah Timur baghayat Shah Alam*; *Majmuha-i Mutfarika*; *Akhbar-ul-Sadiq dar Kafiat Bengala Darj Ast*. Also see details *vide* my Paper on *Some Rare Persian Manuscripts and Documents on*

*India (16th-18th Centuries) in the German Libraries.* Max Mueller Bhavan Publications, 1964 Year Book, New Delhi, pp. 59-73. Also Published in vol. I of this series.

2. *The Fifth Report from the Select Committee of the House of Commons on the Affairs of the East India Company*, July 1812, 2 vol. edited by W.K. Firminger, 1917; (henceforth as *The Fifth Report*), also F.D. Ascoli, *Early Land Revenue History of Bengal*, Oxford 1917.

3. Sayyid Gulam Husain is mentioned to be an expert revenue *Munshi* (official) to the Government. It is not exactly clear as to who this person was. It seems that he was the same writer who was the author of *Siyar-i-Mutaakhirin*.

4. Philip Francis, *'Minutes of the Governor General and Council'*, etc. pp. 30-31; also Firminger's Introduction vide f.n. 2.

5. *The Fifth Report*, pp. 170-198; 205-212; Firminger's Introduction pp. XIV-XX. also F.D. Ascoli vide f.n. 2.

6. Franois Bernier's, *Travels in the Moghul Empire, 1656-1658*, Oxford University Press, 1934, pp. 211-12, 220-26.

7. In the late 18th century revenue literature, some Indian *munshi* read *Ruba* in place of *Ray* described in the Persian text of the *Ain-i-Akbari* in connection with the assessment rate levied by Akbar. See *Ain*, British Museum Add. 7652, fols. 148b -149a; Ms. Hamilton, Berlin, fol. 125b; tr. Jarrett. II. p.72.

8. Moreland, W.H., *The Agrarian System of Moslem India, Appendix G*, Cambridge, 1929.

9. W.K. Firminger, *The Fifth Report*, I. *op. cit.* Introduction pp. XXVIII-XXIV; Compare it with Sir John's Minute dated 18th June, 1789, vide the *Fifth Report*, II, Appendix no. I; also J. Shore; *Minutes of April 1788* in J.H. Harington, *An Elementary Analysis of the Laws and Regulations*, Calcutta, 1814-15 vol. II. pp. 233-34.

10. Major Davy, *Institutes Political Military*, Oxford, 1783.

11. Sir John Shore's Minute, dated 18th June, 1789.

12. Ms. Or. fol. 234, Berlin; Ms. or quart 216, Berlin.

13. Ms. or. oct. 113 J, Berlin. See detailed discussion in my Paper on *Nature of Dehat-i-Taaluqa (Zamindari) Villages and the Evolution of the Taaluqdari System during the Mughal age.* The Indian Economic and Social History Review, Delhi, July-Sept. and Sept-December, 1965, pp. 166-177 and 259-288 respectively. Also

published in vol. I of this series.

14. Mr. Shore's Minute of 21[st] December, 1789.

15. See detailed discussion on the position of the Bengal *Zamindars* and *Taaluqdars* vis-à-vis other portions of North India vide my Paper on *Nature of Dehat-i taaluqa* (*Zamindari*) *and the evolution of the Taaluqdari system during the Mughal Age.* Vide f.n. 13. Published in vol. I of this series.

16. Ms. or. quart. 258, Berlin. In fact, the term *riaya* stood for all the cultivating and revenue paying agricultural families. As such, the *Riaya* comprised the *Zamindari, Chaudhurie, Muqaddami* and *Muzarian* (*Raiyat-i Raiza*) families. But the use of the term *Riaya* has also to be read in the context of a particular narrated passage in which *Riaya* and *Zamindari* families may be differentiated from each other. The *Muqaddams* constituted the principal *Riaya* and in many portions of North India would invariably belong to the *Zamindari* families. But in Bengal, the 17[th] and 18[th]centuries sources insist on putting the *Mandals* and *Muqaddams* etc. merely as *Riaya* distinct from the *Zamindari* class.

17. Also, see details in my Paper, *Nature of Land-Rights in Mughal India*, The Economic and Social History Review, Delhi School of Economics, Delhi, Vol. I. July-September 1963, pp. 2-7. Also published in vol. I of this Series.

18. *Ibid*; also Ms. Or. quart. 258, Berlin, fol. 304b.

19. *Baharistan-i-Ghaybi* of Mirza Nathan, *Baharistan, Histoire de Bengals dequirs*, Ms. no suppl. Pers. 252, *Bibliotheque Nationale*, Paris; tr. 2 vols. by Dr. M.I. Borah, Gauhati, Assam, 1936; *Murraqat-i-Hasan* by Mir Abul Hasan Alamgiri, Ms. 217, State Library Rampur; *Fathiya-i-Ibriya* by Shihab-ud-din Talish, Ms. 98, Lytton collection, M.U. Aligarh; Continuation, Mr. Or. 589, Bodleian Library, Oxford.

20. Francis Gladwin, *Ayeen Akbery*, 2 vols. London 1800.

21. *Ain-i-Akbari*, tr. Col. H.S. Jarrettt, second edition, corrected and further annotated by Sir J.N. Sarkar, vol. II & III, Calcutta, 1949. vol. I had already been translated by Blochmann, revised and edited by Phillot, Calcutta, 1927 and 1939.

22. The *Seir Mutaqherin* or *Review of Modern Times* by Seid Gholam Hossain Khan dedicated to Rt. Hon. Warren Hastings, Governor-General of Bengal. First published in 1789. Reprinted in 1901, 4 vols, Calcutta.

23. *Riyaz-us-Salatin* by Gulam Husain Salim Zaidpuri, *A History of Bengal* written in 1786-88. B. b. Ind., Calcutta, 1890.

24. James Mill, *The History of British India*, 3 vols. London, 1817 3rd edition in 6 vols. London, 1826.

25. A.D. Campbell Esq., *Extracts from the Proceedings of the Select Committee of the House of Commons on the Position of Zamindars and Cultivators in Bengal, from the Records of the East India House, 1820; and from The Fifth Report of the Select Committee,* 1812 (Madras). C. Appendix No.6, pp. 67-96.

26. *Ibid.*

27. See details vide my Paper on *Nature of Dehat-i taaluqa (Zamindari) and the evolution of the Taaluqdari system during the Mughal age* vide f.n. 13. Also published in vol. I of this series.

28. *East India (Parliamentary Papers)*, 1810, *House of Commons*, vol. & page, 5, 13, Paper 363, *East India Company. Second Report of Select Committee*, with Appendix.

29. James Mill, *History of British India*, vol. I, Chapter V, p. 247, vol. IV, Chapter III, pp. 1-23. Erick Stokes, *The English Ulilitarians and India* (Oxford University Press, 1959), pp. 1-139; also B.M. Bhatia, *English Economic Thought and Indian Economic Policy in XIX century* vide Seminar on *History of Ideas*, University of Delhi, 1964 (unpublished Proceedings).

30. *Ibid.*

31. W.W. Hunter, *A Brief History of the Indian People*, 2nd edition London 1833, pp. 125-26.

32. *Ibid.* Orissa, vol. II. p. 206.

33. Mountstuart Elphinstone, *The History of India*, 2 vols. London 1841; 9th edition 1916 with Notes and Additions by E.B. Cowell, chapter II, pp. 66-87; 472-77.

34. See f.n. 27.

35. H.S. Maine , *Village Communities in the East and West* London, 1895. pp. 103-239. For criticism of Maine, see W.J. Ashley, *The Origin of Property in Land*, by De Coulanges tr. by Margaret Ashley and edited by W.J. Ashley, London; 1890. Introduction by William Ashley, VII-XIVIII. For the decline of the village community, see Arthur Phillips, *Land Tenures of Lower Bengal*, Calcutta, 1876; pp. 40-148.

36. Col. Galloway, *Observation on the Law and Constitution of India, of the Nature of the Ceded Tenures and the System of Revenue and Finance as Established by Moohummudun Law and Moughal Government with an Enquiry into the Revenue and Judicial Administration and Regulation of Police in Bengal*. London 1825, p. 191.

37. James Tod, *Annals and Antiquities of Rajasthan*, 2 vols., London, 1829-32.

38. Also see C.U. Wills vide f.n. 41.

39. Kaviraj Shyamaldas, *Vir Vinod*, *Samvat* 15th, *Chaitra* 1943/March 1887 A.D. vol. II, Udaipur Rajyantralaya.

40. See details vide H.L. Singh, *Modern Historical Writing in Hindi* vide *Historians of India, Pakistan and Ceylon*, edited by C.H. Philips. London 1961, pp. 461-72.

41. C.U. Wills, *A Report on the Land Tenures and Special Powers of certain Thikanedars of the Jaipur State,* pp. 7-117. Appendices B, F. D, G.

42. C.A. Elliot, *Chronicles of Poona*, pp. 28-77, 85-120; 146-misprint, 106-112.

43. W.C. Benett, *A Report on the Family History of the Chief Clan of Roy Bareilly District*, Lucknow, 1870; *Gazetteer of the Provinces of Oudh*, vol. I, Introduction I-VIII.

44. John Malcolm, *A Memior of Central India, including Malwa, and adjoining Provinces with the History, and Copious Illustration of Past and Present Condition of that Country*, 3rd edition, vol. II. London, 1823; pp. 1-226; *Report on the Provinces of Malwa and Adjoining Districts*, Calcutta, 1822.

45. C.D. Field, *The Regulations of the Bengal Code*, Calcutta, 1875, pp. 21, 33.

46. P. Carnegy, *Notes on the Land Tenures and Revenue Assessments of Upper India*, London, 1874.

47. Alfred. C. Lyall, *Asiatic Studies Religious and Social*, London, 1899 (1st edition) Reprinted, 1907, pp. 162-264; *Gazetteer of Rajputana*, 1879; *Chief and Leading Families in Rajputana*, Calcutta, 1894, Introduction pp. 1-4.

48. K.G. Keene, *A Sketch of the History of Hindustan from the Muslim Conquest to the Fall of the Mughol Empire*, London, vol. I. 1885;

pp. General Introduction iii-xix; 73-82, 144-45, 159-162, 183-184, 210-213, 238-243, 250-266.

49. Baden Powell B.H, *Land Systems of British India*, Oxford, 1892, 3 vols.

50. J.N. Sarkar, *Mughal Administration*, 1920.

51. See f.n. 36.

52. V.A. Smith, *Akbar the Great*, 1917.

53. W.H. Moreland, *India at the Death of Akbar*, London, 1920; *India from Akbar to Aurangzeb*, London, 1923; *The Agrarian System of Moslem India*, Cambridge, 1929, For details of other books and analysis of Moreland, see J.B. Harrison, *Notes on W.H. Moreland as Historian*, vide *Historians of India, Pakistan and Ceylon*; edited by C.H. Philips, London, 1961, pp. 310-318.

17

# Bamiyan versus Ayodhya in Historical Perspective-Based on Literary and Archaeological Sources (Summary)

Professor B.R. Grover spoke on 'Bamiyan versus Ayodhya in Historical Perspective–Based on Literary and Archaeological Sources.' Having dwelt upon numerous primary sources of ancient, medieval and modern periods on the subject, he underlined the importance of Bamiyan in Afghanistan, both as a commercial and Buddhist cultural centre. Along with various other Buddhist cultural centres, it was situated on the Silk Route well connected with Kandhar, Herat and Iran in the South and West, Khurasan in the North-West as well as other territories of Central Asia across River Oxus, especially Mongolia and even China to the East.

From the very ancient period from the great entrepot of Balkh, the caravans, breaching off from the main trade route from east to west, carried the Chinese merchandise across the passes of Hind Kush to India. Both the routes from Herat and Balkh converged on the Bamiyan Valley. Here, the city of Gulgula served as the resting and the refreshment place for the travelers. From Bamiyan, two routes led to the Kabul plateau, i.e. across the Shaibar Pass and the Ghorband valley–a route followed by the Chinese pilgrim Hieun Tsang (7$^{th}$ Century) and later on by Changhiz Khan (1220 AD) and secondly from Bamiyan turning South crossing the Koh-i-Baba range by Haji Gak Pass and then after crossing route Helmand and the Unai Pass downward towards the valley of Kabul river on the central plateau leading to Kabul itself.

As a matter of fact, the commercial-cum-cultural centre of Bamiyan located about 205 miles (330 Km) North-West of Kabul and 8,200 feet (2,500 meters) above sea level constituted an important route from Balkh to Taxila (then India, now Pakistan). During the ancient and early medieval periods, Bamiyan remained as the main Buddhist Cultural Centre with Buddhist population comprising monks, pilgrims and traders.

The earliest ruined Stupa at Bimaran (near Jalalabad) is of about 1st and 2nd centuries with standing figure of a Buddha, flanked by Indra and Brahma. It had a base with Indian lotus and Buddha in *abhaya-mudra*. Apart from it, at Bamiyan the colossal images of Buddha 35 meters and 53 meters high on the cut-off cliffs of the Hindu Kush Mountain were the wonders of the world art heritage.

The small Buddha, 35 meters high, belonged to second half of the third century. Apart from it, there are hundreds of pilgrim caves along sand stone which face the cliff. The large Buddha, 53 meters high, is of 5th century AD. Some scholars think that these dates are wrong. However, most scholars agree about the site dates in the Kushano-Sasanian period, or 300-700 AD.

The aforementioned statues on the monastic establishment at Bamiyan were hewn out of the rock on the face of the cliff and like the whole community of caves faced South of the valley, an orientation ensuring full warmth of the sun during the long mid-winter. The distance between the erstwhile two colossal images is five-eighth of a mile. On other side of the statues, i.e. on the East and West, the cliff is honeycombed with vast complexes of cave chapels, assembly halls and monastic cells for the monks. Both the statues were equipped with a system of stairways giving access to the summit. However, the crumbling of the great masses of the cliff has destroyed these passages. For the larger statue (53 meters), the top of the edge with its frescos by an artificial path and gallery built along the face of the cliff to the West of the statue. There are further caves opening from behind the feet of the image and other still in the cliff above and behind it.

The higher statue represented *Bodhisattva Maitreya* and his Sakti. Besides this, the art of sculptures, paintings, statues of

Buddha from the 2nd-3rd century AD to the seventh-eighth centuries represents the Hinayana inspiration which is well confirmed by the Chinese pilgrim, Hieun Tsang in the early seventh century. In the significant Bamiyan paintings, many a representation of the Rupananda story characterising the impermanence of the physical beauty vis-a-vis spiritual enlightenment are inscribed. The colours used were manufactured out of the local earth and minerals. The smaller caves of Bamiyan represented various architectural forms of the Sassanian and Gupta styles having been fused together.

The religious community at Bamiyan was flourishing during the period of Kanishka. When Hieun Tsang visited the site in 632 AD, the great Buddha shone in the sun, apparently untouched by the white Huns who had ravished India and the Kabul valley in the fifth century. When later on, another pilgrim Hui-Chao visited the valley in the 8th century, he still found the monasteries well populated. Thereafter, the Arabic Islam overthrew and exterminated both the Buddhist and the Brahmanical settlements in Afghanistan.

At Kakrak, another Buddhist site about 2.5 miles (4Km) South-East of the Bamiyan Buddha statues, had a standing Buddha about 10 meters high and a sanctuary exhibiting frescoes of a centrally seated Buddha surrounded by circles of smaller seated Buddhas of around 5th-6th centuries A.D. or a little later. These represented the Mahayana Buddhist concept of one of the classical Buddhas surrounded by his magic emanations, the *mandla* of esoteric Far Eastern and Tibetan Buddhism.

During the early Christian centuries, the region of modern Afghanistan formed a part of the Kushan empire, the Sasanian Empire and many of its regions were later on a part of the Gupta Empire. Chronologically speaking, the Kushan Empire in Afghanistan ruled in the 1St and the 2nd centuries A.D. The Zegro tribes emerged as an indigenous Persian dynasty, the Sasanian (224-651 A.D.) overthrew the intruder Parthians, Ardshir I (224-41), the founder overran the Kushan states from Sogodina to Punjab. The Gupta rule lasted from 320 A.D. to the 7th century. The Haphthalite Empire in Afghanistan and North-West India lasted a century (450-565 A.D.). The Hindu Shahi dynasty established itself at Kabul and held much of Eastern Afghanistan until the ninth and tenth centuries.

The destruction of all the statues by the Taliban at Bamiyan as well as in other places of Afghanistan, in the name of Islam is a barbaric act and vandalism which has given an eternal blow to the world cultural heritage.

Professor Grover himself equally traced the history of the disputed structure of Ramjanam Bhoomi Baburi Masjid at Ayodhya since the 16th century. He argued that there is considerable literary judicial and archaeological evidence which clearly bears out the fact that the disputed structure i.e. the 'Baburi Masjid' was built on the demolished site of Ramjanam Bhoomi. He stated that for want of time, only a few significant sources may be quoted. He cited that the 18th century theological work by the daughter of Bahadur Shah 1st (1707) son of Aurangzeb, entitled *Sahifa-i-Chilil Nasih Bahadur Shahi* popularly named by Nawab Ali Naqi Khan, the Prime Minister of Awadh (1855) A.D. as *Chilil Nasail Bahadur Shah I* (vide 25th Counsel of the aforementioned work entitled '*the Forty counsels*') stressed the fact even though the mosque was constructed on the state of Sita Rasoi (*Janmasthan*) temple, the Hindus continued to perform image worship and even blew conch shells and that the Friday prayer was not performed by the Muslims in this mosque. The 18th century European traveler, Joseph Tieffernthaler (1766-71), who visited Ayodhya is emphatic that the Hindus practiced their religious ceremonies at both the places, i.e. courtyard of the mosque as well as inside the mosque as they considered that this was the place where Vishnu took birth in the form of Rama.

Time records of the Nawabi rule in Awadh show a long-drawn tussle between the Hindus and the Muslims as well as Shia-Sunni Muslims amongst themselves over the possession of the *Janmasthan*–'Baburi Masjid' site. The intermittent references to the statement of the *Qazis* of Faizabad for the years A.D. 1735, A.D. 1825 are very clear on this issue. A significant Note submitted by Hafizullah, the *Darogha* of Faizabad Court to the Awadh Royal Court (1825) clearly states that the 'mosque' constructed by Babur was situated at the birthplace of Rama, son of Raja Dashrath, and adjacent to the Kitchen of Sita, wife of Rama (i.e. *Sita Ki Rasoi*). Later on in the late 19th century, Maulvi Abdul Karim being himself the *Imam* of Baburi Masjid, in his work on *Gumgashtah-i-Halat-i Ayodhya*, having referred to various medieval and nineteenth century sources, particularly the Sufi literature, gave detailed description of the two halls (*burjs*) and identified the western tower hall (*burj*) as the birthplace of Rama which along with *Sita Rasoi* was demolished by Babur for constructing a mosque thereupon.

During the second half of the nineteenth century, British administration in Awadh, both the legal and expert archaeological opinions confirmed the fact that the *Janmasthan* 'mosque' located in the *Janmaasthan* complex was built by Babur at the very site of the sacred Hindu temple after the latter's demolition. In a landmark judgment in 1886 in Civil Appeal # 27 of 1885 against the earlier judgment in the suit 61/280 of 1885 of *Asthan Janmasthan* vs. the Secretary of the State for India and Mohammad Asghar, the District Civil Judge, Faizabad, Col. F.E.A. Chamier recorded, that on a personal visit to the disputed land in Ayodhya, that to the West and South of the habitation, on the border of the town of Ayodhya, he found that about 356 years ago, a masjid had been built on land held sacred by the Hindus."

Later on, Mr. Akhtar Asan Naqvi, a Muslim Civil Judge, Faizabad, in a regular suit of 1945 between the Shia Central Board of Waqf U.P.V/s Suni Board of Waqf, U.P. having examined the historical issues of the Ayodha mosque, reaffirmed the fact that Babur destroyed the *Janmasthan* temple (1528) and on its site built a mosque using largely the materials of the old structure.

An equally important expert opinion on the archaeological aspect by E.A. Fuhrer of the Archaeological Survey of India in 1891 concluded that on the eve of the Muslim conquest, there were three important temples at Ayodhya, i.e., the *Janmasthan* (birthplace temple of Rama), the *Swargadwar* and the *Treta-ke-Thakur*. On the *Janmasthan* site, Mir Khan (Mir Baqi) built a masjid during the reign of Babur and used therein many of the black stone (*kasauti*) columns. Later on, mosques were constructed on the site of other two aforementioned temples by Aurangzeb.

Professor Grover remarked that even though the demolition of the disputed structure, popularly known since the late 19th century as *Masjid Janmasthan* or *Masjid Waqia Janmasthan* or 'Baburi Masjid' at Ayodhya on Dec. 6, 1992 was unfortunate. The parallelism and drawing an analogy with the Bamiyan cultural heritage is rather misplaced. He contended that the discovery of the foundation stone in Dec, 92 confirms the fact that the disputed structure stood on the erstwhile destroyed temple in the sixteenth century. As such, this inscriptional evidence bears out the fact that around mid-twelfth century, Nayachandra, the Chief of Saket Mandalam with headquarters at Ayodhya, who was the feudatory of Govind Chadra (1114-1154), the ruler of the Gahadavala Kingdom built the Vaishnava temple at this site. It was this temple which was later on demolished. The demolition of this *Janmasthan* temple at Ayodhya and its replacement by a mosque was a sheer act of vindictiveness and vindication of the supremacy of Islam over heathenism (*Kufr*), so dear to Zahiruddin Muhammad Babur, the first Mughal King of India.

Apart from this, *Ramjanam Bhumi*-Baburi Masjid had been all through a place of worship by the Hindu Community till date ever since the Mughal age. Clearly after December 1949, it had never been a functional mosque. The land revenue records since 19th century confirm the ownership of the area under the disputed structure vested with the Hindu *Mahants*. No plot or sub-plot comprising the disputed structure of *Ramjanam Bhumi*–Babri Masjid was under *waqf*. All this is borne out by the three regular Land Revenue Settlements (i.e. 1861, 1893-94 & 1936-37) of court Ram Chandra (Ayodhya) It is further confirmed by the Boundary and Population (*Hadbast & Abadi* ) Revenue Maps appended to the Settlement Reports of 1861 & 1936-37, which show only *Janamsthan* (Birth place of Rama ) and do not indicate any mosque in the *Janamsthan* complex. On the contrary, the Bamiyan Buddhist cultural heritage was not claimed by any other religious community. What is true of the Bamiyan statues is equally true of the Buddhist/Brahamanical statues and artifacts in other parts of Afghanistan. Moreover, the demolition of the Bamiyan statues and all artifacts with gunpowder by a *fatwa* of the religious and the ruling Taliban is absolutely different in character than the demolition of the disputed structure by a mob frenzy due to the delayed judicial process in respect of acquisition of the land by the State rather than any act of religious fanaticism on the part of the Indian State which is secular in character. If there is any parallelism of the destruction of the Bamiyan statues through explosive gunpowder blast, it is to be found only in the 18th century destruction of the Hari Mandir (Golden Temple), Amritsar (Punjab) by the Afghan invader Ahmad Shah Abdali. This temple was rebuilt a few years later by Sardar Jassa Singh Ahluwalia, the ruler of Kapurthala.

As there is no similarity between the two situations, the belated justification of the Bamiyan vandalism by some religious fanatics in Afghanistan, Pakistan and India (Reference Syed Ahmed Bhukhari of Jama Masjid, Delhi) as an act of retaliation against the demolition of the disputed structure (*Ramjanam Bhumi-* Baburi Masjid) at Ayodhya after nearly nine years is nothing short of deceiving the world. The latest declaration by the Taliban at Kabul (March 19, 2001) that as an atonement for the delayed action on the part of the Islamic rulers of Afghanistan for not having destroyed the Buddhist statues and artifacts in Bamiyan and other regions of Afghanistan possessing both Brahamanical and Buddhist artifacts over the centuries, they had slaughtered about hundred cows speaks for itself and needs no further comments. Clearly, it is an onslaught on the sentiments of the Hindu community of India which holds the cow as sacred. Moreover, the slogan of 'Allah o Akbar' 'Mashah Allah' at the time of destruction of the statues and the above declaration by the Taliban leader Mullah Muhammad Omer that the smashing of the two Buddha statues had pleased Allah who as a result had sent rains in the drought hit country for the last four years conveys extreme fanaticism. He proclaimed, "We broke the Idols and Allah sent us rains". All this religious bigotry speaks for the outrage at Bamiyan.

## *18*

# 'Distortions of History – The Current Experience : A Critique

The seminar organised by the Department of Tourism, Government of West Bengal, in Calcutta city on the concluding day of the Indian History Congress Session on 'Distortions of History- the Current Experience' held on December 30, 1995, created more of distortions rather than correcting the distortions of Indian history. The speakers, Prof. R.S. Sharma, Prof. Irfan Habib, Prof. Tapan Ray-Chaudhury and Prof. Barun De venomously and completely misrepresented the facts of Indian history.

Prof. Sharma held that hitherto the medieval Indian history had been communalised as the epigraphic and the Sanskrit literary sources depicted the conflict as one between the invading Turks and the Indian Chiefs rather than between the Muslims and the Hindus. He contended that the term *Turushadanda,* which implied tax levied on the people for defense against the onslaught of the *Turushkas,* shows that the defense was organised by the Indian Chiefs against the foreign Turks rather than against the Muslims as the word Muslim does not occur in the available textual Sanskrit description.

One simply wonders at Prof. Sharma's limited approach for the analysis of early medieval Indian history for understanding the nature of Turkish campaigns during the 11th and 12th centuries. The Arabic and the Persian contemporary sources bring out the real nature of the conflict with the Hindu Chiefs of north India. In this regard, to quote only a few authorities, Al Biruni's *Kitabal-Hind,* Al Utbi's *Tarikh-i-Yamini* and *Minhaj-un-din*-b, *Sirajud-*

*din's Tabaqat-Nasiri* and Ziaud Din Barani's *Tarikh-i-Firoz Shahi,* clearly bring out the motives of Turkish campaigns against India. These sources narrate not only the Turkish designs for territorial conquest but equally emphasise the motives for pillage and plunder of wealth as well as the destruction of the Hindu temples, thereby signaling the triumph of Islam over the heathenic ways of worship and idolatry, customs and manners of the Hindus (Wa Hind/Hanud/Hinduism).

In this regard, it is not out of place to refer to the Pakistani historians who equally claim to be 'scientific' and 'objective' in their approach to the study of medieval history of the Indian subcontinent (what they call 'Indo-Pakistan sub-continent'). They too point out various distortions in medieval history created by the Western or the Indian scholarship. Most interestingly, for the medieval age, they bank on the same Arabic and Persian sources as we do. All the same, based on those sources, they often use terminology like 'Muslim invaders'; 'History of Muslim India'; 'Indo Muslim historiography'; 'Muslim Empire in India'; 'Muslim conquest of India', 'Muslim rule' or 'Muslim Empire in Sind', 'Muslim Bengal', 'Victories of Muslim over large Hindu hordes', 'Army of Islam', 'Consolidation of Muslim India', Hindustan as "Citadel of Islam", 'Muslim historians', 'Hindu Sources' and 'Hindu inscriptions', etc. Some historians consider even the Arab conquest by Muhammad bin Qasim (A.D. 712) as the triumph of Islam' and for Mahmud of Ghazni's campaigns in early eleventh century ascribe motives of not only conquest, pillage and plunder of wealth but even iconoclasm, spread of Islam *(tabligh)* and mitigation of the Indian culture based on Brahmanism. For such historiography, only a few well-known Pakistani historians like S.M. Ikram, I.H. Qureshi, K.K. Aziz, Mian Abdul Rashid, Muhammad Munawwar, Manzoor Ahmed and Rafi Ullab Shehab may be mentioned. We may not agree with various terms used by them but in the face of contemporary or near contemporary evidence for the motives and nature of the Turkish (Muslim) conquest of India, as already stated above, it is not essential to disagree with them.

Prof. Sharms's reflections on the history syllabus of the

University of Calcutta, which had courses on the History of the Jats, the Rajputs and the Marathas, etc. are highly misplaced. In fact, these people had distinctly contributed towards the making of the history and culture of India and by no means reflected only regional chauvanism. Moreover, Prof. Sharma's criticism of the historical writings of Sir Jadunath Sarkar on the Mughal Age, K.P. Jaiswal's on *Hindu Polity* and R.C. Mazumdar's on Ancient and Medieval periods is not only biased but having dubbed them as Hindu communal writers is complete travesty of truth. In fact, based on rich source-material and scientific study, these historians produced monumental works of their times.

Prof. Irfan Habib pointed out that there had been communal falsification of history wherein new complexities and sophistications had been inculcated which accounted for distortion of history. Distinguishing between religion and culture, Prof. Habib criticised the Supreme Court's Judgement (11.12.1995) on Hindutva and regarded it as extremely unscientific. He held that religion was smaller than larger concept of culture. In this respect, both Hindu and Muslim cultures were much larger than their respective religions. He further maintained that during the Ancient period, the word Hindu was not in vogue in the indigenous literature and as such it could not be maintained that medicine, astrology, mathematics or mythology were Hindu in character. In similar manner, one could not talk about Islamic astrology or Islamic science as the use of these terms had been parallel development to the falsfied shibboleths introduced by Hindutva. He concluded that in view of such understanding of Ancient India, the Supreme Court's judgement on Hindutva needed to be condemned. Apart from this, Prof. Habib reiterated the stand on the preservation of the ancient monuments as already spelled out by the Indian History Congress at its 1986 Srinagar Resolution. He rediculed the belief of the millions of Hindus who believe that the Baburi mosque at Ayodhya was built on the site of the Hindu temple. He urged the historians to rake strong position in this regard for to restrict history for a particular religion was tantamount to its falsification and unscientific in character. Prof. Habib also referred to the distortions created by the colonial writers like J.C. Collins and C.A. Bayly in the field of modern Indian History by making general statements which were not borne out by statistics.

Prof. Irfan Habib's criticism of the above mentioned judgement of the Hon'ble Supreme Court on the concept of Hindu/ Hindutva, etc. is completely biased and unwarranted. He himself has miserably failed to understand the judgement, both, in letter and spirit. The judgement does not, in any way, hold religion and culture synonymous and is very clear that culture has much wider content with multi-dimensional aspects than proper religion. The Apex Court held that the words 'Hindutva' or Hinduism' were not confined to mere religion, popularly known today as Hindu religion. But they connoted a way of life, in fact, the entire code of conduct of life *(dharma)* incorporating values of life, i.e. spirit of tolerance, respect for all religions and adherence to secularism. In fact, the terms cover every sphere of human activity, which is well comprised by the culture and *dharma* of the people inherited from ancient times. As such, these days, in the political sphere or during the electoral process, any appeal made in the name of Hindutva does not tantamount to making an appeal on ground of religion and, therefore, is not a corrupt practice.

Looked at the surface, the word 'Hindu' seems to be of foreign origin but as it is a mispronounced form of 'Sindhu' (i.e. the river Indus), it is certainly an indigenous term. As the ancient Iranians pronounced the vowel 'S' as 'H' they called the river Sindhu as 'Hindu' and the people of the Sindhu (river Sind/Indus) and beyond as Hindus. All the same, it cannot be maintained that the word 'Hindu' was not reflected the ancient Indian literature. In fact, during ancient period, the term 'Hindu' was basically geographical and cultural in connotation, the name being pronounced by the Iranians for the people of this subcontinent to the East of river Sindh. According to the Arab and Persian sources, during the ancient and early medieval periods, a person from this sub-continent belonging to any tribal social order or religious sect, etc., Brahmanical, Buddhist, Jain, Shivaite, or Vaishnavite, etc. was termed as Hindu. Even the well-known Indo (till 1947) - Pakistani historian. I.H. Qureshi (*A Short History of Pakistan, Karachi, 1967)* concedes that in Ancient period, the name 'Hindu' stood for the traditions of culture of the people of the Indian subcontinent, though he takes credit that "the roots of this culture lay in West Pakistan, the land of River Sind. He states that as connotation of the term 'Hindu' changed at a much later stage, it came to be associated, even though wrongly, with the religious invocations. He further comments that the society gave a final direction to many of the trends which led to the growth of modern Hinduism and developed a spirit that led to classicism. The Arabs also called the land of Hindus 'Al Hind' and in the Persian literature, it also came to be known as Hindustan. Starting from the regional concept being confined to some territories of North India, or the entire North India, in due course of centuries, these terms viz. Hind or Hindustan came to signify the entire Indian Subcontinent. However, during the Ancient Age in India, the indigenous names used were *Jambu-dvipa, Bharat-Mata, Bharat-Lakshmi* and *Bharat-Varsh*, which too underwent change in connotation from time to time. Ultimately *Jambudvipa* and *Bharat-Varsh* have given place to "Bharat that is India". The name India is derived from the 5th Century B.C. Greek word Indi' which was corrupt form of the 6th Century B.C. Iranian word 'Hindu' used for the people of this subcontinent. This shows continuous philological relationship amongst the words 'Hindu', 'Indi' and 'India'.

In the early medieval period, the Arabs called the Hindus settled in the West Asian Countries as Zatt, Abu Salish bin Jam, the author of an early medieval Arab work, states that this itself was translated work of still an earlier manuscript in Hindwani (Sanskrit) composed around the commencement of the Christian era. He further quotes from the latter Sanskrit manuscript to the effect that the people of this subcontinent knew that as the Hindus, they were also called Zatt by the Arabs. Zatt was the Arbisized form of Jat. However, it is clear from the Arab sources that not only the Jat tribes belonging mostly to Buddhist and Brahamanical orders but all other tribes like the Meds, Gujars, Rajputs, etc. all with all their branches, who had emigrated and settled in the West Asian countries, were called Zatt. The above mentioned version of the ancient Sanskrit manuscript stating that the Hindus of the subcontinent were called *Zatt* by the Arabs is further confirmed by Abu-l-Hasan Ali bin Muhammad al Jali, the author of *Mujmalu-T*

*Twarikh* in Persian (417.AH/ A.D. 1026), who states that his own work was a translated version of the earlier Arabic work of Abu Salih bin Jami, initially translated from the early Christian era Sanskrit work.

Prof. Habib's observations on the association of the word 'Hindu' with the ancient Indian scientific achievements in the fields of astronomy, astrology, medicine and mathematics, etc. are highly misplaced. No doubt, scientific developments are universal in character and cannot be associated with any particular religion. But scientific discoveries and achievements on the part of the people of a particular country can be well attributed to the cultural development of the people. In this case, the development and contribution of the ancient Indian people essentially formed a part of the Hindu culture. In fact, the early medieval Arab accounts pay high tribute to the excellence achieved by the Hindus *(Wa Al-Hind)* especially in the fields of medicine and development of scientific astronomical instruments. To cite only one illustration, for the transmission of Indian medicine to the Arabs and its impact on the Arab medicine especially in the field of pharmacy, the rapenties and, *materia medica,* a part from the contribution of numerous named Hindu physicians stationed at Baghdad, the name of Manka occupies the most respected position. Appointed by the Abbasid Caliph Harun al-Rashid (A.D. 788-814) as the Chief of the Royal Hospital, Manka translated some books from Sanskrit into Arabic/Persian and composed *Kitaba-al-Tafsir Asma-al-Aqaqir* which lists drugs and herbs of Indian origin. Similarly, the translated Shushruta's *Samhita* (Sasrud) comprising ten discourses into Arabic. At the same time, he translated Charaka's treatise and a book on poisons, *Kitab-al-Samum* into Persian (Phlawi) and later on, both these works were rendered into Arabic by Abd al-Allah bin Ali and Abbas bin Said respectively. In Iran too, the physicians keenly studied the Ayurveda. Authentic works on *hikam* comprising chapters on Indian medicine were produced. As such, it was the Arab writers who attributed all this contribution to the Hindu system of medicine. Just as these writers refer to the Greek works, the Arab and the Persian works, in the same vein, the works in Ancient India can be termed as Hindu works. In the early eleventh century, even Al-Biruni referred to the 'Hindu Sciences'.

He considered the Hindus excellent philosophers and very good sound mathematicians and astrologers. While commenting on the utter destructive policy of Mahmud of Ghazni, he states that, 'Mahmud utterly ruined the prosperity of the country,... that is the reason, too, why Hindu Sciences have retired far away from those parts of the country conquered by us, and have fled to places, which our hand cannot yet reach, to Kashmir, Benares, and other places". There is no doubt that as parallel to this, scientific achievements cannot be associated with Islam, which is basically a religion. Despite that, the concept of Islamic architecture has been widely accepted, perhaps more because of common traits of architecture in respect of many a monument, prevalent in the Islamic countries. Even till date, numerous works under the nomenclatures 'Islamic Philosophy' and 'Islamic Sciences' are being published in Egypt and the West Asian countries. Similar is the position about the latest concept of the 'Islamic Bomb', which it is considered, may be used by the Islamic countries in time of crisis against the non-Islamic states. It is not correct to say that the association of the word 'Islamic' with the philosophy and sciences developed in the Islamic countries is a counterpoise to the Hindu philosophy and sciences, etc., for at least, there is no 'Hindu Bomb' so far.

Prof. Habib's viewpoint that the event of the Ayodhya temple *(Janmasthan* of Shri Ram Chandra) having been destroyed by the Mughal monarch Babur for construction of the mosque thereupon, being based upon mere belief of the Hindus, is not only completely erroneous but a deliberate attempt on his part to distort the historical fact for misguiding the body of historians and the gullible public for purely ideological and political reasons. Innumerable examples can be cited from medieval Indian history where the most sacred temples of the Hindus were destroyed and in many a case, mosques were also constructed thereupon. The discipline of history demands that along with political and economic factors, one may equally discern and underline the role that religions played in medieval times. It is the examination of the totality of the then thinking and action which should determine the scientific approach to history. Not to talk about Mathura or Benares temples for which there is ample contemporary evidence for having been replaced by mosques by Aurangzeb. There are most authentic literary and archaeological sources which confirm the fact of the *Janmasthan* temple at Ayodhya being demolished (A.D. 1528) by Mir Baqi, the Commander of Babur for the construction of the mosque upon it. However unfortunate the demolition of the disputed structure on 6th December 1992 was, the archaeological remains at the site have revealed three dedicatory inscriptions in the Devanagri script. Of these three there is one Hari-Vishnu 12th century inscription of 20 lines engraved on a thick slab of buff stone (5'x 2'x 2.5') in Sanskrit verse written in Nagari script which narrates that this temple was built in the temple-city of Ayodhya situated in *Saket mandala.* This Vishnu-Hari inscription mentions Ayuschandra as the composer of the verses and also associates the construction of the temple with Govindchandra, a ruler (A.D. 1114-1154) of the Ghadaval dynasty, whose territorial jurisdiction covered Avadh as well. This inscription certainly proves the building of a magnificent temple of Hari-Vishnu, the killer of Ravana, i.e. Rama. It is the same temple which was later on demolished by Mir Baqi 1528) for the construction of a mosque thereupon. As a matter of fact. the discovery of such a clinching inscriptional evidence should end the entire controversy. But most ironically, the historians with vested ideological interests have turned a Nelson's eye to it.

As regards modem Indian history. Prof. Habib's criticism of the colonial exploitation and colonial approach to history is, by and large, justified. Even when one may not agree with C.A. Bayly's generalisation *(The Rulers, Townsmen and Bazars-North Indian Society in the Age of British expansion 1770-1870,* Oxford, 1983) to the effect that regional considerations and conditions constituted normal state of affairs in the Indian society, the role of the regional or the regional-cum-religious factors even during the 18th century India, howsoever peripheral or significant, cannot be denied. It is not only the economic and agrarian factors that brought about the downfall of the Mughal Empire in the 18th century but along with them, the rise of the regional powers guided by socio-religious and political factors which affected the unified features of the Indian polity.

Prof. Tapan Ray Chaudhary commenting sarcastically on the

heritage of the Hindu culture stated that the Vedic studies which had been established at different places in the world were usually taken for the study of Ayurvedic medicine and herbs and the Vedas were confused with the Ayurvedic centres. What a discovery about the study of the Vedas? Prof. Chaudhary cast aspersions on the 'great' historians of the Vishwa Hindu Parishad, who had indulged in distortions of history by taking up the issues of Hindutva, the fighting Aryan race and completely ignoring the national aspect as in their version of modern Indian history, the *khilafat* and the non-co-operation movements did not figure. Perhaps Prof. Chaudhary does not know that Vishwa Hindu Parishad has no official historians attached to it and all those historians whose scientific writings are not acceptable to the so-called secular historians are, in fact, independent scholars. Even during the course of mutual dialogue between the Vishwa Hindu Parishad and All India Babri Masjid Action Committee in March 1991 and October-November 1992, the Government of India recognised that the expert-historians attached with either side were independent scholars, even though with divergent views. That such historians dubbed as VHP historians, do not keep in mind the national aspects of history, is a gross exaggeration. However, Prof. Chaudhary himself did not agree with the views of Prof. Sharma and commented that the writings of R.C. Mazumdar and N.K. Sinha's Ranjit Singh did not form a part of communal history, as these were produced while fully keeping the national interest in mind.

Having traced the intellectual background and the false perceptions of historical writing to the imperial concept of history initiated by James Mill (early 19th century) and followed up by Elliot and Dowson. Prof. Chaudhury questioned their version of the "Muslim rule in India and the Muslim tyranny over the Hindus". He argued that such a viewpoint had been advanced by the British historians to show that it was the British rule which had emancipated the Hindus from the Muslim rule. He asked, was there a Muslim rule in India? To his mind, there was none as during that period, the State was not theocratic in character. He quoted the oft-repeated conversation between the Sultan Alauddin Khaliji and Qazi Mughis-ud-Din wherein the Sultan remarked that he did not know what was lawful or unlawful according to the *shariat* but he would do what he considered as the interest of the State. As such, as the State was not governed by *Shariat* laws, pure and simple, it did not make any distinction between Muslims and Hindus in respect of property matters, community life and the land revenue assessed on the Hindu and the Muslim peasants.

There is no denying the fact that James Mill analysed the Hindu civilisation with contempt and in his scathing criticism wrote about the Hindus as 'superior to lower animals but not superior to higher animals', in mind and body... 'the most enslaved portion of human race' and in their sensual pleasures, 'very near to that of national animals'. James Mill was equally critical of the Muslim despotic institutions and culture. In fact, in the field of historiography, his main purpose was to show the superiority of the European culture as against Indian culture, whether Hindu or Muslim. But as regards the suppressed position of the Hindus during the Sultanate and Mughal periods. James Mill followed by Elliot and Dowson portrayed the nature of the rule under them, especially the position of the Hindus based on the contemporary medieval Persian sources. Elliot and Dowson in the '*History of India as told by its own Historians*' may have been a little selective in the narration of the excerpts from the contemporary sources but they have done yeoman service to the students of medieval Indian history who do not know Arabic or the Persian languages. No doubt, that in matter of land revenue assessment on the peasantry, there was no discrimination between the Hindus and the Muslims but the real discrimination in respect of the financial burden between the two communities lay in the imposition of *jizya* and cesses, especially octroi and pilgrimage, which formed a part of *sairojihat* of the revenues. It is well authenticated by the sources that right from the inception of the Turkish rule in India, in accordance with the Islamic concept, *jizya* was imposed upon the Hindus, being regarded as the *Zimmis.* Even Amir Khusrau, the great poet-cum-historian, attached to the Royal Court during the period of Alauddin Khalji regarded the imposition of *jizya* on the subjugated Hindus *(Kufar)* as mandatory. Excepting the interregnum of about a little more than a century, when abolished by Akbar and re-imposed by Aurangzeb, it remained in vogue right from the beginning of the 12th Century to the first quarter of the

18th century. In fact, Prof. Chaudury has not appreciated that the conversation between Alaud Din Khalji and Qazi Mughis-ud-Din centered around three main issues to be determined as per *Shariat* viz the position of the *Zimmis* (here Hindus), the punishment to be meted out to the corrupt Government servants and the distribution of the wealth (*mal*) gathered by Alaud-Din Khalji during his Deogarh campaigns in Deccan. While there was controversy over the distribution of the plundered wealth, whether it belonged to the Sultan in person or formed a part of the Royal treasury (*baitulmal*) or to be shared as per *Shariat* and Islamic precedents set by the *Khalifas*, there was no difference of opinion on the question of the position of the *Zimmis* (Hindus) to be subjected to the payment of *jizya'*. During the reign of Aurangzeb, both Raja Raj Singh of Mewar and the great Maratha leader Shivaji fought against the imposition of *jizya* upon the Hindus. For the reign of Aurangzeb (1658-1707), there are reliable contemporary sources, of even archival nature, which bear out the governance of the State was based upon Islamic polity in many a respect. Apart from other causes, the religious factor was quite marked for the rise of the Sikhs, the Jats and the Marathas against the Mughal State and was considerably responsible for the ultimate collapse of the Mughal Empire. Apart from this, the use of terminology like Muslim Rule in India', to which Prof. Chaudury has taken exception, has already been accounted for.

Prof. Chaudhury conceded the fact that certainly there was temple destruction during the medieval age but argued that the question of the destruction of the temple (of Ramjanambhoomi) by Babur or Mir Baqi was not relevant today and would not help the people in any way. He stated that with the demolition of the 'Baburi Masjid', the politics of the middle ages could be seen in the modern times and that in many a respect, the Medieval Age was more civilised than the present era. He further stated that the political communalism of the people in majority was trying to tyrannise the minorities and instead of building up communal forces, one might appeal to reason rather than be guided only by emotions.

Prof. Chaudhury's moral sermon is contradictory in many a respect. The relevance of a particular place of religious worship is determined by the reverence the people have shown to it all through the ages. As a scholar of history, he should have better known that ever since time immemorial, the Hindus have been worshipping Lord Rama, Lord Krishna and Shivji and their deities placed in the sacred temples in Ayodhya, Mathura and Benares respectively. In fact, these gods constitute the very heart and soul of the Hindu religion and these temples are the holiest of the holy places. The historical records show that during the early medieval age, whenever they were demolished by the invading Muslim rulers, they were reconstructed thereafter by the Hindu chieftains. Moreover, ever since the destruction of these temples and construction of the mosques on the same site during the Mughal age, there has been intermittently Hindu-Muslim tussles, both armed and judicial over these sites. For the Hindus, more than the structures of these temples, it is the site, i.e. the sacred *bhoomi* which has been held in esteem for worship of the deities. So the demand for the sacred site of Ramjanma Bhoomi or other places at Mathura and Benares is as much relevant today as it was during the medieval age. Prof. Chaudhury's testimony to the present-day European spirit of tolerance by foregoing the past religious conflicts is not only besides the mark but also exaggerated. Numerous examples can be cited from the East European countries, when after gaining freedom from the Turkish yoke in the $19^{th}$ century, the peoples of these countries rebuilt the churches on the very sites of the mosques. Even the British historian, Arnold Toynbee in *One World and India* commented that after the attainment of Independence in 1918, the Polish people pulled down the Eastern Orthodox Christian Cathedral, earlier built by the Russians in the heart of Warsaw to show their political mastery but the Indian Government, to their credit, did not touch the mosques at Mathura and Benares which had been built by Aurangzeb at the Hindu holy sites, not basically for the purposes of worship by the Muslims but sheerly out of political vindictiveness to "signify that an Islamic Government was reigning Supreme, even over Hinduism's holiest of holy places". But now it is high time that in the interest of communal harmony, which is an essential ingredient of Indian secularism, the wrongs done to the Hindus in the past should be rectified in an amicable manner.

Prof. Barun De in his long winded speech for over an hour attempted to raise issues, both repetitive and stereotyped. He suggested that the historical trends which led to distortions in Indian history, especially those on which communal forces were being built up, needed to be stressed. He said that it was important to understand as to with whom the historians were communicating, whether they were having a mutual dialogue or communicating with the people in the country through any medium viz. English or Hindi or in a regional language, i.e. Bengali, Marathi, etc. He held that a historian might communicate with the people who might not share the same views. All the same, history might aim at common consciousness with the people. In the selection of facts, a historian should avoid bias and prejudice but the selected facts in history might be interpreted in an analytical manner, which would equally aim at reconstruction with a sense of objectivity. History may inculcate consciousness and for this, the touchstone was the standard of the history textbooks, which were being properly looked after by the Board of Studies of the West Bengal Government, and which would combat distortions in history for a free and constructive state and society.

Prof. Barun De dilated on those aspects of history, which he considered to be distortions in New Cambridge History of India and the works of C.A. Bayly and Burton Stein. Prof. De considered that Bayly's theory of regional conditions as the normal way of Indian life and Burton Stein's view that the downfall of the Mughal Empire was not due to economic or agrarian factors but because of the clash with the regional principalities were anomalous in character. Prof. De thought that such versions had been advanced with an eye to the 21$^{st}$ century India, which according to these writers, might come up with regional principalities and sub-states. He further commented that such versions were aimed at rationalisation of the regional conflicts and basis which lay at the root of the Kashmir and Borderland problems. Prof. De held that another proposition of the prevalence of the ethnic wars in the Indian subcontinent was aimed at the accentuation of the regional basis so as to promote the interest of capital transfer. This was tantamount to distortion and was a more sophisticated form of Imperial colonialism aimed at the growth of marketing, which was the beginning of animal politics.

Prof. De ridiculed the writings of Ram Mohan Roy which characterised the Muslim rule as the 'Muslim tyranny in Bengal'. He also jeered at the idea of the 'so-called Ramjanam Bhoomi' having been demolished by Mir Baqi or the earlier Jaunpur rulers. He also referred to the event of 6th December 1992 i.e. the demolition of the disputed structure at Ayodhya, which was being inappropriately shown, as an act of 'Divine Providence. He said that foreign historical accounts had been produced which show that Hindu communalism in India was more important than Muslim communalism for the partition of the country. He stated that the attempt for equating the dynastic chronology was a vulgarised concept and that for the analysis of Indian history, the religious, caste and ethnic factors were being emphasised by these writers. He further pointed out that though in the recent past, especially in 1970's and 1980's, books had been published from the Marxist viewpoint so as to cover the social life and the peasantry, two disturbing elements, i.e. the role of the communal parties like the R.S.S. with P. N. Oak as its historian and the search for a political party which could hunt for the past for the glorification of the Hindus were out to distort history in a crude and vulgar manner. According to him, attempts were being made by these sections, who, on the one hand resorted to character assassination of the historical personality like Akbar with the verdict, 'Who says Akbar was great', and on the other hand, Ram Chandra had been shown as a warrior. At the end, Prof. De regretted that the Indian nation had not come to its own. He also wondered at the people who had elected 'Advani (L.K. Advani) Man of the Year-1995'.

Such a lopsided and maliciously motivated talk on the part of Prof. De needs no elaborate comments. He starts with an ideal theoretical concept of a professional historian for the reconstruction of history in an objective manner, without bias or prejudice and ends with his regrets for the choice of Advani (L.K. Advani) as Man of the Year-1995 by a nation which has not come to its own. His own version of the writing of C.A. Bayly is as well repetitive of the one-sided opinion of Prof. Irfan Habib. In fact, for many an aspect of the pre-colonial era, Bayly even referred to and acknowledged both Prof. Irfan Habib and the present writer (B.R. Grover). C. A. Bayly's remarks on the decline of the Mughal Empire and emergence of the regional principalities as an aftermath of Aurangzeb's religious policy is not unfounded. Bayly aptly remarks, "Aurangzeb had departed from the latitudinarian stances of his predecessors and insisted on a more full-blooded Islamic Policy among his high officials. But in Gangetic north India, where less than 15 percent of the population were Muslims and were concentrated in the cities, this was a hazardous move. Local conflicts over Hindu and Muslim practice became confounded with the tension and periphery over the destination of revenue and resources". Similarly, Prof. De's criticism of Burton Stein for not having accepted the view of the mere agrarian cause responsible for the disintegration of the Mughal Empire is partial. In fact, in this regard, these writers have tried to substantiate what was already written long back by the learned historians J.N. Sarkar, Sri Ram Sharma, W.S. Sardesai and others. One may not agree with the views of Bayly, Burton Stein and the authors of New Cambridge History in many a respect, but to say that they have stressed the religious or ethnic factors leading to the emergence of the independent principalities in the 8th century with a view to inculcate such an apprehension for 21st century India, howsoever despicable, is rather too farfetched an opinion. All the same, it is difficult to agree with any of their views which undermines the role of the Indian Muslim League and Muslim communalism vis. a vis. the Hindu organisations responsible for the partition of India. Prof. De's own remarks about Raja Ram Mohan Roy and the Ayodhya issue are not only misplaced but distort the facts of medieval Indian History. As the case is sub-justice, it is difficult to express opinion about the responsibility for the unfortunate event of 6th December 1992 but for all this, one has to appreciate the mob-psychology for avenging the past wrong done to the cultural heritage of the Hindus during the Medieval Age. As pointed out by Prof. De, the latest trends in the 70s and 80s for an emphasis on the socio-economic aspects for the analysis of Indian history are welcome but to have unnecessarily dragged in R. S. S. in the controversy is unwarranted. One may not agree with P. N. Oak's views on the medieval monuments but in no case does he represent the R. S. S. which is a cultural and national organisation rather than a communal one. The portrayal of Shri Rain Chandra as a national hero is not unhistoric. One can evaluate the achievements and limitations of the Mughal monarch, Akbar and assess whether he was 'great' or not without any communal bias. But any attempt to compare him with Shri Ram Chandra, who is worshipped by the majority of the Hindus as the Vishnu *Avtar*, is rather irrelevant. Anyway, Akbar, the Mughal monarch, equally finds a distinguished place in the Indian Constitution as an eminent historical personality in the history of India.

## Indian History Congress Session 1995: A Critique

The Indian History Congress, one of the oldest bodies of the professional historians of India, aims at the study of history and civilisations of the peoples of India and other than India, in an objective and scientific manner. But it is highly regrettable that for the last few years, it has been reduced to a forum with vested and ideological interests on the part of certain dominant sections who while professing 'secular and scientific' approach to history aimed at serving the 'national' interests of the pluralistic Indian society have been making collective endeavour to distort and misinterpret the history of India. Despite the existence of authentic source-material for an objective analysis of history and culture of India, such an attempt to politicise history is bound to do more harm than serving the national interests.

The 56th session of the Indian History Congress held at Rabindra Bharati University, Calcutta, on December 28-30, 1995, was inaugurated by Shri Benoy Krishna Chowdhury, Hon'ble Minister-in-Charge, Department of Land and Land Reforms, Government of West Bengal. In his Inaugural Address, he underlined the distinctive role of the peasantry and the working class in Bengal in the freedom struggle waged against the British Colonial rule. He has made laudable attempt to trace the impact of the magnitude of land revenue on the peasantry of Bengal ever since the assumption of *Diwani* by the English East India Company in 1765 and the resultant various types of upsurges against the British Colonial rule during the last three decades of the 18th century – a tradition which was followed up in the 19th and

20th centuries. He emphasised that since 1930s, the poor economic plight of the cultivators or share-croppers called the '*bargadar*' or '*adhiar*' or '*bhangchasi*' on account of payment of rent as half the share of the gross produce to the *Jotedars* and the Zamindars as well as heavy usurious rates of interest on the crop-loan, considerable land alienation resulting in the increasing loss of occupancy rights of owner cultivators and the rapid growth of the share-croppers between 1928 and 1940 led to active participation of the Communists and the revolutionaries released from Andaman and other jails (1937-38) in the Bengal Provincial Kisan Sabha. Apart from the contribution of the other workers, the Hon'ble Minister underlined his own role in the Kisan Sabha movement and especially that of Shri Jyoti Basu, then Chief Minister of West Bengal who as the leader of the Communist group in the Bengal Legislative Assembly (February, 1947) championed the cause of the *tebhaga* movement of the peasantry against the *Jotedars* and the police repression. The Hon'ble Minister further claimed that all through the peasant movement had been marked by Hindu-Muslim unity and that even the August 1946 Hindu-Muslim communal riot and the great killings in Calcutta were engineered by the British Government who sought to hide their conspiracy under the code of "Operation Asylum". In his assessment of the 1946 Calcutta communal riots, the Hon'ble Minister did not ascribe any responsibility to the Indian Muslim League for the communal riots. Similarly, there is no denying the fact that like various other national organisations and the people in different parts of the country, the peasant members of the Kisan Sabha of Bengal supported Netaji's I.N.A. movement and Mutiny in the Royal Indian Navy (December 1945- February, 1946), but this was an all India national upsurge and was by no means confined to peasantry and urban sectors of Bengal under the Communist leadership. At the same time, the Inaugural Address gives credit to the Bengal Kisan Sabha for successfully containing the Hindu-Muslim riot in Noakhali but most surprisingly it does not at all refer to the services rendered by Mahatma Gandhi in this regard. In fact, for the 20th century history, the Inaugural Address has exaggerated the role of the peasantry and urban working class in Bengal in the freedom struggle against the British Raj under the

Communist leadership and has completely ignored the signal contribution of the Indian National Congress in this regard.

At the time of inauguration, Shri Satyasaddan Chakraborty, the Hon'ble Minister of Education, who addressed the delegates, while correctly distinguishing between the scientific and fictional history, urged the importance of objective approach to history. However, his reference to Shri Ram and *Sita Rasoi* as a part of fictional history (hence worthy of condemnation) was highly misplaced, erroneous and prejudiced. The Hon'ble Minister should have known that in the well-known case of Vishwa Hindu Adhivakta Sangh vs. Union of India and others (1992), the Lucknow Bench of the Allahabad High Court, in its Judgement delivered by Hon'ble Justice H.N. Tilhari on 1st January, 1993, pointed out that the Indian Constitution as adopted by the Constituent Assembly on 26th November, 1949, enshrined the concept of secularism though the expression itself was introduced by the Constitution in the 42nd Amendment Act. The framers of the Constitution equally emphasised the cultural heritage of India especially through a list of illustrations as contained in the Constitution and engraved in the Chapters 1 to 22. Amongst the various other historical figures/phases which find mention in the above mentioned illustrations of the Constitution are Shri Ram and Sita in a scene from the *Ramayan* depicting conquest of Lanka and recovery of Sita by Rama, Shri Krishna propounding Gita to Arjun, scenes from Buddha's and Mahavir's life, portrait of Akbar with Mughal architecture, portraits of Shivaji and Guru Gobind Singh and portrait of Gandhiji and Dandi March. By depicting these portraits, the Indian Constitution recognises these personages as historical and a part and parcel of Indian history. Here in the portraits, Shri Ram and Sita are as much a real part of authentic Indian history and culture as later on Lord Buddha or Akbar, or Mahatma Gandhi's Dandi March in 1931.

The above mentioned judgement by the Hon'ble Allahabad High Court runs as, "…..the birth and existence of Ram Chandra with Sita and events of their life has been accepted as realities having taken place to establish rule of law and discipline and it has not been left to be taken as a myth. The revelation of Rama in the form of human being, his birth even cannot be denied nor events of life as the same has always been accepted by the children of this land Bharat and framers of its Constitution. The Constitution shows that the Constituent Assembly accepted the history of Rama in relation to the places as a fact, reality and to its national pride and cultural importance... here Rama when we adopted him and his life as part of our constitutional theme to depict certain ideal, he became a Constitutional entity–admittedly a reality of our National culture and fabric and not a myth". As such, the Indian Constitution regards "Lord Shri Rama, a figure constitutionally accepted as Lord of the builders of this nation and its culture."

The above mentioned judgement of the Lucknow Bench of the Allahabad High Court, dated 1st January, 1993, also permitted the Hindus and devotees of Shri Ram Chandraji to have *Darshan* at the make-shift Ram Janmabhumi temple at Ayodhya, constructed at the site of the disputed structure, unfortunately demolished on 6th December, 1992. The Hon'ble Court also directed to preserve and protect the material and articles of historical/archaeological importance which were taken or found on the spot in the debris of demolished structure or in the nearby area.

The U.P. Sunni Central Board of Waqfs & others filed petition for special leave to appeal (Civil) No. 717/93 in the Hon'ble Supreme Court of India against the above mentioned judgement of High Court of Allahabad making Vishwa Hindu Adhivakta Sangh & others as respondents. The Bench of the Hon'ble Supreme Court presided over by Hon'ble Justices U.N. Ray and G.T. Nanavati vide their judgement dated December 11, 1995 did not accept the petition. The Hon'ble Court directed that as per its earlier order dated October 24, 1994 regarding the Reference No. 1/93 under Article 143(1) of the Constitution with I.A. No. 1/94 in T.C. (c) with No. 44/93, made by the President of India in respect of the disputed structure, i.e. Ram Janmabhoomi-'Baburi Masjid', all disputed suits about the latter structure had already been sent back to the Allahabad High Court for adjudication, the above mentioned suit may as well be disposed of by the same court. As the Hon'ble High Court at Allahabad had already decided this suit, its judgement dated January 1, 1993 stands final.

Similarly, by jeering at *Sita Rasoi* as a part of fictional history, the Hon'ble Minister has betrayed complete ignorance of the medieval Indian history and the historical literature published in 1991-92 during the course of the controversy over the disputed structure named Ram janmabhoomi-'Baburi Masjid'. As already clarified in these writings, the Janmasthan temple at Ayodhya, demolished (1528-1529) during the reign of Babur, the first Mughal invader of India, was also popularly known as 'Sita Rasoi' - a fact which is well confirmed by the 18th-19th centuries authentic literary and historical sources, both in Persian and Urdu. Symbolically, the *Chabutra* comprising *chakla* and *belana* of *Sita Rasoi* could be well identified on the northern side of the outer courtyard of the disputed structure demolished on 6th December, 1992. Howsoever considered unfortunate, the event of demolition of the disputed structure brought forth the fresh indisputable archaeological evidence which confirms the fact that at the very disputed site, prior to the construction of the so-called 'Baburi Masjid', there existed a Vishnu Temple. Amongst the discovery of various archaeological remains of the Hindu Temple, the very inaugural stone comprising a 12th century Sanskrit inscription in Nagari Script provides details of the Vishnu temple constructed on this site. This is an eloquent proof of the fact that at the very site of Ram Janmabhoomi at Ayodhya, there stood a Vaishnava temple from at least the 11th-12th which was destroyed by Mir Baqi in Babur's reign, for building a 'masjid' around A.D. 1528-29. It is this Vaishnava temple which was later on described as 'Sita Rasoi' in the Persian and Urdu literature. It is a pity that the Hon'ble minister along with the body of the professional historians should turn a 'Nelson's' eye to the archaeological findings in the aftermath of 6th December, 1992. The details of all these objects, now kept under lock-and-key of the Central Govt., are available with the Allahabad High Court and can be obtained by anyone who so desires.

Professor H.K. Barpujari, the General President, read his Presidential Address on 'North-East India, the Problems and Policies since 1947'. In his Address, he reiterated the noble theoretical concept that the duty of a historian is to lay bare facts or pass a judgment without fear and favour. Under no circumstances should he suppress or distort facts to suit interests, personal, political or communal. He further commented that "Clio has no other interest than the search for the truth, the whole truth," irrespective of national, religious, linguistic or regional considerations. Ironically, in the same breath, he further remarked, while extending the bounds of knowledge, that the historian's "findings must serve the interests of the community" by recording "events with the object of removing misunderstanding, strengthening views and enlightening the public both in its strong and weak points". However, even though the learned President theorised the role of the historian, he made no attempt to comment by way of any illustration, as to how, in practice, majority of the historians in control of the Indian History Congress, were suppressing or distorting facts of history to suit their ideological and political interests.

As a matter of fact, the General President had taken up a topic for the Inaugural Address which pertains to the recent events of contemporary history, for which he could have no access to the archival material or the confidential record of the Government of India. As such, he has simply relied on the annual Quinquennial Reports, official and non-official, as well as secondary sources, viz. monographs, brochures, articles of magazines and journals, media, local and national. To all this, he has added eye-witness account based on personal knowledge. Most surprisingly, the learned President, despite all his scholarship, could not select a topic for analysis on any of the past phases of the pre-Independence period for this region, more especially the lesser known socio-economic and political aspects, for which he could have an access to the more reliable and authentic sources, which could be utilised in an objective manner in accordance with the ideal concept of a historian as outlined by him in the Introduction.

Imitating an experienced journalist and a politician, the General President dealt with various contemporary controversial issues of North-East India, viz. the re-organisation of States, Balkanisation of Assam, boundary disputes, migration of the East Pakistani/Bangladeshi Hindus and Muslims to the Valley of Brahmputra, and its impact on the Assamese society, secessionism, military action and insurgency on the part of the ULFA, SULFA and the Bodos. The Address provides a scathing criticism of the North-Eastern policies of Pandit Nehru, Shrimati Indira Gandhi's Indira-Mujib Agreement (1972) and the present day Government with the result that "the entire North-East region is now in turmoil". The Address ends with an appeal to the present Election Commissioner, Shri T. N. Seshan, to act as the saviour of the people of Assam by removing the names of the foreigner from the voter's list so as to help in the solution of the problems of the migrants into Assam. No politician could have done better than the General President of the Indian History Congress under the garb of a historian.

The sectional Presidents of both Ancient India and Medieval India did not attend the session of the Congress. Nor did they send their Presidential Addresses for the delegates. Such is the sorry state of affairs of academic seriousness in the activities of the Congress. However, Dr. Gautam Sengupta, the Sectional President of Historical Archaeology, Epigraphy, Numismatics and Archives, presented his Address on 'Archaeology in India: Some Urgent Issues'. Having traced the history of the development of the Archaeology in India since the late 19$^{th}$ century (1861), more especially since the period of Lord Curzon, the Viceroy of India (1899-1905), he dealt with the establishment of the Archaeological Survey of India at the centre and the various archaeological departments in the Universities and the Provinces before and after Independence of India. The speaker has criticised the Archaeological Survey of India on the plea that it has not been able to define its own policy in respect of excavation and exploration and that there is near total lack of co-ordination with different archaeological organisations in India as the Central Advisory Board of Archaeology has not been very effective. He has also pointed out that even though the Archaeological Survey of India has identified pre- and proto-history as its priority area, it has not paid any serious attention to historical archaeology and more especially, medieval archaeology.

The authoritative articles published by Dr. Y.D. Sharma on the Exploration of Historical Sites and A. Ghosh's Fifty Years of Archaeological Survey of India published in '*Ancient India,* Bulletin of Archaeological Survey of India (November 1953), R.N. Mehta's Mediaeval Archaeology,' 1979 and the annual numbers of Indian Archaeology–A Review, with effect from 1954-55 to 1988-89 (published in 1993) bring out the importance of the explorations relating as much to the other periods as for the medieval age. In this regard, to cite a few examples, the extended explorations at Hampi, Fatehpur Sikri, Thaneswar (Haryana) and Lalkot as well as Siri Fort in Delhi are quite significant. In 1957-58, the already explored mound at Thaneswar, locally known as 'Harsh-Ka-Quila', representing the capital of King Harshavardhana, was further examined. Surface finds of pottery confirmed its early mediaeval date, though possibly going back to the pre-Gupta Period. In 1959-60, in the course of repairs to the Sultan-Ghari monument, at Delhi (Mehrauli Palam road), i.e. the tomb built by Iltutmish (1231) for his deceased son Nasirud-Din Mahmud, the dismemberment of the lime-concrete roof of the octagonal chamber of the tomb, lying on a square platform retained by ashlar-stones and filled with earth and debris in the centre, brought to light several beautifully carved lintels from Hindu temples, approximately of the seventh century. Included among these sculptured slabs was the reused marble *yoni patta* (base slab for a *linga),* the upright of a railing with medallions in front and the mortice holes on a side to receive cross-bars. This clearly brings out the fact that the tomb was built on the very site of the Hindu temple and after destruction, its rubble was used in the construction of the tomb.

Similarly, in 1961, during the course of repairing and replacing the red stone-slabs of the casing walls of Qutab Minar, above the surface, which has been damaged due to natural weathering, Hindu sculptured deities used as rubble in the big walls were found. However, apprehending any communal tension, further work in this regard was stopped by the Government. Very recently, two sculptural pieces, one with an Islamic inscription on the upper side and Hindu deity at the back, and another, a doorjamb with Hindu designs fell apart from the main body of the Quwwatul-Islam mosque. These are being preserved by the Archaeological Survey of India in the premises of the office of the Qutb Minar. All this further confirms the contents of the inscription at the Eastern end of the Quwwatul Islam mosque that it was built with the material of the twenty seven Hindu and Jain demolished temples situated on the same site. Apart from this, in the same Lalkot area, a four armed Samkarshana image of Vishnu in blackstone, with a Sanskrit inscription below the feet of the image, dated *Samvat* 1204 (AD 147), has been found to the south-east of Qutb Minar. Close to the find spot of the image was a stone platform, on which was marked the exterior plan of a *pancha-ratha* shrine. The excavations at Lalkot (Delhi), the city of the Tomars and the Chauhans, the last Hindu rulers and the first capital of the Turkish rulers, have brought to light many an architectural and sculptural aspect of the Tomar-Chauhan monuments, further modified by the Turkish rulers.

At the end, the Sectional President offers a sermon that archaeology may not be politicised so as to be used for issues which are non-archaeological, which according to him has given a serious jolt to plural society in the recent years. However, he has not afforded any instance of the misuse of archaeology. The concluding para of the Address shows that the learned speaker himself wants to make use of archaeology for political ends for strengthening the plural society as envisaged by him rather than purely for scientific purposes and for unearthing the pattern of civilisation which has governed the Indian life through the centuries.

The Indian History Congress at its Annual Business Meeting held on 30th December, 1995 moved two resolutions regarding the preservation of monuments. In the first Resolution, the Congress cautioned the Central Government against any damage likely to be done to an ancient fortress at Kasargod by using it as centre of tourism. The second Resolution noted that there were "continuing attempts of a section of people to attack places of worship" and called upon the Central, State Governments and the Archaeological Survey of India to protect monuments by "fully implementing the Ancient Monuments Act." The Congress also reiterated its earlier Resolution passed at its 47th Session held at Srinagar in October 1986 which has also decried the attempt to convert centuries old places of worship of one community into those of another on the alleged ground that they had been originally built on sites over which sacred structures of the other community had once stood. The Resolution regarded these allegations of "dubious kind" and exhorted the concerned "parties to establish worship in monuments under the control of the Archaeological Survey of India, wherever such worship has ceased long ago."

After the Resolutions were moved, the present writer B.R. Grover took exception to the manner the Resolutions had been moved. He pointed out the procedural flaw in this regard as the Resolutions had not been circulated along with other papers of the agenda. He argued that in the past, as per proper procedure, the Resolutions were always circulated in advance to the delegates so as to give them proper opportunity to go through them minutely. But for a couple of years or so, this practice had been arbitrarily dropped and the resolutions were just verbally read out. This irregularity was pointed out even in the past sessions of the Indian History Congress but no action was taken by the Executive Council of the Indian History Congress in this regard.

The writer, Prof. Grover, further stated that even though the contention of the first Resolution was quite valid, no report has been sought from the Archaeological Survey of India as to the steps it has taken for safeguarding the misuse of the ancient fortress of Kasargod as centre of tourism. It was essential to have taken this report and known the exact position of the case before unnecessarily criticising the Government in this regard. At the same time, the writer argued that the second Resolution relating to any apprehended attack on the monuments was too vague as it did not spell out as to when and where the attempt of attack was made on the place of worship of any community. Moreover, any reference to the October 1986 Srinagar Resolution was irrelevant as much water has flown down the River Jhelum at Srinagar since then. In the course of discussion on the Resolutions moved from time to time since then, reference had always been made to the disputed structure named 'Ram Janmbhumi-Baburi Masjid". But it was not realised that ever since the Srinagar resolution, the legal position had undergone a tremendous change. The Parliament Act of the Places of Worship (1991), the demolition of the disputed structure in Ayodhya on 6th December 1992, the acquisition of certain area at Ayodhya Ordinance, 1993, the reference to the Supreme Court regarding the issue as to whether a Hindu temple or any religious structure existed prior to the construction of the Ram janmabhumi-'Babri Masjid' in the area on which the structure stood, the judgement of the Supreme Court dated 24th September 1994 directing that all suits relating to Ayodhya Ram janmabhumi may be taken up by the Allahabad High Court and the present day proceedings going on at its Lucknow Bench have rendered all issues relating to the Ayodhya structure sub-judice. As such, no resolution relating to the Ayodhva monument could be, as per law, adopted by the Congress. The writer contended that historically, it was incorrect to say that during the mediaeval age, no places of worship of one community were converted to places of worship of another community at the former's site. Apart from the most reliable evidence on the Ayodhya disputed structure and various such cases, there is irrefutable contemporary evidence to show that the Keshav Dev temple at Mathura and the Gyanvyapi Vishwanath temple at Benares were destroyed by the Mughal emperor Aurangzeb in A.D. 1666 and A.D. 1669, respectively, and the mosques were constructed on the same site. This fact was even acknowledged by the expert historians of the All India Babri Masjid Action Committee during the course of dialogue with the Vishwa Hindu Parishad in October-November 1992. The demand on the latter's part for the restoration of these two sites either voluntarily by the Muslim community based on mutual goodwill or through legislation by the Government of India is neither unreasonable nor does it tantamount to any attack on the places of worship. Prof. Grover also pointed out that none of these monuments had been declared as protected monuments under the protection of the Archaeological Survey of India, or the State Government under the Ancient Monuments Act. So the reference in the Resolution to the latter organisation was rather inapt. Prof. Grover maintained that in view of all these facts, the Resolutions could not be accepted and be better withdrawn.

# 19

# Distortions and Bias in History with Special Reference to the History of India

## What is History? Is it a Science?

The word "history" derives its origin from a Greek word meaning "enquiry" or "learning by enquiry". Enquiry of what? It is an enquiry and analysis of the events of the past.

In defining history, Edward Hallett Carr stated: "The historian without his facts is rootless and futile; the facts without their historian are dead and meaningless... (History) is a continuous process of interaction between the historian and his facts, an unending dialogue between the present and the past" (*What is History*, p. 24).

History is a record. It is a record of the political regimes and empires and their rise and fall. It is equally a story of civilizations, their social, economic and cultural fields, ever changing with elements of continuity also. The term history today is generally used for that field of study which treats history as "actuality" or history as a "science". It has been defined as the "science of man in time." In so far as it seeks the truth, history is a science.

History seeks truth. Yet history has been sufficiently used as an effective instrument of "brain washing", calling for periodic accusations of partisanship. In the selection of facts, a historian should avoid bias and prejudice but the selected facts in history might be interpreted in an analytical manner, which would equally aim at reconstruction with sense of objectivity. History may inculcate consciousness and for this, the touchstone was the standard of history textbooks to combat distortions in history for a free and constructive state and society.

However, the task of a historian is not limited to a mere assembly of facts. Facts require interpretation. A historian reconstructs the past and makes it intelligible through analysis and interpretation of facts. In the selection and interpretation of facts, a historian should avoid bias and prejudice. It is the duty of a historian to search for truth and relay the whole truth, irrespective of personal, political, cultural, social, ideological and religious considerations. However, many historians suppress or distort facts of history to suit their ideological and political interests. Once the narrative is geared to an objective with personal bias and group prejudice, it gets reduced to mere propaganda.

In history, the subjective element plays a significant role in the process of acceptance, selection and interpretation of facts. Not all historians can claim to have the same scientific approach, and even with a scientific approach, it is not always possible for them to arrive at one set of interpretation. In the interpretation of historical facts, it is possible to distort facts and figures, details and descriptions. Distortions of facts assume many shapes and forms. Significant omissions, particularly the contributions of other people, can speak volumes about the prejudices of the historian. Quoting facts out of the context can change the course of historical events.

Furthermore, the discipline of history demands that along with political and economic factors, one may equally discern and underline the role that religion has played through times immemorial. This factor cannot be altogether ignored. It is the examination of the totality of the then thinking and action which determines the scientific approach to history. History plays a vital role in the understanding of the ways of life, cultures and religions of people, their contribution to human civilization through the ages and their present day interdependence. It presents the vast panorama of man's progress through the ages. It is a continuous social process.

Historians tend to view evidence from a certain angle or vision. These different angles of historians living in the same or different periods or social milieu lead to inevitable biases and/or preconceptions. All the same, it is important to get the different angles or perspectives on the same facts to enable us to pursue our search for the truth, the whole truth. This is a hard talk. As Oscar Wilde said: "Anybody can make history; only a great man can write it."

**Is Rewriting of History Necessary?**

The rewriting and re-interpretation of history is not a new or modem phenomenon. It has been going on from one age to another. Goethe remarked that history must be rewritten from time to time not only because new facts have been discovered but above all because every generation comes forward with new interests and new ways of looking at things and consequently observes the past from different angles than theretofore.

D. P. Singhal, a professor of history at the University of Queensland,Australia, states that "The involvement of the elements of human perception in recording events and interpreting them makes historical narratives, even when based on the same data, so varied. Hence a discovery of new material, a change in outlook, values or society brought about by a revolution or advancement of knowledge, must lead to re-writing of history" ("Battle for the Past", *History Today*, vol. 1, 2000, pp. 5-14). Indian history is no exception. The changing concepts of history alone require periodic revisions.

Constant research is needed to uncover more facts and offer new interpretations. Critical investigation of the work of others can result in the formulation of more correct interpretations. Every age brings with it some new ideas about the historical thinking on the part of the people in respect of their past life. Thus history is to be rewritten not only because new facts and data have been discovered but because the life and culture of the people has to be looked upon from a different and proper angle than done in the past and new aspects have to be taken into account. It appears that of all the ages in the past, the present age is perhaps the most historical-minded. Today, in India, historiography is in deepening crisis. It is well accepted that what has happened in the past cannot be changed –even the Almighty God cannot do it.

All the same, there is a danger that through distortions, a historian can alter the past. One has to be equally cautious against the "command conclusions" and of making history as an instrument of propaganda for the vested ideologies or groups in a community or a nation. Writing history, therefore, is a task of requiring high moral standards as well as high intellectual capabilities.

The operation for rewriting history has to aim at the analysis of the cultural aspects in the society in a proper scientific manner.

For the socio-economic analysis, social and political ideas as well as institutional set-up have to be studied and worked out.

Apart from trends of historiography, emphasis has also to be laid on the inscriptions, archaeology, regional languages, literature, speculative ideas, art, architecture, music, science, technology and medicine.

In addition to the continuation of work on traditional line of political history, it is necessary to make further breakthrough in the analysis of social and economic history, more so at the regional level. In countries like India, one has to concentrate on rural society, the agrarian set-up, the tribal structure, the role of the tribes, clans, castes and landed intermediaries, the condition of the peasantry, the concept of the village community, handicrafts and industries in the rural and urban society.

An objective and scientific writing of history has to be encouraged. Aspects to be taken into account include polity, economy, social organisations, religion, philosophy, art and literature, science and technology, legal institutions, etc.

**Periodisation of History**

There has been some controversy about the periodisation of history in India. Basically, the division is in three periods but definitions have changed. Earlier, the periods were defined as Hindu, Muslim and British periods of Indian history. The earlier criterion was based on religion. This nomenclature, devised by the British, was found to be inappropriate. Since then the periods have been renamed as Ancient, Medieval and Modern after the European model. This, too, according to some historians, is not considered as very appropriate as they feel that the European criterion does not apply to India. It is felt that Medievalism connotes certain social, ideological and political attributes perceived in European cultural history which do not really apply to the Indian realities which are different. As such, the whole question needs re-examination.

British writers who laid emphasis on diversities and were lukewarm on compositeness of Indian cultures, also gave categories like North and South India which are still continuing.

**Distortions of British Historians and Their Angularities**

Many British writers during the British rule over India had misconceived notions about Indians and Indian civilization. Being the paramount power in India, they were somehow convinced of their own superiority over Indians and continued to rely on Mill and Macaulay who held the Indians and their literature in low esteem. James Mill analysed Hindu civilization with contempt. He held "Hindus as superior to lower animals but not superior to higher animals – in mind and body the most enslaved portion of human race". Even Edmund Burke's philosophical assertion of the supremacy of Indian traditions and his criticism of the British "drain" of wealth of India did not make much difference in British thinking about Indians. They considered the degenerate conditions of eighteenth century India as its normal condition holding their rule as struggle between East and West, between liberty and despotism and termed their rule as "the march of civilization", their power having been employed to dethrone "oriental despotism" to ensure growth of civilised communities. Seeley applauded the Englishman's conquest of India. He held that the British, who had a "higher and more vigorous civilisation than the native races", founded the Indian Empire "....partly out of philanthropic desire to put an end to enormous evils" of the "robber states of India".

Marxist angularities about India are equally biased and distorted.

Marx's view of India's past was also 'Europe-centered'. He, too, saw British rule a "double mission to India", one destructive and the other regenerating. He wrote in 1953: "Indian society has no history at all, at least no known history. What we call its history, is but the history of successive intruders who founded their empires on the passive basis of that unresisting and unchanging society."

"England has to fulfill a double mission in India: One destructive and the other regenerating – the annihilation of old Asiatic society, and the laying of the material foundation of Western society in Asia." Most nationalist/imperialist historians ignored the aspect of economic exploitation of India by Britain. Historians such as Vincent Smith, Dodwell, Coupland and others – all wrote on the same lines holding that India was merely a geographical expression and would relapse into old state of degeneration if the firm hand of benevolent paramount power was withdrawn. Lord Bryce topped them all in pronouncing that "Take away the British Raj and the idea of unity (of India) will vanish like mist". What a forecast!!

As far as unity of India is concerned, let us see what was actually achieved by free India after Independence in 1947. A move on the part of the British Government, no less than a mischievous move (and perhaps deliberate in the light of the above quoted remarks of Lord Bryce) was that while relinquishing power of supremacy of what was called British India to the Indian Government, in regard to the princely states in India numbering more than 525—big and small they announced that as published in the Stafford Cripps Mission's Memorandum on States on May 22, 1946, that when independent government was established, "The British would cease to exercise the power of paramountcy and the relationship of the States with the British would no longer exist and all rights surrendered to the States to the Britishers would return to them. The States could enter into a Federal relationship with the successor government or enter into any political arrangement". This meant recreating so may pockets of privately held territories within India and thus hitting at the unity of the country. This act of the outgoing British government was, in fact, a very mischievous move on their part which could have created utter chaos in the newly independent country had the position been allowed to subsist. The British were perhaps either trying to be too legalistic or did not want the freedom of India to succeed. However, the astute handling of the situation by the Government of India, in particular, the iron hands of Sardar Patel, free India's first Home Minister, who adopted a carrot and stick policy towards the princely states, solved the problem, and the government succeeded in merging all the princely states in India, thereby consolidating the country.

So much for the prophecy of Lord Bryce – "unity of India vanishing in the mist".

**Distortions and Bias by Indian Historians**

In the recent times, the canvas and scope of history has been sufficiently widened so as to cover the culture of the people with its multi-dimensional aspects and phases of life. The methodology of historical research demands not only coordination with the other social scientists for analysing the cultural and institutional aspects of the people but to develop scientific and objective approach for the mitigation of historical biases and distortions which have crept up from time to time. Notwithstanding these well-cherished ideals, it is most unfortunate that in the recent times, the Indian historiography has developed a serious crisis and is passing through a very crucial stage. The present-day democratic and social structure based on the concept of 'secularism' has considerably affected the historical thinking. However, it is a pity that for many an issue, inspired more by ideological publicity, far from having frank and fearless viewpoint based on historical facts and removing the past distortions in Indian history, attempt is being made to create more distortions rather than to rectify them. The analysis of the past events has been, unfortunately, linked up even with the false concept of secularism and political electoral vote-bank.

Prof B.R. Grover, who had been closely associated with the Indian History Congress for more than five decades, was deeply distressed to see this August forum of historians being used for narrow sectarian purposes and personal ends. He stated that "The Indian History Congress, one of the oldest bodies of the professional historians of India, aims at the study of history and civilizations of the peoples of India and other than India, in an objective and scientific manner." He observed: "It is highly regrettable that for the past few years, it has been reduced to a forum with vested and ideological interests on the part of certain dominant sections who, while professing 'secular and scientific' approach to history aimed at serving the 'national' interest of the pluralistic Indian society, have been making collective endeavour to distort and misinterpret the history of India. Despite the existence of authentic source material for an objective analysis of history and culture of India, such an attempt to politicise history is bound to do more harm than serving the national interests."

Referring especially to a Seminar on "Distortions of History – The Current Experience", organised by the Department of Tourism, Government of West Bengal, held in Calcutta on December 30, 1995, he observed that it created more of distortions rather than correcting the distortions of Indian history. He gave a critique referring specially to the following points:

Prof R.S. Sharma held that hitherto the medieval Indian history had been communalised as the epigraphic and the Sanskrit literary sources depicted the conflict as one between the invading Turks and the Indian Chiefs rather than between the Muslims and the Hindus. He contented that the term '*Turushadand*' which implied tax levied on the people for defence against the onslaught of the *Turushkas,* shows that the defence was organised by the Indian Chiefs against the foreign Turks rather than against the Muslims as the word Muslim does not occur in the available textual Sanskrit description.

However, it is to be noted that the Arabic and the Persian contemporary sources bring out the real nature of the conflict with the Hindu chiefs of north India. In this regard, to quote only a few authorities, Al Biruni's *Kitabal-Hind,* Al Utbi's *Taraikh-i-Yamini* and *Minhaj-un-din-b,* Sirajud-din's *Tabaqat-Nasiri* and Ziaud Din Barani's *Tarikh-i-Firoz Shahi*, clearly bring out the motives of Turkish campaigns against India. These sources narrate not only the Turkish designs for territorial conquest but equally emphasise the motives for pillage and plunder of wealth as well as the destruction of the Hindu temples, thereby signaling the triumph of Islam over the heathenic ways of worship and idolatry, customs and manners of the Hindus (Wa Hind/Hanud/Hinduism).

In this regard, it is not out of place to refer to the Pakistani historians who equally claim to be "scientific" and "objective" in their approach to the study of medieval history of the Indian subcontinent (what they call 'Indo-Pakistan sub-continent'). They too point out various distortions in medieval history created by the Western or the Indian scholarship. Most interestingly, for the medieval age, they bank on the same Arabic and Persian sources as we do. All the same, based on those sources, they often use terminology like 'Muslim invaders'; 'History of Muslim India'; 'Indo-Muslim historiography'; 'Muslim Empire in India'; 'Muslim Conquest of India'; 'Muslim Rule' or 'Muslim-Empire in Sind', 'Muslim Bengal', 'Victories of Muslim over large Hindu hordes', 'Army of Islam', 'Consolidation of Muslim India', Hindustan as "Citadel of Islam", 'Muslim historians', 'Hindu Sources' and 'Hindu inscriptions', etc. Some historians consider even the Arab conquest by Muhammad bin Qasim (A.D.712) as the triumph of Islam' and for Muhmud of Ghazni's campaigns in early eleventh century ascribe motives of not only conquest, pillage and plunder of wealth but even iconoclasm, spread of Islam *(tabligh)* and mitigation of the Indian culture based on Brahamanism. For such historiography, only a few well known Pakistani historians like S.M. Ikram, I.H. Qureshi, K.K. Aziz, Mian Abdul Rashid, Muhammad Munawwar, Manzoor Ahmed and Rafi Ullah Shehab may be mentioned. We may not agree with various terms used by them but in the face of contemporary or near contemporary evidence for the motives and nature of the Turkish (Muslim) conquest of India, as already stated above, it is not essential to disagree with them.

Prof. Sharma's reflections on the History syllabus of the University of Calcutta, which had courses on the History of the Jats, the Rajputs and the Marathas, etc. are highly misplaced. In fact, these people had distinctly contributed towards the making of the history and culture of India and by no means reflected only regional chauvinism. Moreover, Prof. Sharma's criticism of the historical writings of Sir Jadunath, Sarkar on the Mughal Age, K.P. Jaiswal's on *Hindu Polity* and R.C. Mazumdar's on Ancient and Medieval periods is not only biased but having dubbed them as Hindu communal writers is complete travesty of truth. In fact, based on rich source-material and scientific study, these historians produced monumental works of their times.

Prof. Irfan Habib pointed out that there had been communal falsification of history wherein new complexities and sophistication had been inculcated which accounted for distortion of history. Distinguishing between religion and culture, Prof. Habib criticised the Supreme Court's Judgement (11.12.1995) on Hindutva and regarded it as extremely unscientific. He held that religion was smaller than larger concept of culture. In this respect, both Hindu and Muslim cultures were much larger than their respective religions. He further maintained that during the Ancient period, the word Hindu was not in vogue in the indigenous literature and as such, it could not be maintained that medicine, astrology, mathematics or mythology were Hindu in character In similar manner, one could not talk about Islamic astrology or Islamic science as the use of these terms had been parallel development to the falsified shibboleths introduced by Hindutva. He concluded that in view of such understanding of Ancient India, the Supreme Court's judgement on Hindutva needed to be condemned. Prof. Habib also referred to the distortions created by the colonial writers like J.C. Collins and C.A. Bylay in the field of modern Indian History by making general statements which were not borne out by statistics.

Prof. Irfan Habib's criticism of the above mentioned judgement of the Hon'ble Supreme Court on the concept of Hindu/ Hindutva, etc. is completely biased and unwarranted. He himself has miserably failed to understand the judgement, both, in letter and spirit. The judgement does not, in any way, hold religion and culture synonymous and is very clear that culture has much wider content with multidimensional aspects than proper religion. The Apex Court held that the words 'Hindutva' or 'Hinduism' were not confined to mere religion, popularly known today as Hindu religion. But they connoted a way of life, in fact, the entire code of conduct of life *(dharma,)* incorporating values of life, i.e., spirit of tolerance, respect for all religions and adherence to secularism. In fact, the terms cover every sphere of human activity, which is well comprised by the culture and dharma of the people inherited from ancient times. As such, these days in the political sphere or during the electoral process, any appeal made in the name of Hindutva does not tantamount to making an appeal on ground of religion and, therefore, is not a corrupt practice.

Looked at the surface, the word 'Hindu' seems to be of foreign origin but as it is a mispronounced form of 'Sindhu' (i.e. the river Indus), it is certainly an indigenous term. As the ancient Iranians pronounced the vowel 'S' as 'H' they called the River Sindhu as 'Hindu' and the people of the Sindhu (River Sind/Indus) and beyond as Hindus. All the same, it cannot be maintained that the word 'Hindu' was not reflected in the ancient Indian literature. In fact, during ancient period, the term 'Hindu' was basically geographical and cultural in connotation, the name being pronounced by the Iranians for the people of this subcontinent to the East of River Sindh. According to the Arab and Persian sources, during the ancient and early medieval periods, a person from this sub-continent belonging to any tribal social order or religious sect etc. Brahmanical, Buddhist, Jain, Shivaite, or Vaishnavite, etc. was termed as Hindu. Even the well-known Indo (till 1947). Pakistani historian, I.H. Qureshi *(A Short History of Pakistan,* Karachi, 1967) concedes that in Ancient period, the name 'Hindu' stood for the traditions of culture of the people of the Indian subcontinent, though he takes credit that "the roots of this culture lay in West Pakistan, the land of River Sind, the 'Indus' of the Greeks &". He states that as connotation of the term 'Hindu' changed at a much later stage, it came to be associated, even though wrongly, with the religious invocations. He further comments that the society gave a final direction to many of the trends which led to the growth of modern Hinduism and developed a spirit that led to classicism. The Arabs also called the land of Hindus al Hind and in the Persian literature, it also came to be known as Hindustan. Starting from the regional concept being confined to some territories of North India, or the entire North India, in due course of centuries, these terms viz. Hindu or Hindustan came to signify the entire Indian Subcontinent. However, during the ancient age in India, the indigenous names used were *Jambu-dvipa, Bharat-Mata, Bharat-Lakshmi and Bharat-Varsh,* which too underwent change in connotation from time to time. Ultimately *Jambudvipa* and *Bharat-Varsh* have given place to "Bharat that is India" (The Constitution of India). The name India is derived from the $5^{th}$ Century B.C. Greek word 'Indi' which was corrupt form of the $6^{th}$ Century B.C. Iranian word 'Hindu' used for the people of this subcontinent. This shows continuous philological relationship amongst the words 'Hindu', 'Indi' and 'India'.

Prof. Habib's observations on the association of the word 'Hindu' with the ancient Indian scientific achievements in the fields of astronomy, astrology, medicine and mathematics, etc. are highly misplaced. No doubt, scientific developments are universal in character and cannot be associated with any particular religion but scientific discoveries and achievements on the part of the people of a particular country can be well attributed to the cultural development of the people. In this case, the development and contribution of the ancient Indian people essentially formed a part of the Hindu culture. In fact, the early medieval Arab accounts pay high tribute to the excellence achieved by the Hindus *(Waal-Hind)* especially in the fields of medicine and development of scientific astronomical instruments. To cite only one illustration, for the transmission of Indian medicine to the Arabs and its impact on the Arab medicine especially in the field of pharmacy, the *rapenties* and *materia medica,* part from the contribution of numerous named Hindu physicians stationed at Baghdad, the name of Manka occupies the most respected position. Appointed by the Abbasid Caliph Harun al-Rashid (A.D. 788-814) as the Chief of the Royal Hospital, Manka translated some books from Sanskrit into Arabic/Persian and composed *Kitaba-al-Tafsir Asma-al-aqaqir* which lists drugs and herbs of Indian origin. Similarly, the translated Shusruta's *Samhita* (Sasrud) comprising ten discourses into Arabic. At the same time, he translated Charaka's treatise and a Book on Poisons *Kitab-al-Samum* into Persian (Phlawi) and later on both these works were rendered into Arabic by Abd al-Allah bin Ali and Abbas bin Said respectively. In Iran too, the physicians keenly studied the Ayurveda. Authentic works on *hikam* comprising chapters on Indian medicine were produced. As such, it was the Arab writers who attributed all this contribution to the Hindu system of medicine. Just as these writers refer to the Greek works, the Arab and the Persian works, in the same vein, the works in Ancient India can be termed as Hindu works. In the early eleventh century, even Al Biruni referred to the 'Hindu Sciences'. He considered the Hindus excellent philosophers and very good sound mathematicians and astrologers. While commenting on the utter destructive polity of Mahmud of Ghazni, he states that, "Mahmud utterly ruined the prosperity of the country...that is the reason, too, why Hindu sciences have retired far away from those parts of the country conquered by us, and have fled to places, which our hand cannot yet reach to Kashmir, Benares, and other places". To give other instances: Writing about the advancement in the knowledge of astronomy in Ancient India, the European writers have recorded:

R.A.S. of Great Britain and Ireland – Vol. 11, p. 138, 139

*"The Brahmin obtains his result with wonderful certainty and expedition in Astronomy."* Prof. Bailley – Famous French Astronomer

*"The Hindu systems of Astronomy are by far the oldest and from them, the Egyptians, Greeks, Romans and even the Jews derived their knowledge."*

W.W. Hunter – Brief History of Indian People – Page 53

*"The Brahmins had advanced far in the Astronomy before the Greeks arrived in India in 327 B.C... The fame of the Brahmin astronomers spread westwards and their works were translated by the Arabs about 800 A.D. and so reached Europe.*

Monier Williams – Indian Wisdom – Page 189

*"A very strange theory of planetary motion is expounded at the commencement of Surya Siddhanta, Chapter II, which is unknown outside India."*

Weber's Indian Literature – Page 255

*"During the eighth and ninth centuries, the Arabs were the disciples of Hindus."*

There is no doubt that as parallel to this, scientific achievements cannot be associated with Islam, which is basically a religion. Despite that, the concept of Islamic architecture has been widely accepted, perhaps, more because of common traits of architecture in respect of many a monument, prevalent in the Islamic countries. Even till date numerous works under the nomenclatures "Islamic Philosophy" and "Islamic Sciences" are being published in Egypt and the West Asian countries. It is not correct to say that the association of the word 'Islamic' with the philosophy and sciences developed in the Islamic countries is a counterpoise to the Hindu philosophy and sciences, etc.

Prof. Tapan Ray Chaudhary, commenting sarcastically on the heritage of the Hindu culture, held that the Vedic Studies which had been established at different places in the world were usually taken for the study of Ayurvedic medicine and herbs and the Vedas were confused with the Ayurvedic Centres. Does this reflect any depth of knowledge of the Vedas and Vedic philosophy which has attracted serious scholars of philosophy from all over the world?

Further, having traced the intellectual background and the false perceptions of historical writing to the Imperial concept of history initiated by James Mill (early 19$^{th}$ century) and followed up by Elliot and Dowson, Prof. Chaudhary questioned their version of the "Muslim rule in India and the Muslim tyranny over the Hindus". He argued that such a viewpoint had been advanced by the British historians to show that it was the British rule which had emancipated the Hindus from the Muslim rule. He asked, was there a Muslim Rule in India? To his mind, there was none as during that period, the State was not theocratic in character.

There is no denying the fact that James Mill analysed the Hindu civilisation with contempt and in his scathing criticism wrote about the Hindus as 'superior to lower animals but not superior to higher animals', 'in mind and body....the most enslaved portion of human race' and in their sensual pleasures, 'very near to that of irrational animals'. James Mill was equally critical of the Muslim despotic institutions and culture. In fact, in the field of historiography, his main purpose was to show the superiority of the European culture as against Indian culture, whether Hindu or Muslim. But as regards the suppressed position of the Hindus during the Sultanate and Mughal periods, James Mill followed by Elliot and Dowson portrayed the nature of the rule under them especially the position of the Hindus, 'based on the contemporary medieval Persian sources'. Elliot and Dowson in the '*History of India as told by its own Historians*' may have been a little selective in the narration of the excerpts from the contemporary sources but they have done yeoman service to the students of medieval Indian history who do not know Arabic or the Persian languages. No doubt, that in matter of land revenue assessment on the peasantry, there was no discrimination between the Hindus and the Muslims but the real discrimination in respect of the financial burden between the two communities lay in the imposition *of jizya* and *cesses,* especially octroi and pilgrimage, which formed a part of *sairo-jihat* of the revenues. It is well authenticated by the sources that right from the inception of the Turkish rule in India, in accordance with the Islamic concept, *jizya* was imposed upon the Hindus, being regarded as the *Zimmis.* Even Amir Khusrau, the great poet cum historian, attached to the Royal Court even during the period of Alauddin Khalji regarded the imposition of *jizya* on the subjugated Hindus *(Kuffar)* as mandatory; whether it belonged to the Sultan in person or formed a part of the Royal treasury *(baitulmal)* or to be shared as per *Shariat* and Islamic precedents set by the *Khalifas*, there was no difference of opinion on the question of the position of the *Zimmis* (Hindus) to be subjected to the payment of *jizya.* During the reign of Aurangzeb, both Raja Raj Singh of Mewar and the great Maratha leader Shivaji, fought against the imposition of *jizya* upon the Hindus. For the reign of Aurangzeb (1658-1707), there are reliable contemporary sources, of even archival nature, which bear out that the governance of the State was based upon Islamic policy in many a respect. Apart from other causes, the religious factor was quite marked for the rise of the Sikhs, the Jats and the Marathas against the Mughal State and was considerably responsible for the ultimate collapse of the Mughal Empire.

Prof. Barun De rediculed the writings of Ram Mohan Roy which characterised the Muslim rule as the 'Muslim tyranny in Bengal'. He said that foreign historical accounts had been produced which show that Hindu communalism in India was more important than Muslim communalism for the partition of the country.

All the same, it is difficult to agree with any of their views which undermine the role of the Indian Muslim League and Muslim communalism vis a vis the Hindu organisations responsible for the partition of India.

Shri Benoy Krishna Chowdhury, Hon'ble Minister-in-Charge, Department of Land and Land Reforms, Government of West Bengal, in an Inaugural Address of the 56$^{th}$ session of the Indian History Congress, claimed that the peasant movement had been marked by Hindu-Muslim communal riots throughout and the great killings in Calcutta were engineered by the British Government who sought to hide their conspiracy under the code of "Operation Asylum." In his assessment of the 1946 Calcutta communal riots, the Hon'ble Minister did not ascribe any responsibility to the Indian Muslim League for the communal riots. Similarly, there is no denying the fact that like various other national organisations and the peoples in different parts of the country, the peasant members of the Kisan Sabba of Bengal supported Netaji's I.N.A. movement and Mutiny in the Royal Indian Navy (December 1945-February 1946), but this was an all Indian national upsurge and was by no means confined to peasantry and urban sectors of Bengal under the Communist leadership. At the same time, the Inaugural Address gives credit to the Bengal Kisan Sabba for successfully containing the Hindu-Muslim riot in Noakhali but most surprisingly it does not at all refer to the services rendered by Mahatma Gandhi in this regard. In fact, for the 20$^{th}$ century history, the Inaugural Address has exaggerated the role of the peasantry and urban working class in Bengal in the freedom struggle against the British Raj under the Communist leadership and has completely ignored the signal contribution of the Indian National Congress in this regard.

**Some Historians' Views About Nanak Panth**

In the recent times, a few Pakistani historians have revived the well-trodden concept about the so-called 'Bhakti Movement' resulting from interaction of Islam and Hinduism. To them, Guru Nanak, Kabir and Dadu were the founders of the syncretic sects for the reform of the Hindu society which, according to them, was essentially due to the impact of Islam which changed the character of Hindu society. Even though most of the ideas of Shankara,

Ramanuja and Ramananda could be traced to ancient Indian thought, in their totality and characteristic emphasis in medieval India, appear to indicate Muslim influence. Many a scholar in India, based on the original ancient Sanskrit texts, have already done away with this traditional Indo-Pakistani viewpoint. Most recently, another Pakistani scholar, Manzoor Ahmed Manzoor, has viewed the ideas and thought of Guru Nanak Dev and the emerging Sikh Movement with consideration and sympathy. He considers Nanak's Movement as a peaceful, silent revolution. Nanak's rejection of religious asceticism or renunciation was to upgrade the Hindus in beliefs and practices. To face the onslaught of Muslim rule, he compares the Hindu's position of Guru Nanak Dev with that of Sayyid Ahmad Khan of 'Muslim India' of later days, who wanted to upgrade Muslims in view of their backwardness with reference to the better culture offered by the English. Such a comparison is rather odious in character as Guru Nanak, far from being a mere reformer, founded the 'Nanak Panth' which ultimately commanded the mass support of the people in the Punjab. All the same, Manzoor Ahmed Manzor pays tribute to the high intellectual caliber of Nanak's followers and the succeeding Gurus.

In a seminar on Sikhism and Inter-Religious Dialogue held in Chandigarh (India) from January 4-6, 1992, Mr. Noel Q. King, Professor Emeritus of history and comparative religion, University of California at Santa Cruz, expressed the view that Sikh teaching shares many features with Jewish, Christian and Islamic views and stated that there is much in common with the teachings in Christianity and Islam. This view completely ignores the facts and reality regarding the emergence of Nanak Panth – a Hindu sect and its emergence unto the Khalsa.

In the annals of Indian History and Culture, Guru Nanak Dev, the founder of the *Nanak Panth* occupies a unique position in the socio-religious life of the people of India. He was a great Hindu religious thinker and revolutionary both in thought and action. Though basically devoted to the Bhakti school of thought, he evolved afresh socio-religious philosophy and code of conduct to be pursued both by the elite and the common people.

In the Punjab, Guru Nanak (fifteenth-sixteenth centuries) also took inspiration from the Sant *panth.* However, Nanak's approach to monotheistic religion based on experience was clearer, more consistent and comprehensive. Nanak's thought revolves as much around God as man and the social order. Kabir and Nanak are strict monotheists and their monotheism is strictly related to man and his society. Everything that happens is in accordance with His Law (*hukum*). The whole creation is in Him. He existed in the heart of every man.

Nanak rejected caste distinctions, religious asceticism or renunciation to face the onslaught of Muslim rule. The cardinal principle of this teaching was the unity of God and the equality of all men before Him. He preached against caste distinctions. He also urged that the object of human life was purity of mind, and declared that asceticism or renunciation of the world was unnecessary.

Notwithstanding its pacific nature in the initial stages, impelled by political circumstances, there was gradual transformation of the *Nanak Panth* during the course of the 16th and 17th centuries of the Mughal rule. In this respect, the two landmarks, which ultimately changed the very character of the *Panth,* were the execution of the fifth Guru Arjun Dev at the hands of the Mughal monarch Jahangir and the execution of the ninth Guru Tegh Bahadur (1675) during the reign of Aurangzeb. Jahangir mentions in his Memoirs, "...In Goindwal...there was a Hindu named Arjun, in the garment of Sainthood and sanctity, so much so that he had captured many of the simple headed Hindus, even of the ignorant and foolish followers of Islam. They call him Guru.... For three or four generations they had kept this shop warm. Many times it occurred to me to put a stop to this vain affair and to bring him into the assembly of Islam." After the execution of Guru Arjun Dev, the sixth Guru Har Gobind (1606-1644) kept up the tradition of the latter for arrangement of horses and retainers. He also wore two swords of "Miri" i.e., temporal power and "Piri" i.e., spiritual power. Next to the Harimandir Sahib, he also raised a platform called 'Akal Takht', the seat of temporal authority. He had also a few conflicts with the Mughal State.

Guru Gobind Singh wrote in his own biography *Bachittar Natik* that he had taken birth for the purpose of spreading the faith, saving the saints, and extirpating all tyrants.

The importance of *Dasam Granth* of Guru Gobind Singh from the perspectives of religion, history and literature is undeniable. As the *Dasam Granth* also comprises some of the major systems of religious beliefs in India, especially the *Shakta,* the *Vaishnava* and the *Shaiva,* these can be well related to the Guru's own beliefs and faith. The recently discovered manuscript of the *Dasam Granth,* compiled during the first half of the nineteenth century, comprises forty illustrations and paintings of the Kashmiri school." Apart from the paintings of Guru Nanak and Guru Gobind Singh, they cover Lord Shiva, Hanuman and various other Hindu deities. These equally reflect the conceptual relationship and faith of the Guru in them. It is also well accepted that before launching the institution of the Khalsa and waging a concerted and effective war against the Mughals, Guru Gobind Singh offered prayers at the Naina Devi temple and sought blessings from the goddess Naina Devi for success in his mission *of Dharam Yud.*

Ahmad Shah Batalia attributes the beginning of the Singhs *(Singhan)* to the institution of the Khalsa. He calls the Singhs *(Singhan)* as a group of the Hindus who also claimed to be followers of the earlier faith of Baba Nanak Bedi *(Nanak Panth).*

Ganesh Das Badhera's description of the Sikhs, the Khalsa and Singhs *(Singhan)* and the role played by them during the course of the eighteenth century and that of Maharaja Ranjit Singh is more apt and objective than many of the writers. He calls the community of the Sikhs *(quam-i-sikhan)* as a part and parcel of the Hindu society. He equally considers the Khalsa community *(quam-i-Khalsa)* as synonymous with the Sikhs. According to him, the Hindus were inseparable from the Singhs, Khalsa and its organisational set up which were essentially a part of the Hindu Society *(ahl-i-Hunud).*

Another scholar of the nineteenth century, Pandit Raja Ram Tuti makes the Hindus as the basis of the Khalsa and the Singhs *(Singhan)* who played crucial role in the eighteenth century, both against the Mughals and the Abdalis.

Mufti Ali-ud-din, a resident of Lahore in his *Ibrat Nama* (1854) has dealt with the social life of the common people during the reign for Maharaja Ranjit Singh and thereafter in a comprehensive manner.

As regards the Sikhs, the author comments, they generally shook off the rituals that the Brahmanas fostered on the other Hindu society.

At the end, it may be reiterated emphatically that right from the sixteenth century down to at least the mid-nineteenth century, the *Nanak Panth* was regarded as an integral part of the Hindu society. Even though distinct from the other Hindu faiths, viz., the Brahmnical order, Vaishnavism, Shivaism, other bhakti cults and the socio-religious orders like the Jains, *Jogis (faqirs,* i.e., *Kanphattas* and *Augars*, etc.), it remained within the Hindu socio-religious structure. As a matter of fact, right from the eighth century onwards, the Muslim writers used the term Hindus *(Hunud)* in India in contrast to the followers of Islam *(Musalmin).* In the early medieval age, even though Buddhism was well established in Sindh, Multan and other parts of the west Punjab, despite special tension between the Buddhists and the Brahman, the Arab accounts insist on covering both as a part of the Hindu society. From thirteenth century onwards, the Persian sources maintain this concept of the Hindus and Muslims and consider all religious sects in Hindustan which were outside the Islamic religion and its people *(Musalmin)* as the Hindu people *(Hunud).* It is clear from the hymns of Guru Nanak and the writings of Guru Gobind Singh that when they appeal for social cohesion and composite human culture, they only mention the Hindus and the Muslims as the two main religious classes in Hindustan and regard their own socio-religious order as a part of the larger Hindu society with multifarious sects.

At the same time, the numismatic evidence clearly bears out that apart from the use of the words Khalsa, Nanak and Gobind Singh, the *Pipal* tree leaves are also inscribed on the coins which clearly shows the traditional Hindu/Brahamanical impact on the currency. For the period 1840-49, Hindu symbols like *Trisul, Om, Chattar, Sat,* Shiv and Ramji were inscribed on the Sikh coins which were struck in the name of the Sikh Gurus.

20

# Problems of Social and Economic History of India

Professor B. R. Grover, during his tenure at the Indian Council for Historical Research (ICHR), first as a Director and later as its Chairman, was deeply concerned with the problems in the method of the study of the social and economic history of India. His views about such problems and the reconstruction of the society are given below:

Professor Grover often stated: A great challenge which faces the Indian history is its reconstruction. An important fact to be borne in mind is that the vastness of the Indian sub-continent offers regional variations because of the diversities in the geographical situation and the habits of the people settled in different regions. In the course of centuries, the socio-economic and political phases have affected the growth of different regions in a variety of ways. The scattered source material is equally disproportionate in relation to time and areas. For some regions, ample source material is forthcoming which shortens the time gap for gathering consecutive information, while for others the data is sufficiently time-gapped. However, for the 19$^{th}$ and the 20$^{th}$ centuries, there is abundant source material for the reconstruction of the society. For the earlier centuries, the abundance or paucity of the available source material with regard to time and area is bound to affect the methodology in the technique of historical research so as to avoid generalization. As a precaution, it is worthwhile to note that though we have to be fully conversant with the methodology of historical research in Europe, we cannot transplant it en-block in the Indian history. Though certain rough parallelism can be drawn, the problems in the method of the study of the social and economic history of India are quite different. The generalization is based on different factors and theorization is still impossible. We have to be equally cautious against the use of European terminology in the Indian context. We may better use our own contemporary regional terms connoting their socio-economic significance, believed Professor Grover.

For the socio-economic analysis, social and political ideas as well as institutional set-up have to be worked out. Apart from the trends of the historiography, emphasis has as well to be laid on the inscriptions, archaeology, regional languages, literature, speculative ideas, art, architecture, music, science, technology and medicines. Notwithstanding the continuation of work on the traditional line of political history, in the recent years a breakthrough has been made in the analysis of the social and economic history at the regional level. All the same, we have to concentrate more on the rural society, the agrarian setup, the role of caste and landed intermediaries, the condition of the peasantry, the concept of the village community, rural trade, handicrafts, and industries in the rural and urban society. Unless we exploit the full range of source material available to us, we can never reconstruct a proper perspective of the socio-economic development at regional and all-India level through the course of the centuries. The internal trade, the local agricultural and industrial products, the export commodities, the river system for transportation, the organization of the mercantile communities, the commercial organization in the urban centres, the inter-provincial and foreign trade and the role of the trading castes can be well constructed from the source material in hand.

According to Professor Grover, "With an objective approach and disciplined methodology of research, we can construct a fairly accurate and dependable picture of the social and economic life of the people at various levels of historical development in the course of the centuries."

To make the scholars of history aware of the problems of social and economic history of India, Professor Grover, as Director of

ICHR, undertook to organise some seminars. Since the objective of ICHR is to organise, sponsor and support seminars, workshops and conferences for promoting historical research and facilitating utilization of historical knowledge, Professor Grover undertook the task of organising some seminars on regional basis. The theme of all the seminars was "Problems of Social and Economic History of India", but in each seminar the emphasis was mostly on the socio-economic history of the region in which it is held. In a majority of these seminars, Professor B. R. Grover reflected on the approach to the study of the socio-economic problems of various regions in India. Under the sponsorship of ICHR, the first such seminar was held at the Department of History, University of **Poona**, from March 29 to March 31, 1976. The objective of this three-day seminar was to make young scholars aware of some of the problems of the social and economic history of India, and to direct their attention to specific problems both of the content of methodology. The seminar was inaugurated on 29th March, 1976 by the then Governor of Maharashtra, Honourable Shri Ali Yavar Jung. In his inaugural speech, the Governor emphasized the need for an in-depth study of the various problems that confront a social historian. He urged upon the young scholars to abandon the traditional concept of dynastic history and to pay more attention to the history of people, to the social stresses and strains which form the basis of any social history. He urged the scholars to avoid periodization of history and look upon history as an integrated whole. "We are," he said, "Indians first and foremost, and, as such, we must study the centrifugal and centripetal forces of Indian history within the national framework." "It is dangerous," he warned, "to dismiss factors such as religion or customs lightly since they, in their turn, shaped the attitudes of societies at some given time in history." He urged the scholars to study scholars like Amir Khusro and Malik Ambar in greater detail. He drew the attention of the scholars to the fact of the existence of a large body of documents, private or semi-official, that are available in all parts of India, and stressed the need for collecting, organizing, preserving and indexing them, before they are lost to the country forever. He welcomed the idea of regional seminars and regional histories, and assured the support of the Government of Maharashtra to a Centre for Western Indian History at Poona, if and when the ICHR opened such a centre at Poona. The Vice-Chancellor of Poona University, Professor D. A. Dabholkar, while welcoming the Governor, emphasized the role played by the city of Poona in the general historical activity of the nation and recalled the services of such great scholars as Rajwade, Parasnis, Khare Shastri, G.S. Sardesai, Kosambi, and others. He appealed to the ICHR to set up a Centre for the Study of Western India at Poona.

At this academic session, several scholars spoke. Professor B. R. Grover, Director of ICHR, emphasized the need for regional seminars and workshops. If the research work was not done on a regional basis, the regional potentials would never be tapped, nor the regional resources fully utilized, he said. He also underlined the fact that a separate methodology for dealing with the specific problems of Indian social and economic history will have to be devised. He urged the young scholars to apply their minds to the task, and help reconstruct the history of India on scientific lines.

A total of fifteen seminars sponsored by the Indian Institute of Historical Studies (ICHR) were held at different places in India. The second seminar was held at Gorakhpur from December 8-10, 1976 on **Uttar Pradesh**, the largest state in India. The topic was: **"Problems of Socio-Economic History of Uttar Pradesh from 1526 to 1947".** During the Mughal age, the regions of the present state of Uttar Pradesh formed a part of the *Subah* Delhi and the other *Subahs* of Agra, Awadh. According to Professor Grover, under the British rule in India, considerable reshuffling from time to time was done in the territorial divisions for the purposes of administration. This equally affected the state of Uttar Pradesh. However, in the course of centuries, the importance of cultural links of Uttar Pradesh amongst various regions within the province and the adjoining territories of the other provinces cannot be underestimated. The students of medieval history are well aware of the fact that even though the Turkish and the Mughal institutions have left their impact on the Doab and other regions of this province, the indigenous elements, both amongst the Hindus and the Muslims have equally remained imbibed in the culture of the people. The reciprocal impact in many an aspect of the society has led to the evolution of the composite culture which cuts at the root of the monstrous two-nation theory. For the medieval ages and even for the British colonial rule, we can by no means concentrate merely on the political currents and cleavages in the society. The thesis of the Muslims, being a separate cultural entity and a nation, is the result of imperialist concept of historiography developed during the British Indian period.

In the post-independence period, there has been considerable intellectual temper and historiography is in deepening crisis. Of all the ages, the present age is the most historical minded and the historian is well equipped with multifarious tools in the operation of rewriting the history of India. This has thrown a great challenge to the concept of partisan history based on misunderstanding of the past and falsification through the suppression of truth. The understanding of the concept of culture for a proper scientific study of history is essential as culture exists within the society and not outside it. In the socio-economic study of a region, there cannot be rigidity in periodisation as there is no continuity in the socio-economic life and the methodology of research involved therein. In fact, elements of continuity and change have to be taken in conjunction, more especially in the Indian social order. Moreover, even the vastness of the Uttar Pradesh province offers regional variations both because of the geographical situation and social values and traditions of the people in different regions. The abundance or the paucity of source-material in the course of centuries both with regard to time and areas is bound to affect the methodology in technique so as to avoid sweeping generalisations. Notwithstanding all rough analogies and rough parallelism with the evolution of the European society and its conceptual values, the Indian social plane remains at a different level. As such, the *enblock* adoption of the European terminology in the Indian context is bound to give a distorted view of the Indian society.

Ethnic and land problems relating to the agricultural produce, sharing of the surplus produce, nature of land rights and the evolving concept of property provide a sufficient guideline to the socio-economic analysis of the agrarian structure and society. Looking at it from the historiographical aspect, most of the works on the agrarian problems undertaken by the English administrators, administrator-scholars and historians (English, Indian and others) right from the close of the 18th century down to the recent times relied largely on the English records. As such, the analysis remains partial. The various categories of the revenue documents from the 17th down to the 20th century throw considerable light on the concept of ownership of land and nature of land holdings on the part of the various agricultural classes in the village community. For the 17th-18th centuries, some of the village documents give details of the holdings, the castes of the cultivators and even the agricultural population of the village. The composition of the agricultural population and the nature of the land tenures of the villages varied from one region to another. Based on tribal and clannish order, the dominant rights of the *Zamindari* class undergo a change in the course of centuries. There was considerable reshuffling in the clannish structure for the imposition of the superior rights for the enjoyment of a share in the surplus produce. Thus the social picture on an ethnic plane in the agrarian society is by no means static. The evolution of the *Taaluqdari* system since the 17th century and its conceptual change in respect of land ownership during the British rule fundamentally affected the position of the primary *Zamindars*, the peasant proprietors and other classes of the agriculturists. The very concept and nature of the village community undergoes a change and its working is quite different from the *Taaluqdari* territories to the non-*Taaluqdari* areas. Thus based on contemporary documentary evidence, the entire concept of the village community in the Uttar Pradesh needs to be recast.

The concept of self-sufficiency of the village in the developed regions of Northern India has already been well explored. On a commercial plane, there is an integrated pattern during the 17-18th centuries and the pre-British era. The linkage of the commercial products of the villages with the *qasbas* and the main commercial centres in the rural areas as well as the urban centres within and outside Uttar Pradesh is a marked feature of the commercial sector. The internal trade, the local industrial and commercial products, the export and import commodities, the river system for transportation, the organization of the *banjara* communities, the commercial organisation with *hundi* and *bima* system, the revenues from the commercial items, the commercial organisation in the urban centres, the inter-provincial and foreign trade and the role of the trading castes can be well constructed from the available contemporary sources.

For the medieval ages, we cannot appreciate the culture of the people of Uttar Pradesh without going into detail into the various aspects of socio-economic pattern in an integrated manner. Though important works based on regional source material covering archaeology, epigraphy chronicles and archival literature have been produced, an Indian scholar could not possibly work on these regions without proper knowledge of the regional languages. Only a beginning has been made in this direction. The methodology of research needs more of coordination on the part of the historians and scholars of other disciplines in the social sciences for analysing the cultural and institutional aspects of the people of these regions. The role of the Hindu saint-poets, *panths*, the Muslim Sufis and their *Jamat Khannas* and *Khangahs* in the socio-religious life of both the communities, Hindus and the Muslims, needs further analysis. Notwithstanding all religious tensions and cleavages, the socio-economic factors served as common bond for an integrated and composite culture of the people of the Uttar Pradesh during the pre-British era.

At the Seminar in **Hyderabad** (September 7-9, 1977), the topic was: "**Socio-Economic Studies in the Deccan (15$^{th}$ to 19$^{th}$ Centuries).**" Professor Grover stated: Needless to stress that Hyderabad is a historic city which has played a significant role in the political and cultural history of the Deccan and India as a whole. The states comprising Deccan are repositories of rich archival source-material. To mention only a few, the erstwhile *Daftar-i-Diwani-wa-Mal* and now the Central Records Office, Government of Andhra Pradesh, Hyderabad; the Maharashtra State Archives, Bombay; the Bharat *Itihas Samshodak Mandal*, Poona; The Goa State Archives; the *Salar Jang* Family Collection at Hyderabad and National Archives of India, New Delhi, the manuscript collections of the rich libraries are the treasure houses of source-material for the reconstruction of the social and economic history of the Deccan and Western India.

Notwithstanding the fact that many a scholarly work has been produced by eminent scholars on the Deccan, for the socio-economic analysis, social and political ideas as well as institutional set-up need to be worked out in detail.

At the **Bhubneswar Seminar** in September 1976, Professor Grover felt that of the Eastern India, Assam and Meghalayn had not found adequate treatment and as such, it was imperative to have a separate seminar on this region with regard to its social and economic history. After fruitful correspondence for nearly a year, Professor Grover was able to achieve this purpose and held a seminar in **Shillong** from October 10-12, 1977 on the "**Socio-Economic Change in North-Eastern India**." Gradually, we are shifting our focus on the regional study at a microscopic level while at the same time its linkage with the wider cultural aspects of Indian society remains equally marked, said Professor Grover at the seminar in Shillong.

Regardless of regional bias, elements of continuity and change in the socio-economic formation from one phase to another may be equally discerned. For the sake of illustration, an instance may be quoted from the medieval agrarian structure of Assam which may be very much pertinent to the present seminar. During the 17th and 18th centuries, major portion of Assam felt the impact of the Mughal land revenue administration. There is no denying the fact that in respect of concept of land ownership, village community, methods of assessment, the pre-Mughal features continued as such but at the same time, the Mughal State replenished the agrarian structure with new features so as to incorporate with the political and revenue structure of the Mughal State. Despite regional variation, the *Zamindari* pattern and *Jagirdari* system are operative in Assam. Of course, one must distinguish between such *amli* regions where there is the direct impact of the Mughal system and the *ghair-amli* areas, especially the hilly regions where there is only the indirect impact. All the same, both *amli* and *ghair-amli* practices form a part of the Mughal pattern of governance.

For the early 17th century, Mirza Nathan's *Baharistan-i-ghaybi* associates the term *Zamindar* both with the princely chiefs and the landed intermediaries. The picture can be clearly drawn.

As a general rule, the Mughal Imperial policy aimed at forcing the local *Zamindars* to submission for the payment of the revenue (*peshkash*, fixed, nominal or assessed periodically) rather than to extinguish them completely. Under the terms of submission, two-fold principles were followed towards the *Zamindars*. Ordinarily, such of the *Zamindars* who submitted either voluntarily or without fighting after getting the ultimatum were given back their *Zamidaries* as *jagirs*. Secondly, usually after the failure of the armed resistance on the part of the *Zamindar*, a major portion of the erstwhile *Zamindari* was annexed to the Mughal territory and some portion was assigned to him as maintenance *Jagir*. If a *Zamindar* became rebellious, on reduction a major portion of his territories was assigned in *tankhwah-jagir* to the Mughal *Mansabdars*. In any case, whatever be the position of the *Zamindars* as *Jagirdar*, all loyal *Zamindars* had to render military service for the expansion of the Mughal Empire and some were even enlisted in the regular Imperial service. They had essentially to pay *peshkash*, though some paid fixed amount as stipulated in the treaty while others as regular revenues for the *Zamindari* areas other than the *watan* or maintenance *jagir*.

The *Zamindari* of *Sylhet* was totally annexed to the Mughal State and was placed under the management of a Mughal administrator. Though *Baharistan-i-ghaybi* mentions about the submission of the *Zamindars* of Kachar, Tippera and Balwa, it does not say anything about the nature of their *jagirs*. The very fact that the Mughal *thanas* were established therein suggests that either like *sylhet* they were totally annexed or major portions of their territories were put under direct administration and leaving the money with small *jagirs*. As regards land revenue administration, it is clear that such of the *Zamindaries* which were entrusted in *jagir* in entirety were declared *ghair-amli* and the *Zamindars* were left with autonomy for revenue administration. But such *Zamindaries* whereof only small portions were assigned for personal *jagirs* to their Chiefs were declared *amli* subject to Mughal pattern of assessment and collection of the revenues. The major portions of the *Kamrup* territory were brought under the pattern of the Mughal administration. Some *paraganas* were reserved in the *khalisa*, while others were assigned in the *tankhwah-jagir* or assigned to the revenue-farmers (*Mustajirs*) for the collection of the revenues. Later on, the *Zamindari* of the Kuch Bihar was annexed to the Mughal State in 1661 A.D. Shahbuddin Talish bears testimony that the land revenue administration, in general pattern, was brought in line with the other provinces. All other petty *Zamindaries* of Kuch Bihar, though continued in existence, were inevitably brought under the Mughal pattern of administration. The contemporary evidence of late 17th and early 18th centuries reveals that usually their territories were assigned in *tankhawah-jagir* to the Mughal State officials. The Mughal policy towards the chiefs of Kuch Bihar, Kamrup and Assam Hills suggests that, by and large, the *Zamindars* were left with only a portion of their *Zamindari* territory in personal *jagir* and the final position was the same as in the other consolidated regions of the Mughal Empire. In principle, the *Zamindari* system in Assam worked on the same lines as in the other Mughal provinces.

Similarly, one may underline the agrarian changes that took place during the British Raj. The Settlement Regulations of the Bengal Code, supplemented by rules framed by Government, were enforced in Assam. The concept of the Permanent Settlement and the *raiyatwari* system fundamentally affected the agrarian structure and the life of the peasantry in Assam and the hilly regions. A minute analysis would reveal the elements of continuity as well as change leading to the emergence of new concept of land ownership and rights, feudal concept based on the reshuffling of the agrarian relationship amongst the various social classes.

The seminar at **Jabalpur,** (held from September 16-19, 1978) covering **"Rajasthan and Madhya Pradesh"** was sixth in the series. In this seminar, Professor Grover did not deal with the socio-economic history of the regions for the ancient period, but spoke about the pre-Mughal era of the medieval age. He stated: For the pre-Mughal era of the medieval age, an illustration based on the coordination of the epigraphic and literary sources with the Persian and the regional chronicles may be offered for an analysis of the agrarian structure for these regions. The problem of agrarian administration did not rest simply upon the direct relationship between the Delhi Kingdom on the one hand, and the

Rajput chiefs and the petty *Zamindars* on the other. Same may be said about the Malwa Sultanate and the other Rajput chiefs. A microscopic study of these regions shows that there was a recurring clannish warfare among the Rajput clans themselves, between the Rajput and other low-caste Hindu agricultural tribe and above all, between the Rajputs and Muslim tribal communities who had settled around these territories. The main issues in such conflicts were the disputed villages and *parganas* settlement, acquisition of agrarian lands or imposition of the *Zamindari* rights on the suppressed clans. At times, a stronger Rajput clan would push out another weaker Rajput clan from certain villages or might drive out a lower caste Hindu tribe or a Muslim tribe from a certain region. It would also forcibly impose its *Zamindari* or *Chaudhari* rights over other Hindu or Muslim clans in the settled villages. At times, a powerful Muslim clan overpowered a Rajput clan and acquired a few villages or the *Zamindari* of a disputed *pargana*. The motive of social action and regional conflict was not essentially religion. Bloody feuds based on clannish rivalry might continue for generations and the disputed villages and the *Zamindari* rights of dominant clan might also change hands after the victory of one clan over another. The revenue collectors of the Sultanate posted in provinces had no option but to accept the regional reshufflings in the agrarian possessions and the *Zamindari* rights provided the State revenues were paid by the *Zamindars* with established authority.

In both the regions of Madhya Pradesh and Rajasthan, not only the old Hindu states continued but many a Rajput family fleeing from the plains after the Turkish invasions settled and carved out new states by suppressing the local non-Rajput chiefs and indigenous tribes. They were considerably helped by the geographical features of these regions to withstand the Muslim penetration and were able to continue their independence till Akbar's age. In line with the past Hindu tradition, the Raja asserted a theoretical claim over the land ownership (known as *Prathvipal*, *Bhupal, Adeshatu*) though in practice, the hereditary and transferable rights of the peasants were fully recognised.

The agrarian lands were possessed and cultivated by the joint families. The Raja claimed complete ownership over the waste lands and jungles and could alienate them as he pleased. The Raja also made both secular and religious assignation of revenues as well as rent free grants of land. In Rajasthan, a sovereign Raja claimed military service and tribute from the vassal chiefs. The process of the establishment of the now Rajput states, subduing the weaker rulers of the Rajput clans as vassal chiefs through mutual warfare, at times fighting the Muslims states of Malwa, Gujrat and Delhi Sultanate, the suppression of the lower caste Hindu chiefs as well Muslim tribal chiefs and communities on the part of the Rajput Rajas for the extension of their own states continued throughout the medieval age till the merger of these territories in the Mughal Empire under Akbar. Within the state, the revenue-free grants (*sasan*) of the villages were made to the Brahmans, the *Bhats*, the temples and their attendants (*Charnas*). The revenue-free grants of the waste cultivable lands were also made to the above mentioned beneficiaries. In line with the old Hindu tradition, these grants were regarded as hereditary and perpetual in nature. The donees possessed the further right of alienation. The assignment of land was made in terms of measured units of land against the cultivable capacity of plough-oxen (*hala)*.

On the secular side, small scale grants of villages in *bhum* were made to the *Bhumias* who paid small quit rent (*bhum barar*) and rendered local service of watch and ward of the villages and other miscellaneous services to the State. Based on the caste system, the caste groups played important role in the socio-economic life of the village communities (*Gosthi*, *Sherathi*, *Sangh)* based on clannish character and casteism was well organised. The main agricultural classes were *Gujars*, *Jats* and *Patels*. At times, even Vaishyas and Brahamans cultivated lands. The village headman (*Mandapika*) functioned on behalf of the ruler for the fixation of land revenue assessment and collection of revenues. The village headman worked under other revenue officials of the State. The government always gave due consideration to the elders of the village community and the revenue assignments or revenue free grants of waste cultivable land were made in the presence of few village elders. The assessment on the joint family holdings was based on sharing and appraisement (*lata*) methods. The land was often measured through the *hala* method. The exact incidence of State demand for this period cannot be traced but it is clear from the epigraphic sources that a differential scale of State share was based on a detailed classification of the agrarian lands in accordance with the means of irrigation. Besides the land revenue, the State claimed various *cesses* on the agriculturists.

From the 16$^{th}$ century down to the early 19$^{th}$ century of the pre-Britishers covering mainly the Mughal age and the Maratha phase, for the territories of Rajasthan and Madhya Pradesh, we have perhaps the largest source material of varying categories in comparison to any other region of India. Descriptive lists and catalogues of some of the valuable records have already been published. Apart from the State Archives, there are repositories with the private landed families. With limited financial resources and available talent, it may take years for any institution or organization even to docket them or to prepare hand lists.

The mine of available information throws a challenge to the historians for reconstruction of the social order during these centuries. As the source material on polity, administration, social ideas, urban life and agrarian relations is of technical nature and of numerous types, any reliance on partial or fragmentary material based merely on either of the languages, Persian or regional, i.e. Hindi, Rajasthani and Marathi or accounts in English is too risky to give a fully reliable and comprehensive picture of the subject in hand. For any social structural analysis, the examination of the sources on comparative basis and resort to cross examination is rather essential. A disciplined technique of the study of the sources may as well help in bridging the gap in our knowledge to the largest possible extent. For the study of any subject in hand, it is the principle of priority and the importance of the selection of the source material which has to be essentially kept in mind. Some important works covering polity administration and agrarian history of these regions have already been produced in recent years.

The huge source material covering revenue and judicial papers at the village, *Pargana* and higher units of administration like the *Sarkar* and the *Subah*, the correspondence amongst the local officials addressed to the higher officers and vice-versa requires a careful sifting based on seasoned methodology of historical research. Interestingly, utilization of the source material at the bottom and moving upwards from the village to the *Pargana, Sarkar, Subah* and the State has yielded better results for the social stratification and agrarian structure than the mere utilization of sources material pertaining to the Imperial Court, the provincial administration along with fragmentary use of the consolidated abstracts of the *Sarkar* and the *Pargana* units of administration. In this respect, apart from the scholarly contribution of a few other historians including the present chief guest Professor S. Nurul Hasan and Professor Satish Chandra, Professor Grover has already contributed towards the analysis of the rural life. The vast 18th century source material especially pertaining to the *Mahratta* phase of these regions is so far mostly untapped. Its proper utilization for the portrayal of the social and economic aspects of these regions is bound to dispel many a generalization based on the contemporary chronicles and English writings.

At the seminar at **Ahmedabad** (September 28-30, 1979) that covered **Western India**, especially the modern states of **Gujarat** and **Maharashtra**, Professor Grover had this to say: During the last four centuries, considerable political and territorial changes have taken place in these regions. The change from the independent Sultanates to the Mughal rule was effected during the 16th and 17th centuries under the Mughals. These regions formed a part of the *Subah* Gujarat, a portion of *Subah* Ajmer and the Deccan *subahs.* From around the middle of the 18th century to the early 19th century, they formed part of the Maratha Empire. Under the British rule in India, most of these regions constituted part of the Bombay Presidency. Of course, under the British rule in India, considerable reshuffling from time to time was done in the territorial divisions for the purposes of administration. However, in the course of centuries, the importance of cultural links of these regions and the adjoining territories of the other provinces cannot be underestimated. The students of medieval history are well aware of the fact that even though the Turkish and the Mughal institutions have left their impact of these territories, the indigenous elements, both amongst the Hindus and the Muslims have equally remained imbibed in the culture of the people. The reciprocal impact in many an aspect of the society has led to the evolution of the composite culture which cuts at the root of the monstrous two-nation theory. For the medieval ages and even for the British colonial rule, we can by no means concentrate merely on the political currents and cleavages in the society. The thesis of the Muslims, being a separate cultural entity and a nation, is the result of imperialist concept of historiography developed during the British Indian period.

At the **Udaipur** Seminar (November 8-10, 1979), the topic was: **"Reflections on the Approach to the Study of the Socio-Economic Problems Especially of Rajasthan and Madhya Pradesh since the Medieval Age."** Professor Grover stated that ever since the medieval times, considerable political and territorial changes have taken place in these regions. The change from the independent or semi-independent principalities to the Mughal rule was affected during the $16^{th}$ and $17^{th}$ centuries. Under the Mughals, these regions formed part of the *Subah* of Ajmer and Malwa. From around the middle of the $18^{th}$ century to the early $19^{th}$ century, they felt the impact of the Maratha Empire.

In the socio-economic study of a region, there cannot be rigidity in periodization as if there is no continuity in the socio-economic life and the methodology of research involved therein. In fact, elements of continuity and change have to be taken in conjunction, more especially in the Indian social order. However, even the vastness of these territories in Rajasthan and Madhya Pradesh offers regional variations both because of the geographical situation and social values and traditions of the people in different regions.

In Rajasthan and Madhya Pradesh, ethnic and land problems relating to the agricultural produce, sharing of the surplus produce, nature of land rights and the evolving concept of property provide a sufficient guideline to the socio-economic analysis of the agrarian structure and society. Looking at it from the historiographical aspect, most of the works on the agrarian problems undertaken by the English administrators, administrator-scholars and historians (English, Indian and others) right from the closing of the 18th century down to the recent times have relied largely on the English records. As such, the analysis remains partial. The various categories of the revenue documents from the 17th down to the 20th century of which Rajasthan has the largest archival repository in India throw considerable light on the concept of ownership of land, nature of land holding on the part of the various agricultural classes in the village community. For the 17th-18th centuries, some of the village documents give details of the holdings, the castes of the cultivators and even the agricultural population of the village. The composition of the agricultural population and the nature of the land tenures of the villages varied from one region to another. In recent years, important work in this respect has been done by Professor Satish Chandra and a team of his students. For the last two decades, I have also endeavoured to analyse the agrarian problems to some extent.

The seminar at **Chandigarh** that was held from October 2-4, 1980, was according to Professor Grover, more specialised and extensive so as to cover **Socio-cultural History of India during the 11th-12th Centuries A.D.** "It is highly significant as at least for North India, excepting Sind and West Panjab, it is the last phase before the impact of the Turkish rule is felt," said Professor Grover. Sind was occupied by the Arabs in the beginning of the 8th century but with the decline of the Abbassid Caliphale, the kingdoms of Multan and Mansurah became independent local states side by side with the other Rajput kingdoms in the North. In early 11th century, as a consequence of Mahmud of Ghazni's raids, Panjab was annexed to the Ghaznwid Empire. After their defeat at the hands of the *Seljugs,* the *Ghaznwid* rulers took refuge in the Panjab which remained their sole possession. During the 12th century, the South-East frontiers of the Panjab remained quite unstable and the Rajput rulers made steady incursions. The fact that Sind and Multan broke away from the Arab Caliphate of Baghdad and came to be ruled by the local converted Muslim tribes suggests that the indigenous notions of socio-economic must have continued to predominate. The *Ghaznwid* occupation of the Panjab was mostly a military occupation. All of this points towards the continuance of the early medieval village communities based on Clannish order. Of course, Islam and its Sufi order made an impact on the cultural life of the people. From the close of the 12th and beginning of the 13th centuries, the major portions of Northern India came under the domination of the Delhi Sultanate. All the same, even this cannot be taken as a dividing line in the socio-cultural history of the people of India. It is doubtful if the Islamic theory of laws in *dar-ul-harb* were enforced in India at all. It may really be wondered if at all the theoretical Islamic ideas relating to State polity and administration were really enforced in actual practice even in such regions of North India which were under the direct control of the Sultanate. It could not have been enforced in India which had its own socio-economic and cultural pattern enrolled in the course of centuries in accordance with the regional geographical features and clannish customs of the people settled in different parts of the country.

At the **Simla** Seminar on **"Regional Historical Writings in India with special reference to Western Himalayas"**, Professor Grover stated: Except for medieval ages and pre-British era, the present speaker is not competent to deal with all the cultural aspects of the Western Himalayas during the course of the centuries. However, a few case studies can be picked up where further scientific research can be taken up by the Indian scholars. In the latter half of the 19th century, valuable works were produced on the Western Himalayas, both by the English and the Indian scholars but the main trend in historiography remains political and dynastic. The works in vernacular by Hakim Paras Ram, Twarikh-i-Maharajagan-i-Katoch, Twarikh-i-Kotlehr, Twarikh imandir Shri Jawal; Hardyal Singh, Twarikh-i-Rfyasathi Kohistan Punjab; Sarbdayal Diwan, Twarikh-i-Rajgan Zilaha Kangra and Twarikh-i-Sirmur more or less follow the same pattern. However, some of these works have published the original Mughal documents which serve as a useful source material for further analysis. With the advancement of methodology and research during the last two decades, a few important works have been produced which depict various aspects of the history of this region. In his book on Chieftains in the Mughal Empire during the reign of Akbar, A. R. Reza Khan has devoted three significant chapters on the *Subahs* of Kabul and Lahore which make significant contribution to our knowledge in the political and institutional set up during the Mughal Age. M.S. Randhawa's Kangra paintings of Bhagvate Purane add a fresh dimension to the cultural heritage of this region. The major breakthrough comes with Professor J.S. Grewal and B.N. Goswami's works on 'The Mughal and Sikh Rulers' and 'The Vaishnayas of Pindori' and miscellaneous articles with the publication of the original source material along with introduction and commentary. Indu Banga's 'Agrarian system of the Sikhs' covers such areas of the hilly regions which came under the Sikh rule. It is a well-documented and scholarly contribution. All the same, it may be surmised that the socio-political problems of the periods covered by the above scholars have been looked at mostly from the Delhi or the Lahore angle. The other side of the coin still needs to be better appreciated.

In the post-independence period, a number of works have been produced on Kashmir. Notwithstanding the scholarly contribution, Mohibbul Hasan's 'Kashmir Under the Sultans', R. K. Parmu's 'A History of Muslim Rule in Kashmir (1320-1819)' offer a combination of the dynastic history and social portrayal. P.N.K. Bamzai's 'A History of Kashmir' gives good insight into the cultural aspects of the people of Kashmir. M.L. Kapur's 'A History of Medieval Kashmir', 'Studies in History and Culture of Kashmir' and 'History of Jammu and Kashmir State' equally offer a combination of political and social history. However, the later aspects, even though well analyzed, form only a small portion of the works in line with the traditional historical writings. For the modern period, Mohammad Ishaq Khan's 'History of Srinagar (1846-1947)' adds a new dimension – well analysing the socio-economic features in the development of the capital of Kashmir. G. S. Charak, in his work 'History and Culture of Himalayan States', has well summed up the researches carried on these regions hitherto.

Kashmir lies en-route to Central Asia via land route and thus has been a meeting place of different nations. It has Tibet in the North and USSR and Chinese Turkistan in the North East. Due to its geographical situations, it was in the ancient and middle ages, a commercial centre between India and Central Asia. A large number of coins found here bear a testimony to this fact.

Despite the difficulty of its route through Kashgar over Kuenlin range, the wandering pilgrim monks took the philosophical ideas beyond its borders and attracted foreign pilgrims and students to India. These frequent meetings resulted in the transfusion of Indian and foreign culture. For the ancient Indian period, further archaeological excavations are needed to identify the venue of the Buddhist conferences. During the *Kushan* period, Sarla Khosla's work, 'The History of Buddhism in Kashmir', throws significant light in this regard – by identifying *Kunsana* (*Kun-sa-na)* with the above conferences. However, the latest investigations of the Japanese scholars identify it with the village Kundalvan which could be confirmed only through further excavations.

Buddhism in China was introduced by a number of enterprising Kashmiri scholars. The activities of Buddhist monks created great interest for this region in China which produced great Buddhist scholars and philosophical works. China has preserved our literature which has been lost in India. Similarly, Tibet, Ladakh and Khutan are indebted to Kashmir for Buddhism, Buddhist literature and Indian culture and civilization.

The controversy about whether Buddhism died in India because of the onslaught of Islam or its inherent weakness and revivalism of Brahmanism can be well tested in this region where it died in the north-western areas as well as in Kashmir but continued to subsist especially in Ladakh and Tibet. Much further useful work can be done with the help of the Ladakhi and Chinese works as well as archaeological excavations in Kashmir.

For medieval and the modern age, there is ample source material relating to Western Himalayas in Persian, English and the regional languages on the basis of which detailed analysis on the various aspects of polity, administration, agrarian set up and cultural life can be well analysed in details as independent monographs.

It is very fortunate for the students of history that the Bhuri Singh Museum at Chamba has preserved historical source material of various types covering the history of this region from the early medieval ages down to the 19$^{th}$ century. A fairly reliable catalogue of this Museum compiled by J. Ph. Vogel was published in 1909

A.D. Thereafter, two additional items have been collected by the Museum, which still remain un-catalogued. This is undeniably one of the richest repositories in India which throws immense light on the socio-economic and cultural life of the people of the hilly regions during the course of the centuries. Apart from the stone inscriptions, sculptures, metal inscriptions, wood carvings, wood work, textiles and embroideries, paintings, there are large number of copper plates and documents which cover the socio-economic and institutional aspects of this region. The present writer, having worked on this region, has collected photographs of all the epigraphic and archival documents of the Museum. There are 36 copper plates dealing mostly with the land grants from around 10th century to the mid-19th century. One copper plate also covers the treaty between the two local chiefs (1788 A.D.). Apart from this, there are in all 128 documents of which 72 have been catalogued by Vogel whereas 56 '*Tankari*' documents covering the latter half of the 18th and early 19th century comprise *sanads,* letters, agreements, title deeds, statements and treaties, etc. The un-catalogued '*Tankari'* documents cover more or less the same aspects. Apart from this, there are 28 Persian documents covering viz. *sanads*, *mazars (*declarations*), khatut* (letters), *hakum* (orders) and *parvanas* issued from time to time from around the middle of the 17th century to 1846 A.D. In addition to this, there are two documents in *Nagari,* one in Gurumukhi and one in English which cover the first half of the 19th century till 1846 A.D.

It must be acknowledged that of these, the texts of six Persian documents along with English translation have already been published as an appendix to the catalogue of the Bhuri Singh Museum. Of course, as a pioneering researcher, credit must be given to Vogel who incorporated this portion in the catalogue after having got the Persian texts translated into English by eminent Persian and Arabic scholars of the time. All the same, it is evident to any expert working on administrative and agrarian history of the region that the translation is rather inept and extremely defective in respect of many a technical term used in the documents. This was perhaps inevitable as the translators, even literary experts, had the least idea about the territorial connotation and revenue terminology available to us today from the Persian archival sources in other parts of India. Credit may also be given to Hutchinson and Vogel who have utilized the epigraphic and the Persian translated documents in their well-known work on the history of the Punjab Hill States as well as other articles published earlier in *The Journal of Punjab Historical Studies.* All the same, Hutchinson and Vogel could hardly appreciate the technical institutional aspects outlined in the Persian documents due to inept translation as well as due to lack of understanding of the broad framework of the Mughal administration and institutions. They were equally inhibited by the limitation to the approach of the study of local history emphasizing mostly the political and the military aspects and regional glorification. It is only in the recent years that the methodology of historical research on local history while underlining the integrating economic and institutional factors with other parts of the *Subah* and country as a whole has been developed so as to have a concerted approach to the analysis of the administrative and the economic history of India.

As a matter of fact, despite parochial hesitation for admission, most of these hilly regions were brought under the *Zamindari* pattern of the Mughal administration for the purposes of the realisation of the revenues. This is equally true of the Afghan and Sikh periods for the territories under their control. The *Tankari* documents are extremely useful for working out internal socio-economic aspects of the hilly regions. They very well bring out the fact that the medieval society in these regions was neither closed nor archaic in character as depicted by the foreign travelogues and writings of the British administrators. There is no denying the fact that the concept of the village community, land ownership and land tenures stood at a different level than those of the planes but all this needs a further examination and elucidation.

It may be further added that apart from the above mentioned sources, the Indian scholars have not so far been able to utilize the Nepalese sources especially for the first 15 years of the 19$^{th}$ century when many a portion of the hilly regions in the Western Himalayas, especially the areas of the Hill Chiefs, Himachal Pradesh, Gharwal and Kumayon came under the temporary occupation of the *Gurkhas.* Some Nepali scholars have already published some documents with a bearing on the political aspects for this period. However, there are vast number of revenue papers available at the Revenue Department, Kathmandu, which, when analyzed properly, would throw much fresh light on the economic life of the people during this period.

I am sure that the present seminar will highlight many a problem which will help in the re-construction of the social, economic and cultural history of Western Himalayas through the ages.

# 21

# Indo-German Understanding As a Means For Promoting International Stability

International stability is the major concern of the present world politics. The ever-increasing complexity of the international problem since the 2nd World War possesses a concern for peace as much to the politicians as to the academicians and the journalists. How a historian might look at the problem may be quite different from the standpoint of a politician or a political scientist or a journalist. Though national ends and international peace may be the determining factors for the framing of a country's programme or policy, one section of an intelligentsia may differ from another with regard to the means of pursuit and realisation of these aims. A politician or a journalist looks at the current problems mostly from the immediate end in view, a political scientist is more concerned with the norms of the political organisations and analysis of the international relations, a historian is basically governed by the discipline of historical research. The discipline emphasizes the sifting of the facts with an analytical mind so as to reach the proximity of objectivity. The past background, the present-day political realities and hope for the future shape the mind of an historian.

Indo-German relations have their roots in the economic ties and cultural relationship of the past. Though India and Germany have developed strong economic ties for the last twenty years, they had fairly good commercial intercourse during the 16th-18th centuries. On cultural plane, the German romanticism of the 19th century was greatly inspired by the Orient and more especially, the Indian spiritual and cultural heritage. This led to the establishment of regular philosophical and Indological studies at the German University. Goethe's humorist approach in search for 'light' responded to the Indian Sanskrit literature of which his quatrain "Sakontala" of Kalidasa is a classical contribution to the German literature. Though Max Mueller is certainly more well-known amongst the Indian and the European indologists, another fascinating personality who felt greatly interested in the East and especially in India was Friedrich August Graf Von Noer (1830-1881).[1] A born Prince turned into an exile, paid three visits to India sheer out of his fascination for the dreamland – India, the goal of his dominant enthusiasm. He was as much impressed by the ancient Indian culture as by the medieval Indian-Muslim culture. He learnt Sanskrit to study classic Hinduism and acquired working knowledge of Persian to discover Akbar's mind. He visited the temples in South India, attended the religious sermons, placed a wreath of flowers at the tomb of Akbar the Great at Sikandra not only out of his love for the great Indian culture but to identify his own soul with the spirit of the respective ancient and medieval India. To Von Noer, the most appealing aspects of the Mughal India were its cultural contribution and the development of the concept of liberal state by Akbar. He interpreted Akbar's philosophical and religious trends of mind in the light of Schopenhauer's philosophy as to how a man seeks truth by his personal intuition and how a boiling point is reached on the thermometer of civilization at which all faith, all revelation and all authority volatilizes. To the ancient Hindu mind and the medieval Sufi concept, man's metaphysical cravings are as inextricable as physical. This is as well true of Schopenhauer's mind. Despite all its shortcomings for limited use of contemporary Persian sources, Von Noer's study of Kaiser Akbar is a remarkable testimony to the Indo-German philosophical rapproachment. Even though Max Mueller never visited India, his publication of the *Rigveda*, scholarly editorship of the *Sacred Books of the East* and many other writings on comparative philology, religion and mythology revealed India's past even to the Indians themselves. These examples illustrate how the German mind responded to the Indian culture. During the interregnum of the two World Wars, the popular welcome to Rabindra Nath Tagore on his German visit and the German sympathy with the Indian struggle for freedom afforded fresh emotional ties with India.

During the course of the 19th century, a keen interest was taken by the German scholarship in India's ancient and medieval culture. It is very little known that some of the German libraries have valuable collections of the oriental manuscripts in Sanskrit and Persian dealing with various aspects of the Indian society and culture right from ancient times down to the 19th century.[2] Before the 2nd World War, an extremely valuable collection was made by the Staatsbibliothek Berlin but during the course of the war, most of the manuscripts were removed to two small towns, though important University centres, namely Marburg and Tuebingen. At present in Germany, a good collection of the Sanskrit and Persian manuscripts covering Ancient and Medieval Indian history is available at the Universitaetsbibliothek (University Libraries) of Bonn and Tuebingen, Bayeriche Staatsbibliothek, (Ehemalige Preussische Staatsbibliothek) Marburg and Staatsbibliothek (State Library) Berlin East. The valuable collection in the Staatsbibliothek Berlin was made in the course of the 19th and 20th centuries before the 2nd World War. A detailed catalogue of the Persian manuscripts in the Koenigliche Bibliothek, Berlin, published in 1888 A.D., is known in all the important libraries in Europe and India. But the rich collection made after the publication of the catalogue was compiled in a comprehensive 'Handlist' which is available only in the Staatsbibliothek Berlin (EAST) whereas the manuscripts lie scattered at the above mentioned libraries in Tuebingen and Marburg. At present, a scholar could work on these manuscripts only after having consulted the Handlist in Staatsbibliothek Berlin (East) which involves either way the crossing of the Berlin Wall. What an irony of fate.

A proper understanding amongst the countries is not possible unless their respective histories were to be read in proper and balanced perspectives. This is equally important for fostering international morality which is the best way to check an international disturbance. To associate epithets like 'Barbaric', 'uncivilized', 'jingoist', and 'war-mongering' with the people of any country for having brought about a war in the course of history without trying to understand the various socio-economic and political factors responsible for it is not justified. An historian has to sift the archives of all the belligerent parties before coming to any conclusion about the problem of the war-guilt. The problem may not be looked only from the viewpoint of the victors. Similarly, in a struggle against an Imperialist power, the viewpoint of the colonial peoples has to be equally analysed on the basis of the archival literature. The ideas and aspirations of both victors and the vanquished, the Imperialist countries and the exploited colonies require a thorough examination before an historical verdict can be passed. Though the German universities have taken a keen interest in India's past culture, their studies of Modern Indian History, especially for the $19^{th}$ and $20^{th}$ centuries, have been mostly influenced by the British writings on the Indian problems. It is very recently that the German scholarship has devoted itself to the study of the Indian Archives for the evaluation of the British colonial rule in India. The study of India's national struggle for freedom known from the Indian authors and Indian Archives is finding due place in the study of Indian history. It may be frankly admitted that the Indian interest in the study of German culture and history at the University level is extremely limited. Germany is studied as a part of the history of Modern Europe and that too through the spectacles of the English authors. There is an urgent need at the post-graduate level in the Indian universities to introduce specialized courses in German history. At the same time, the study of the German language may be further encouraged amongst the Indian students. The Indian teachers who have proficiency in German language and have also specialised in European history may be induced to write about the history and culture of the German people from the German sources. This would enable the post-graduate Indian students to evaluate both the English and the German viewpoints for properly understanding the European history. So far as India and Germany are concerned, till present the Indian intellectuals learn about the German people through English newspapers and periodicals published in London. This is a serious handicap as the published news may be coloured or offered with a little slant. It is high time that translations of the best German and the Indian works are undertaken on reciprocal basis. At the same time, the presses of the two countries have to devote more space for covering each others' news and problems than they have done hitherto. It is all the more important for Indian news agencies to get news directly from Germany rather than through London or Washington.

The image of Germany as a war-mongering nation has been based upon the fact that from 1865 to 1939 A.D., i.e. nearly seven and a half decades, she fought five wars in Europe. The first three wars were fought by Bismarck against Denmark (1865), Austria, (1866), and France (1870-71) in order to unify Germany and to make it a nation state. The others were the two World Wars which broke out in 1914 and 1939 respectively. This image still scares both the blocks, i.e. Soviet Union and the Western Powers and is one of the main psychological factors which obstructs the unification of Germany. A serious-minded student of history cannot accept the war-mongering fact on the part of the German people. The occurrence of every war has to be analysed in its background and the accumulative factors as well as the diversified responsibility of the powers involved is always a matter of opinion.

In the annals of Modern World History, there has hardly been a problem more controversial than the premises and the responsibility for the outbreak of the First World War in August, 1914.[3] Even though more than half a century has passed and during this period the world has experienced another Great War, the academic debate on the factors responsible for the 1914 crisis has ever remained with undiminished historical interest. The controversy over the responsibility for the First World War started immediately after the outbreak of the war itself as the Government heads and politicians of the belligerent countries continued to accuse their adversaries for the catastrophe. After the war was over, the Versailles Treaty (1919) contained a clause (Article 231, the so-called 'War Guilt' Clause) which held Germany and her allies as aggressors having started the war and responsible "for causing all the loss and damage." The underlying idea of this clause was to impose obligation upon the Central powers to pay enormous reparations. More than this, the Versailles Treaty gave the 'War Guilt' clause a legal shape under an international treaty. The 'revisionist' school in Germany, other European countries and U.S.A demanded a more judicious review of the background factors responsible for the outbreak of the war. However, the 'War Guilt Lie', the economic crisis consequent on the payment of heavy reparations, the loss of colonies by Germany exerted considerable psychological impact on the German mind and this fact was fully exploited by the Nazi regime of Hitler. After the 2nd World War when West Germany had proclaimed itself a Democratic State aligned to the Western 'Free Society', most of the historians of the United States and the Western European countries have adopted a more liberal interpretation so as to accept the divided responsibility for the outbreak of the 1st World War. For the 2nd World War, the guilt of the Nazi regime in Germany is undeniable. Here, too, it may be argued with legitimate validity that the lack of support of the Western powers to the Weimar Republic in Germany to forge a customs union with Austria incapacitated the newly born democracy to strike firm roots. On the other hand, the initial support to Hitler in Anglo-German naval agreement and passive attitude towards her repudiation of the Versailles Treaty gave a fresh lease to the National Socialist upsurge and German economic recovery. This helped Hitler to gain popularity with working class people. Moreover, the Nazi-Soviet Non-Aggression Pact (August, 1939) precipitated the immediate crisis for which Soviet Union cannot be exonerated in its responsibility.

An academic approach underlining the past Indo-German cultural relations and to understand each other in proper perspective affords an excellent premise for mutual understanding. However, more emphasis on the past cultural relationship would mean airing nothing unless supported by the present day economic ties and political understanding. In the complexity of the present day world politics, economic collaboration and diplomatic support could give a concrete shape to a political understanding. This will not rule out healthy difference of viewpoints on the various world issues but an appreciation of each other's viewpoint and basic support to each other on the fundamental issues concerning the national life and security of country are essential. Judged from this standard, India and Germany have had good mutual understanding but they have still to go a long way before they could effectively serve each other in the political field and to contribute jointly towards the international stability. Both India and Germany have their respective problems. India being an under-developed country needs economic aid and collaboration for its agricultural and industrial development. It also needs security against aggression. Germany accepts defeat in the Second World War but wants final settlement of the Peace Treaty, reunion with East Germany and above all, national security. It is for the last eighteen years that India gained independence in 1947 and/the Federal Republic of West Germany have developed diplomatic relations at an ambassadorial level. Both India and West Germany are parliamentary democracies. As the 2nd World War had resulted in the division of Germany and the Eastern portions of Germany remained under the 'Iron Curtain', India did not recognise East Germany as a Sovereign State. Though the Federal Republic of Germany has entered the Western European Union and the NATO, and India is a non-aligned country, both the states are members of the United Nations and as well are wedded to the cause of international peace. For the last two decades, India and Federal Republic of Germany have developed strong political bonds. The German 'miracle' has made West Germany economically one of the leading countries in the world. It has provided enormous economic assistance (nearly Rs. 900 crores) for the development of India. It has offered technical and financial collaboration with nearly 450 industrial ventures in India. The Rourkela Steel and Fertilizer Plant, the Neyveli mining scheme, the Durgapur Power Station, and the expansion of the Mysore Iron and steel Works have been undertaken in the Indian public sector with German collaboration. West Germany has also given valuable aid in the agricultural package programme at Mandi (Himachal Pradesh) and in the Nilgiris. It has also offered collaboration for the running of school for training foremen in technical trades at Bangalore. These are only few examples of the German collaboration for the development of the Indian economy. However, in the sphere of trade and commerce, India has still adverse balance of trade with West Germany. It has caused serious concern to the Indian economy. This can be remedied to a great extent, if West Germany were to import the Indian goods directly rather than through third countries in Western Europe.

The problem of German reunification is a hard one and in the present day circumstances, the possibility of such an accomplishment is a remote one. The Ostdam Agreement (1945) placed the northern part of East Prussia under Soviet administration and put the other German territories lying to the East of the rivers Oder and Neisse under Polish administration. This is subject to the conclusion of a peace treaty with Germany which has never been signed so far. For all practical purposes, Germany has lost to Soviet Union and Poland the Prussian Provinces of East Prussia, the eastern Provinces of Pomerania, Mark Brandenburg, the free city of Dazing and the Provinces of Lower and Upper Silesia. The other portions to the east of the present Federal Republic of Germany form a part of "German Democratic Republic" whereas the erstwhile capital of the German Reich, i.e. Berlin is equally divided. It is for the first time in the history of Modern Europe that a defeated nation has paid such a huge price in the loss of its national territories and population without even having been obliged to sign an international treaty. The "Germany Democratic Republic" has already agreed to cede to Poland the German territories under the latter occupation since 1945. However hard it is to surrender national territories, despite all reluctance, the Federal Republic of Germany may accept the Oder-Neisse border for Germany as a whole but under no circumstances would it agree to the permanent creation of the two German states on the ashes of the old German Reich. The policy of the Soviet Union is to perpetuate the dismemberment of the German nation and to keep the "German Democratic Republic" as its satellite state in the Communist block. Equally surprising is the fact that notwithstanding the passage of nearly 22 years, the Western powers have paid only a lip-service to the idea of the unification of the two Germanies and have not taken any positive step to open dialogue with Soviet Union for this purpose. It seems that even the Western powers, more especially Great Britain, have a lurking fear about the emergence of hegemony of united Germany in the heart of Europe. There is no denying that a unified Germany shall be more powerful than at present. That chiefly distinguishes the present-day polity from the pre-1939 situation is the Franco-German rapproachment an event of great significance in the modern European history. Apart from this, West Germany is not only a member of UNO and NATO but fervently subscribes to the ideas of European Community and the European Common Market. West German is already a leading industrial country and the union of the two portions of Germany would not maternally alter the economic aspects of European politics. West Germany is also on the way be a nuclear power. A unified Germany may develop a strong military state with all the prospects of being a nuclear power but it could not act in opposition to either of the Super Powers which too have great nuclear sanction behind their respective political policies. The emergence of German hegemony on the $19^{th}$ century and pre-1939 pattern is simply impossible. At present, the Western and the Communist blocks are keeping up an equilibrium and balance of power in the world politics. The nuclear sanction is serving as a guarantee for the separate existence of the States and international peace. The non-aligned States are mostly developing and militarily weak nations. With unified Germany and even as a nuclear power, it may emerge to be a 'middle power' so as to serve tongue of the pendulum and may as well help in the maintenance of healthy equipoise between the two major blocks. A complete rigidity and crystallisation of either of the blocks is impossible in the present day world polity. It is only when West Germany successfully follows a policy of reconciliation with East Germany, the East European states and the Soviet Union for the finalization of the Peace Treaty that the prospects of unification of Germany could emerge.

The problem of German unification is essentially human. The traditional historical spiritual, intellectual and cultural unity of the German people has been completely disrupted since its partition. A unified Germany is an asset to the human culture on which the international stability basically rests. When in reality there is no self-governance and external freedom on the part of the people in the so-called "German Democratic Republic", there is no justification for its political entity. In the present circumstances, there is absolutely no chance of free elections and plebiscite which could determine the fate of the people. For the prospects of unification, the socio-economic reforms effected on the socialist pattern in East Germany would not serve as an obstruction. Nor is it possible to reverse the hands of clock. In case of unity based on federal structure, the landers in East Germany could decide of their own free choice about the fate of the socialist legislation already accomplished. The co-existence of two different concepts of economic patterns in the Western and Eastern portions of Germany would be a unique example in history. This would equally create healthier atmosphere between the two world blocks upon which rests the prospects of an international stability.

There is an opinion in some of the Indian political circles that India should recognise the "German Democratic Republic" as a Sovereign State and establish diplomatic relations at an ambassadorial level. India has had already commercial ties at an official level and very recently it has decided to have consular relations. In some circles, both in India and Germany, it is thought that it is a pointer to the next logical step which may establish regular diplomatic relations between India and "German Democratic Republic". The late Indian Prime Minister, Pandit Nehru, did not recognise the latter at diplomatic level for he was convinced that in reality, this Government did not represent the East German people and that its recognition by India would help in the perpetuation of the German division than in the solution at the German problem. He wanted to leave the solution to the German people themselves as well as the Western powers and Soviet Union. The situation has been rather a stalemate. Not with-standing some emotional feelings and ideological learning towards East Germany in some of the Indian political circles, it does not seem that any fresh vital factor or national interest has emerged which may demand a deviation from Nehru's policy on the German problem. The partition of India in 1947, howsoever unfortunate and against Mahatma Gandhi's better conscience, took place under entirely different circumstances. As such, no analogy can be drawn between the partition of India and the division of Germany. The German problem can be solved only through peaceful method and based upon a European understanding. Even though the Federal Republic of Germany is committed to achieve German unification through peaceful means, the unsettled situation on this issue in the heart of Europe definitely possesses an element of instability which is detrimental to the interest of international stability. In the interests of Indo-German amity and world peace, India as a non-aligned country can play a more positive and dynamic role. India herself is on the threshold of a nuclear power and bound to command better respect and more influence with the super powers. It can considerably help in the creation of the world opinion sympathetic toward the reunification of Germany. It can throw feelers to the Western powers and Soviet Union to open dialogue on this issue. India's positive attitude towards German reunification would definitely give moral weight to the issue. It may not have much immediate effect but it is bound to influence the world politics in the long run.

India equally expects of the German people not only economic assistance and facilities for export market but also a reasonable support for her political problems. The German press needs looking at the Kashmir issue from a more realistic angle than it has viewed hitherto. The people of Kashmir have already acceded to the Indian Union of their free choice and they are running their own government based on free general elections within the framework of the Indian Constitution. The continuation of Kashmir as an integral part of India is of vital importance because to a great extent this determines the secular character of the Indian state. Any further loss of Kashmir territory would give an incentive to the communalist feelings in India. It would be very unfortunate to have India and Pakistan in hostile camps based on purely communal considerations. Such a state of affairs would be extremely dangerous for the Asian and international stability. The German press can go a long way in emphasising this fact for the creation of the world opinion on this issue. The West German government can do its best to impress this fact upon the Western powers so as to appreciate properly India's viewpoint. The German government has done well to dispell all Indian fears about its association with the sale of arms to Pakistan. It can inspire confidence in India that the latter can equally bank on the German support to contain any further Chinese threat. Both West Germany and India have the potentiality of developing as nuclear powers in the near future and are destined to play a vital role in the world politics. Indo-German understanding can definitely go a long way for the maintenance of an international stability.

## References


1. Friedrich August, Prince of Schleswig-Holstein-son-Derburg-Augusturburg, (Graf Von Noer), Altes and Noues aus den Landern des o stens ( Things New and old from Eastern Lands), Hamburg, 2nd edition, 1870; Kaiser Akbar, ein versuch nber die Geschichte Indians in Sechzehnten Jahrhundert *(The Emperor Akbar, an Essay towards the History of India in the 16th century),* Leiden, 1880; Brief and Auzeichnungen ans seinem Nachlass, herausgageben von Carmen, Grafin von Noer (Letters and Extracts from Papers left by the Count Von Noer) edited by Carmen, Countess of Noer, Nordlingen, 1886.
2. For details, B.R. Grover, *Some Rare Persian Manuscripts and Documents on India (16th -18th centuries) in the German Libraries*, Max Mueller Bhavan Publications, New Delhi, 1964, pp. 59-72.
3. For detailed discussion, see B.R. Grover, *Reflections on the Outbreak of the First World War*, Max Mueller Bhavan, New Delhi, (under publication).

# 22

# Eighteen-Fifty Seven-A Landmark in Indian Historiography

Nomenclature – Till recently, Indian historiography meant only the development of historical studies by some Indian Orientalists, Medievalists and European writers, Bhandarkar, Beveridge, Buhler, Max Muller, Sardesai, Jadunath Sirkar, Smith, Sylvain Lavi, H.H. Wilson and the like who held the field. But with the focus on the centenary celebrations of Eighteen-fifty-seven in 1957, the vast literature that grew after the "Mutiny" or the 'Sepoy War' has come to the forefront. As pointed out by Dr. Tara Chand, most of the English writers on the subject toed the line of Earl Stanley, the then Secretary of State, who used the term 'Mutiny' while reporting the events of 1857 to the Parliament in U.K. Consequently, Charles Ball, G.W. Forest, T.R. Holmes, M. Innes, J.W. Kaye, G. F. Macmillan, G.B. Malleson, C.T. Metcalfe, Earl Roberts and a host of others used the term 'Mutiny' to describe the 1857 War. Sir John W. Kaye, however, used the word 'Sepoy War' also. Dr. Alexander Duff preferred to call it "the Indian Rebellions"; and Dodd termed it as 'the Indian Revolt'. Inspite of a lapse of 124 years, the very title of the outbreak is still an open question.

*Earliest works* :- One of the earliest books to be written on the subject was one by W.H. Carey, in 1857, and published from Roorkee. It termed the outbreak as "*The Mahomedan Rebellions*", Subsequently, the Government of India ordered complication of *Mutiny Narratives – District-wise* that constituted one of the earliest source-material printed on the subject under official patronage. These were based on the deposition and evidences submitted to or got by the officials. On the basis of these and dispatches from the Governor-General to the Secretary of State for India, the *Parliamentary Papers* were compiled and presented to the British Parliament.

Much had been said about Col. G.B. Malleson's work under the title – "*The Mutiny of the Bengal Army: By one who served under Sir Charles Napier*" commonly alluded to as *Red Pamphlet*. This is no doubt a narrative and a commentary on the 1857 revolt, but lacks the definitive assertion which is contained in Carey's work. So it is difficult to accept S.B. Chaudhari's assertion that "In a sense it laid the foundation of British historiography on the Indian Mutiny." As more and more contemporary works have come to light, it would be too much to attribute such importance to the *Red Pamphlet* alone. Recently published memoirs of Emily entitled *Golden Calm*, profusely illustrated, give a unique insight into the pre-Mutiny Delhi and the Mughal Durbar during the British residents' hegemony.

Amongst the earliest comprehensive histories of the Mutiny, the following deserve mention i.e., (i) *The History of the Indian Revolt etc.* by G. Dodd published by W & R Chambers, in 1859-60; (ii) '*History of the Indian Mutiny*' by Charles Ball in two volumes, 1859.

The latter work is by far the most prodigious and voluminous of all the works on the Indian Mutiny; but as pointed out by S. B. Chaudhari, it is doubtful if the second volume could have been published even by the end of 1859. No doubt most of these early works seem to have been predated somehow or the other and the translation of the Delhi Proclamation published by Charles Ball in the original edition is incorrect and misleading, in spite of the fact that the correct version had been published by the *Illustrated London News* in its issue of September 5, 1857 – (p. 242). So much reliance cannot be placed on such works, however comprehensive and elaborate they might have been.

*Biographies and Memoirs:*— The post-1857 literature was mostly reflective or explanatory but not so largely narrative as it dealt with the exciting events culminating in the failure of the revolt and fullest establishment of the rule of the British. The British rulers in India thereafter established High Courts, Legislative Council; expanded University education and a wave of anglicisation swept the country. Quite naturally, this period abounded in the colourless biographies and memoirs of the officials and high-ups. Lives of most of the post-Mutiny Viceroys, their autobiographies and reminiscences provide a useful source of information about the events. Their speeches at the Durbars, luncheons or University convocations were at times policy statements. Lord Roberts' *Forty-one years in India* is unique in the respect that it is autobiographical as well as informative. G. Campbell's *Memories of My Indian Career*; Sir Hugh Gough, '*Old Memories*'; G.M. Mallesons's *Recreation of an Official* and Lt. Col. V. Mallesons's, *The Revolt in Central India- (1857-59)* are unique in their composition.

Besides biographies and memoirs, books like Shepherd's, *A Personal Narrative of the Outbreak and Massacre at Cawnpore*, Trevelyon's *Cawnpore* and Kavanagh's *How I Won the Victorias' Cross*, are almost eye-witness accounts. John Longs book, *Wanderings in India*, is also excellent in this respect; it affords the only authentic pen-portrait of Rani of Jhansi and others whom he met during his wanderings. Over and above all, there is the *Diary in India in the year 1858-59* of W.H. Russell, the correspondent of the then *London Times* who was in India at that time. His day-to-day accounts were published in the newspapers, and several British historians compiled or wrote their earliest works on the Mutiny, on their basis, without caring to verify them from records.

*Contemporary Newspapers*:- The resuscitation of dangerous and unauthorised doctrines and dissemination of alarming though unfounded rumours by the press caused consternation in the minds of the officials of the East India Company at Calcutta. Among the contemporary journals at Agra and Delhi, the *Mofusslite*: the *Sirojul-Akhbar* the *Sadique Akhbar*, *Delhi Urdu Akhbar* and the *Delhi Gazette* deserve mention. At Lucknow, the *Tilisme*, the *Ashruf-ul-Akhbar*; and the *Sehre-Samri* were prominent before the outbreak. But the Calcutta newspapers like the *Doorbeen* and the *Sultan-ul-Akhbar*, the *Hindu Intelligencer, the Hindoo*

*Patriot*, the *Friend of India* and the *Bengal Harkaru* afforded one of the best coverage of the 1857 war. They naturally afforded a valuable source-material for the study of the great upheaval and its aftermath.

Contemporary journals and newspapers in England, or even in other foreign counties were not silent spectators. The *Illustrated London News* during 1857-59 was quite alert in not only publishing narratives, but also sketches, e.g. the holocaust at Allahabad, i.e., the burning of the town by Neill and the fort as well as the river in the background. The American newspaper *Washington Union* comments on the crisis in India in 1857 were reproduced by the *Englishman* (Calcutta) in its issue of October 15, 1857 Supplement. Recently, comments from some U.S.S.R. and continental newspapers have also come to light. In short, these contemporary records of news and comments afford refreshing material for evaluation of the events of 1857.

*The other side of the medal* :- It is a pity that the massive literature that came up on 1857 during the nineteenth century did not focus attention on the other side of the medal. Eminent writers like J.J .Mcleod Innes were satisfied with publishing only Indian Mutiny Cuttings from newspapers published during Mutinies; which gave only one-sided picture. *The Mutinies and the People* or *Statements of Native Fidelity* - exhibited during the outbreak of 1857-58 by a Hindu, was first published in London in 1859 and in Calcutta two years later. It is a handy volume of newspaper cuttings. The monumental work of Kaye and Malleson is at best a description of engagements, battles, army manoeuvres and the commissariat, based on official dispatches which abound in incorrect statistics about their rebel forces, casualties etc. In short, their history of the Sepoy War is nothing more than the narrative of the achievements of the British Army in action, the Highlanders and Fusiliers and the Naval Brigades. It is a one-sided picture and after the publication of the Source-Material in *Freedom Struggle in U.P.* – Five Volumes - its one-sided nature has come to the fore all the more. It is pity that the great historians completely ignored the trial proceedings of the non-sepoy leaders of the revolt, which had been lying buried in the U.P. Collectorate Records Rooms till the year 1957. And due to this the work of the three famous historians of the Indian Mutiny, Kaye, Malleson and Forrest had remained unchallenged for a century. They constituted the crux of British historiography on the Indian Mutiny, although from a 'partisan spirit'.

Vinayek Damodar Savarkar in his book *History of the War of Independence* questioned the bonafides of the British historians for the first time. But he did so with the object of inspiring the people to rise again and wage a second and successful war to liberate their motherland. What he wrote from sentiment could only be substantiated by the documents after the centenary publications in 1957 and thereafter.

*First Re-appraisal*:- Ever since the first commemoration of the Indian National rising of 1857 was held in London on the 9th of May 1905, the anniversary celebrations became an annual affair. For the revolutionaries abroad, the 1857 became a nucleus of inspirational literature, which came to be inducted into India, even though banned after the Sea Customs Act. Veer Savarkar's book produced in 1909 was banned. It was originally written in Marathi, and its translation in English was printed in London and Holland. Even after its confiscation, it was printed in Paris and appeared in the Indian book stalls. Its publication proved to be a turning point in the historiography of the Modern Indian History.

*The Free Hindustan* and the *Indian Sociologist*, revolutionary journals, heralded the 1857 outbreak as a national uprising. On the other hand, the Britishers celebrated in their own way the 50th anniversary of the martyrdom of the *Firungees*. In this way, neo-literature on 1857 grew rapidly during the next four decades i.e., 1907 to 1947. San Francisco, *Hindustan Ghader*, *Yugantar Ashram* brought out books and pamphlets like *Anjan Di Gavahi* (1915); Indian National Party, London and Geneva published, *British Rule in India Condemned by the British Themselves* (1915), H.M. Hyndman, in 1911, had already published *The Emancipation of India* from London; Har Dayal from San Francisco published two essays on the enslavement of India by the British, entitled *Ghulam Za Zaher*, *Ghulam ki Atma*; and in 1929, Pandit Sunder Lal came out with his famous book, *Bharat Mein Angrezi Rajya* (Hindi). In this he portrayed the 1857 outbreak as the first united effort to free India. The climax to such a literature came with the martyrdom of Bhagat Singh in 1931. Detailed biographies, poems, dramas etc. grew in abundance and formed part of banned literature. Bhai Parmanand also followed suit and his book, *Tarikh-i-Hind* in Urdu was published from San Francisco in 1918. His chapter on 1857 was judged as especially dangerous so the book was banned.

The Hindustan Socialist Republican Association published its *Fourth Manifesto* i.e., *War of Freedom of 1857* with the 1921 non-cooperation campaign. Even as late as 1942, the Jyoti Publishing House, Baroda, brought out a book on *The Revolt of 1857*, based on the Gujarati edition of *Bharat Mein Aggrezi Raj* by Sunder Lal. Books, pamphlets, poems and dramas on *Jhansi ki Rani* have been appearing in almost all regional languages, besides Hindi. In the same strain, books like *The Devotees of Freedom*; *Shahidon ki Toli* had been appearing in English and Hindi. Of all the mass of banned literature, the pamphlets of the Hindustan Socialist Republican Association like the *Rise, Awake, Be Ready* (1933); and *Ghadar ki Gunj* (San Francisco, 1914), the *Ghadar Birthday*, *Echo of Mutiny* had kept the legend of 1857 very much alive in the pre-Independence days.

*Post-Centenary Appraisals*:- Hardly had the ink dried on the emergence of Free India, the uprooted humanity from Pakistan, the Gandhi martyrdom and Nehru Panchsheel, the decision to publish History of Freedom Movement in India in 1950 sparked off a new wave in Indian Historiography. A committee was appointed under Dr. Tara Chand to supervise the collection of necessary material from all possible sources. Consequently, Dr. S.N. Sen at the All-India level and provincial committees attempted either to publish histories of the Freedom Struggle or publish source material. While Dr. Sen, R.C. Mazumdar produced their works on 1857; Bihar and Madhya Pradesh got histories of Freedom Struggle published in several volumes; Bombay (new Maharashtra) and U.P. decided to publish the source materials. Punjab has also followed suit.

*New Source-Materials*:- As a result of the above mentioned efforts, the publication of *Source-Materials: the History of Freedom Movement volume I (1818-1885)* from Bombay; and

*Freedom Struggle in U.P. (1857-1859)* – five volumes from U.P. made a dent in the Indian historiography. The records in The National Archives) New Delhi, as well in the India Office, U.K. were known to most of the scholars. But the unexpected and sensational discovery of District Court Records in U.P., titled as 'Mutiny Bastas' or *Basta be illat-e-Ghadr*, added a new dimension to the source-material and its publication. Although they were lying in a neglected condition in almost all the districts of U.P., they were in a state of preservation. Most of them contained trial proceedings, of non-sepoy leaders, like Mummoo Khan, Raja Jey Lall, Raja Drig Vijal Singh, Khan Bahadur Khan, Maulvi Liaquat Ali Khan and a host of others. These proceedings could not or were not included in the Foreign Political Proceedings of 30th December, 1859 due to their being recorded subsequently or due to other reasons. But as they contained not only the statements of the top leaders, charges of rebellion against them, judgments passed on them, but also their revealing original correspondence which could have exploded the myth of a Sepoy Mutiny, so they were allowed to gather dust for a century. Anyhow, it was creditable on the part of British officers that they allowed them to be preserved as '*nuissance records*'; resuscitated by the History of Freedom Movement Committee, U.P. in 1956-57. Thanks to the orders of the then Chief Minister Dr. Sampurnanand, all such *Bastas* were handed over to the Committee Office within two months and as their publication was to take time, they were exhibited at Kaiserbagh Baradari, Lucknow and Phoolbagh, Kanpur, both arenas of revolt in 1857. In the meantime, only biographical sketches of seven leaders were published on May 10, 1957, under the caption – *Sangharsha Kaleen Netaon ki Jiwanian*.

**Spurt of Publications:-**

The publication of the source-material unearthed along with original telegrams and bulletins of 1857 preserved in the strong room of the U.P. Secretariat, Lucknow, was done between 1957-63 in five volumes entitled 'Freedom Struggle in U.P.' Ever since their publication, a spate of works on "*The Other Side of the Medal*" had come up in India as well as abroad. E.Thompson's book *The Other side of the Medal* (London, 1930) came into limelight. Michael

Edwards brought out the *Red Year* in 1973. Quite recently, Mrs. Doleres Domen had brought out her book on the *Role of Sikhs in the Peoples' Rising*, (Berlin, 1977); and Christopher Hibbert's popular work *The Great Mutiny, India 1857*, had been published in the Penguin Series in 1980. R. Hilton got printed his book *The Indian Mutiny: A Centenary History* from London in 1957. M.E. Yapphas also highlighted the military importance of 1857 in his work *Strategies of British India* (Oxford, 1980).

Historians of U.S.S.R. and France were also not wanting in enthusiasm for writing on 1857. E. de Valvezen's book written in 1883 had been translated into English and published under the title, *The English and India: New Sketches* – (Los Angles at l' Inde etc.). In this the heroic role played by the British had been applauded. Another French writer, M. de Montalombert in his book – *Un debat sur l' Inde an Parliament* – had discussed the Indian Mutiny on the basis of discussions in the British Parliament.

In 1960, Karl Marx and Frederic Engelo's book entitled *The First Indian War of Independence* was printed from Moscow. Besides this important work, an article written by N.A. Dorolyubor (1836-1861) had also been published by N. Turehinov in *Soremenik* (Moscow) in September 1957; under the title – *A View of History and Present Condition of East-India.*

It is evident from the Continental writers that the 1857 War had aroused interest in countries other than U.K. Even *The Washington Union* (U.S.A.) did not lag behind, and commented on the crisis in India-1857. The comments were reproduced by *The Englishman*, Thursday, 15th October 1857 Supplement and that said, "we do not believe that the rebellion in India will eventuate in successful revolution..." and English never was so powerful as she now is, and never so well prepared to carry on war in a distant theatre. Her immense System Navy, aided by rapid communication by mail and the telegraph, makes it less difficult for her to conduct a war now in India than to have carried on one in America 40 years ago..." The then Calcutta newspapers have reproduced comments in the contemporary international press on the 1857 war and they form an excellent Source-Material. A study of such varied accounts, comments and reflections make the 1857 mode of warfare, the role of the Sepoys, The rebel leaders and the part played by the Sikhs, the Bengalees, the Goorkhas and the like is as fresh today as it was hundred years ago.

*Multifaced Studies:-* Apart from biographical studies, works on the nature of the Revolt; the military aspect had recently attracted attention of writers, Commander W.B. Wowlothan, R.N's work on *The Naval Brigades in the Indian Mutiny, 1857-58*, printed by the Navy Records Society is a work of great importance. The Russian War in the Crimea, on the results of which Azimullah Khan and his master Nana Saheb were banking upon much, had come to an end on March 30, 1856. And within the next six months, several of the Naval officers, who had achieved distinction in the Baltic and the Crimean Brigades, were re-appointed to the East Indies. Naval Brigades played an important part in the Indian Sepoy war and its suppression.

The Shannon's Brigade under the command of Capt. William Peel played a crucial role in the Battle of Kanpur in December 1857 and was attached to the main Army under General Sir Colin Campbell. The Pearls' Brigade was assigned a role in the east of the Ghagra in the Gorakhpur district. Requisitioning of Naval Brigades made up the deficiency of heavy mobile artillery and trained artillerymen in the Sepoy Army under British command and with their assistance, they effected an internal blockade of the revolutionary forces and their top leaders, so much so, they had only one route left to them i.e., retreat to the fastnesses of the Nepalese Terai. All other routes were closed to them. The British Navy was mobilised to the full against then so much so that the projected China operations were put off.

Mrs. Doleres Domen's latest book from Berlin Academy on the *Role of Sikhs in the National Uprising of 1857* and Dr. A.B. Ganguley's book on Tantya Tope entitled *The Guerilla Chief of the First War of Independence* are good attempts in this direction. In the former, an analysis has been given of the comparative strength of the British occupation forces in the nearly annexed province of Punjab, and in the latter publication of Parobs and Orders of Tantya Tope from *Sir Owen's Collections*, India Office throws floodlight on the military aspect of 1857. In this connection, the original correspondence which passed between Maulvi Ahmad Ullah Shah, and Rana Banoo Madho of Baiswara, published in the 2nd volume of Freedom Struggle in U.P. is of the highest importance to a historian. The shortage of lead and sulphur due to British blockade was a major cause of the defeat of the Begum's forces at the fortified towns of the Lucknow and later on at Bareilly.

The crucial role played by Maharaja Sir Jang Bahadur of Nepal and his 10,000 Gorkha soldiers in 1858 at Lucknow, has been highlighted by the publication of Perceval Landons' book on Nepal in 1973; his *Under The Sun* in 1906; Pudma Jangs' biography of the Rana in 1909; and the source-material in U.P. *Freedom Struggle,* Vol. III in 1959. The publication of extracts and references from the Resident at Nepal's correspondence with the Government of India in 1861 in the latest book, *Architects of Indian Freedom Struggle*, throw floodlight on Nana Saheb, and Indo-Nepalese relations.

*Regional and Local Studies*: During the post-centenary period, a good many books have come out in various States and Provinces. K.K. Datta's *Biography of Babu Kunwar Singh and Amar Singh*; Dharaiya's book on *Gujrat in 1857*; K.C. Yadav's book on *Revolt of 1857 in Haryana*; K.K. Srivastava's book on *Revolt of 1857 in Malva* are some of the outstanding works. Besides, these, good many works have appeared in Hindi, Marathi, and other regional languages. They are of equally great importance. With the opening of immense treasure in Local Record Room, the Punjab Government Records; the Delhi State Archives; the Malwa, (M.P.) records of the old Gwalior and other States' records a new vista has opened for further studies on 1857.

Socio-economic disruption caused after 1857, especially in the erstwhile North West Provinces of Agra and Oudh is another aspect which is engaging the attention of scholars. The masterly 'Famine Report of 1861' by Colonel Baird Smith with Maps and Statistics; and the voluminous Report on the Oudh Salt Question submitted by E.N.C. Braddon, Excise Superintendent of Oudh in 1867 preserved in the Record Room of the Lucknow District Collectorate; compiled with the district records in Oudh about confiscation and disposal of unclaimed lands in the post-1857 period are likely to throw immense light on the land revenue policies, settlement reports etc.

Col. G.B. Malleson once remarked that "In the history of the World" there was no more wonderful story than "that of the making of the British Empire in India". But even in this process, 1857 played a most important part as it saw the end of the rule of the East India Company and assumption of Government by The Crown. The change-over sparked off an interesting debate in the British Parliament and the Parliamentary Reports amplified by the Debates can throw still further light on the aftermath of 1857. The role of Press Agents, the distribution of prize money and the igonomous quarries about their sharing as recorded in *Banda-Kirwee Booty* have yet to be published.

The retribution meted out to the revolutionaries, the treatment meted out to the thousands transported to Andamans and Nicobar Islands, the sack and slaughter at Jhansi, Lucknow, Delhi and other places is being projected in a number of works that are coming up in English as well as in other languages. The publication of *Manjha Pravas* Hindi version by Amritlal Nagar has thrown floodlight on Jhansi and Gwalior during 1857-58. Bholanath Chunder's *Travels of a Hindoo*, 2 vols., published from London in 1869 has left behind a gruesome account of the butchery at Allahabad perpetrated by Colonel Neill. A special chapter on this has been devoted by the author in his book: *History of Modern India*, published in 1970; revised edition in 1977.

*Survey of Records in India and Abroad:-* A detailed note on the Source-Material available in India was published as an Introduction to the volumes *Freedom Struggle in U.P.* by S.A.A. Rizwi. Since then the I.C.H.R. has also brought out a small book on the same, written by Kalyan Das Sen Gupta, S.B. Chaudhari in his work an English Writings on 1857 has attempted a broader survey although incomplete.

# Index